Frederick

The Life of My Missionary Grandfather in Manchuria

MARK O' NEILL

Editor   Henry Lee
Designer   Kacey Wong

First published in May 2012
Second impression in June 2016
Published by Joint Publishing (H.K.) Co., Ltd.
20/F., North Point Industrial Building, 499 King's Road, North Point, Hong Kong
Printed by C & C Offset Printing Co., Ltd.
14/F., 36 Ting Lai Road, Tai Po, N.T., Hong Kong
Distributed by SUP Publishing Logistics (HK) Ltd.
3/F., 36 Ting Lai Road, Tai Po, N.T., Hong Kong
Copyright ©2012 Joint Publishing (H.K.) Co., Ltd.
ISBN 978-962-04-3200-2

All photographs in this book were kindly provided by Mark O'Neill (unless otherwise stated).

Contents

Frederick and Annie O' Neill with church members in front of their house in Faku in the 1930s.

How it all began...

It was a warm spring day in Beijing in 1986. I was sitting in the office of Reuters news agency and reading that day's edition of the *People's Daily*. It was one of our first duties in the morning, as journalists. On an inside page, I found a list of 240 towns and cities which had just been opened, that is, made accessible to foreigners. I looked at the list for Liaoning Province in the Northeast, and found, to my surprise, the name of Faku (法庫). This small town, 100 kilometres north of the provincial capital of Shenyang, has a special place in my heart and in the history of our family.

It was there that my grandfather, Frederick O'Neill, spent forty-five years of his life, from 1897 until 1942, as a missionary of the Irish Presbyterian Church. My father spent the first six years of his life in the town and spoke of it with affection. Then he could speak Chinese but forgot it all in later life, because he had no occasion to practise; all he could remember were two words – one a swear word which he would not repeat and *jiaozi*, dumpling, which was his staple food as a child. I had heard stories about the town from elderly relatives and read the three books which Grandfather wrote about his life there.

But, growing up in Britain in the 1950s and 1960s, Faku and China were a long way away. When Chairman Mao and his new government took over in 1949, they expelled missionaries and closed the country to the western world. The missionaries would not be allowed back and we were not permitted to visit. China was far away and inaccessible; we knew and understood nothing about it. Almost no-one in Britain studied Mandarin because they could not use it, except as a scholarly pursuit.

So it was for me as I attended school and university and got my first jobs, as an assistant to an author in Washington D.C.

and a researcher at a television station in Manchester. The city has a sizeable Chinese community and a branch of the Bank of China, where I would see them go to pay and collect money. Then, in 1975, the opportunity came to work in Belfast, the capital of Northern Ireland; it was Grandfather's hometown and the headquarters of the Presbyterian church to which he belonged. The "Troubles" – the conflict between the two communities in Northern Ireland which had turned violent – had begun in 1969 and developed into a low-level guerilla war. Few people wanted to go there; but, for me, it was a welcome opportunity, both to report on an important story and to learn something of Grandfather and his history.

Not many applied for the job as a reporter in the Belfast office of the British Broadcasting Corporation, so I was selected. I found a room with four other young men in a Victorian red-brick house close to Queen's University. Grandfather's footprints were all around me. He was born in a similar red-brick house a few streets away and attended Queen's University; after that, he studied at Assembly's College, now Union Theological College, where the church trained and continues to train its ministers. Built in 1853, it contains a magnificent library with 45,000 books. The college and many of the university buildings were just as they were a century before, when Grandfather lived and studied there. It is not hard to imagine him cycling to his classes along the tree-lined avenues and sitting in the library, surrounded by volumes going back several hundred years.

My first moment of revelation came several months later when I interviewed the Reverend Jack Weir, then General Secretary of the Presbyterian Church. His office was in the church's imposing Victorian headquarters, opened in 1905, in the centre of the city. The subject of the interview was peace talks between the two warring sides in which the Reverend Weir was involved. At the end, I said that I was the grandson of Frederick O'Neill. When he heard this, the gloomy expression on his face changed into a big smile. He explained that his father had also been a missionary in Manchuria for many years and that he had followed in his footsteps, before leaving China in 1950. Then he took me into a large room; on the walls hung the photographs of all those who had been Moderators (head) of the Church, a post which the incumbent holds for one year. He took me to the year 1936 and pointed at the picture of Grandfather; he had a high forehead, a solemn expression and piercing eyes. For the first time, I had a feeling for him and the strength of the convictions that took him across the world to China.

I stayed in Belfast for three and a half years. While reporting took up most of my time, I had the opportunity to meet some of those who had served as missionaries in Manchuria. I remember especially two elderly ladies; of the 91 Irish Presbyterian missionaries in Manchuria between 1869 and 1951, 48 were women, of whom 14 were doctors. The two described their lives in the towns and cities of Manchuria in the 1930s and 1940s – church services, travelling over the countryside in horse carriages, the freezing winters in which the temperature would fall to minus 30 degrees Celsius and the kangs, the brick stoves on which people slept to combat the cold. They spoke of terrible plagues and bandits who kidnapped people, including foreigners.

In the modern comfort of Belfast, with cars, shopping centres and central heating, it was almost impossible to imagine how people lived in such a place; it was so remote from the life we lived. It was also hard to imagine why these ladies, and the other missionaries like them, could choose to give up the life they had at home and settle in Manchuria. In Belfast, I also saw Chinese people, many of them in the restaurant trade. They did an excellent business, because Belfast was a semi-war zone. Few British people or foreigners would go there, let alone invest in a business. So the Chinese who invested found that they were in a market with strong demand for restaurants but limited supply. We sometimes interviewed them, when we wanted good news. I admired their resilience and hard work.

After three and a half years, I began to consider a move elsewhere, abroad if possible. One of my bosses in Belfast had worked at Radio Television Hong Kong; he told me that it would be a good experience to work there and that I should seize the opportunity. He was kind enough to write me a letter of recommendation and I was able to get the job as reporter and editor in the radio section. China was getting closer.

I landed at Kai Tak airport in Hong Kong in November 1978. It was already one of the most prosperous cities in the Far East — densely populated and with a tropical climate. It was China, but completely different to the one I had heard about from the missionary ladies. A month later, the Communist Party held its historic Third Plenum in Beijing, at which Deng Xiaoping announced the reform policies. The door that had been closed for thirty years was unlocked.

In 1980, I made my first visit with a tour group to Beijing and Shanghai. In Beijing, I visited a Scottish lady who was working for the British trading firm, Jardine Matheson, and lived in the Beijing Hotel; the doors had no locks and there were no keys. She took me to a local restaurant where we ate *jiaozi* — one of the only two Chinese words which my father could remember. We were the only two "big noses"[*] there, among about sixty

---

[*]"Big noses" is a popular slang used by Chinese to describe Westerners. It is humourous rather than impolite but is not used in official language.

diners. All were wearing blue cotton suits and had never seen "big noses" before; they surrounded our table and stared intensely at the two strange creatures that we seemed. But we felt comfortable, since theirs was a friendly curiosity. My friend spoke Chinese well and conversed a little with them. Beijing was not so far from Manchuria, I thought, a day's ride in the train; the people in the restaurant looked like those I had seen in the photographs shown to me in Belfast. When Grandfather went for a meal in a restaurant in Shenyang or Dalian, he would have seen people like those.

Back in Hong Kong, I occupied myself with my work and studying Cantonese. There was so much to learn, about history, society, business and language; it was like throwing a person into the ocean and forcing him or her to swim. After I finished my two-and-a-half-year contract at the radio station, I moved to Taiwan for intensive study of Mandarin. If I wanted to stay in the region for the long term, this seemed to be a pre-condition. Since China had opened its doors, it would allow foreigners to go there to work, including journalists like me. I studied at a language school in the morning and worked as an editor of an economic magazine under *United Daily News* in the afternoon. The teachers and the ordinary people were most kind and gracious; it was a wonderful experience.

In 1983, I applied for a job in Reuters news agency; Reuters had been allowed to re-open its Beijing bureau, which had been closed in the Cultural Revolution, and badly needed people who could speak Chinese, however imperfectly. After six months of learning the basics on the editorial desk in Hong Kong and a fourteen-month stint in the New Delhi office, I was assigned to the Beijing bureau in the summer of 1985. So it was that I came to be reading the *People's Daily* that spring day in 1986.

Faku

As I read the paper, I decided at once to visit Faku; this was a precious opportunity, the first in nearly forty years. I agreed with my bureau chief to arrange a reporting trip to Shenyang, to visit companies and factories, and then go to Faku for one or two days. I went on the reporting trip with my Hong Kong Chinese wife Louise, also a journalist; it went well and, on the last evening, we invited to dinner the young man from the city's Foreign Affairs Department who had organised it, as a gesture of thanks. We told him of our plan to go to Faku the next day. He became uneasy and said that it might not be a good idea. I showed him a copy of the article from the *People's Daily*, which said that the town had been open to foreign visitors. Yes, he said, it was legal to go there but the town had had no experience of receiving foreigners, so it might be better to go another time. We could see the reasons for his anxiety. He was the official responsible for our visit to Liaoning; if anything unexpected happened, he would be held responsible. We said that it was a visit of filial piety, to show respect for Grandfather. He could have forbidden us from going but finally agreed, because he was a kind person.

Early next morning, we hired a car and set out from our hotel in Shenyang. Gradually, the factories and apartment blocks of the city gave way to rolling hills of corn and wheat, dotted with clumps of one-storey brick houses with chimneys. As the car drove on, the number of vehicles became fewer and fewer. Most people traveled by bicycle, horse-or mule-cart or by foot; they were dressed in the same blue cotton jackets and blue trousers I had seen in the Beijing restaurant and many wore flat caps. This was the landscape which Grandfather had seen for so many years; in his diaries, he described long journeys over the Manchurian countryside to visit rural churches and communities, sometimes by bus, but more often by horse-cart. He did not have the luxury of travelling in a Toyota and on paved roads.

It was a beautiful day – a clear blue sky and the undulating hills spreading into the horizon. After a journey of two hours, we arrived in Faku. Here the roads were not so good – a narrow strip in the middle and earth on each side, on which people walked or cycled. The driver took us into the courtyard of the state guesthouse in the town, where we found a committee of welcome. The officials were friendly but nervous – they had not received a "big-nose" for many years. We explained that we only wanted to stay for a short time, to see places and people connected with Grandfather. They gave us a comfortable room in the guest house and prepared a delicious lunch.

After the meal, we walked around the town. It was small; it had few factories and relied on agriculture. Most people lived in one-storey brick houses built close together as protection against the fierce winter. They walked, rode bicycles or on horse-or mule-carts, with sacks of grain loaded on the

Faku in spring 1986

back. On a street corner, I found a woman with a wooden stall selling soybean curds, white and shaking like jelly; she cut it with a knife and handed portions to her customers. Grandfather would have seen such vendors every day.

He built a church in the town in 1907; was it still standing? Residents kindly guided me to the site, a large courtyard with the church in one corner. It was instantly recognisable, like the Presbyterian churches of Ireland, a rectangular design with a sloping roof. The windows had been bricked up, with the revolutionary slogan "In Agriculture, learn from Dazhai" written on them. Inside, I found ping pong tables and the boxes which gymnasts jump over as part of their training. The residents told me that the government had taken over the building in the 1940s and used it for sports. Next to the church was the school which Grandfather built, a sturdy two-storey structure still in use as a school.

Then I went to look for Grandfather's house and, astonishingly, it was still there too: a spacious one-storey brick structure, with a sloping roof and two chimneys, larger than the homes of most Faku residents, with open space around it. In his time, it would have had a large reception room and dining room and several bedrooms, where his children or visitors stayed. I went inside and found not a home but a small plastics factory with people at work. When I explained who I was, the staff reacted with great warmth. One gave me part of an envelope addressed to Grandfather, with a stamp of the British king worth 2½ pennies; how had it survived more than forty years and ended up in the hands of one of the workers that day? Residents showed me other houses in which missionaries had lived in – not so large as that of Grandfather but spacious and comfortable, with open ground and trees in front. So, despite the passage of so many years, there was much physical

Grandfather's house

A portion of the envelope addressed to Grandfather

evidence of Grandfather and his fellow missionaries.

Next we went to look for people. Grandfather had a cook named Mr Zhao; residents told me that he worked in a bakery in the town. The next morning I got up early, went to the bakery and asked for him. To my pleasant surprise, Mr Zhao, in his sixties, was sleeping next to a window sill. Although it was before six in the morning, I woke him up and said that I was the grandson of Minister Ni (Grandfather's Chinese name was Ni Feide). Despite the early hour and the shock, Mr Zhao immediately sat up and understood the situation. We sat down at a table and I asked him about his work for Grandfather. He took out a piece of paper and wrote a list of the dishes he made. He said that while Grandfather and Grandmother lived in China for so many years, they liked to have Western food at home; so he had to learn to make it. Among the things he had to learn to make were cakes and biscuits which, like most Irish people, my grandparents adored but are unfamiliar to the Manchurian diet. They did not drink alcohol but liked tea — not Chinese tea, but the Indian variety which most Europeans prefer, adding milk and sugar.

Every three months, Mr Zhao had to make the long journey to Shenyang, the nearest place where he could buy this kind of tea. It meant a trip by horse-cart from Faku to Tieling, a day's journey to the nearest stop on the South Manchuria Railway which led to Shenyang. Mr Zhao spoke of my grandparents with affection – politeness perhaps or, I hope, proof that they treated him well. The next morning, the manager of the guesthouse where we were staying came to see me and ask for my advice: "Now that Faku is open to foreigners, we can expect more visitors like you," he said. "Tell me what it is that they like to eat." He was like Mr Zhao in those early years – learning to adapt to the strange tastes of the "big-noses".

My next task was to see if there were any believers in the town. Residents pointed me to a small compound with a sign on the entrance that read "Faku Protestant Association". Inside the compound was a small room with a table and several elderly people sitting around it. I went in and introduced myself. They were extremely surprised to see such a person, but were very hospitable and invited me to sit down at the table. They described how life had been for the church and its members since Grandfather left the town – escorted by Japanese police in a military vehicle in April 1942. Since he was a British citizen, he was arrested as an "enemy combatant". One of the people, an elderly man whose dark, tanned skin made him look like a farmer, said: "We thank very much your grandfather for coming to Faku. If he had not come, we would not have learnt the good news of Christianity." I was very moved and lost for words.

I also went to visit the local mosque; the town is home to a substantial number of *Hui* (Muslims). The imam and his colleagues received us very warmly; he spoke of the positive contribution which Grandfather and the church had made to the town, building schools and a hospital, and the good relations which it enjoyed with the mosque. There was no Islamic-Christian war here!

I was curious to see if anyone could remember Grandfather in person; this was unlikely since he had left the town forty-four years before. When I saw old people on the streets, I asked them if they could remember an elderly "big-nose" with the white collar which ministers wear around his neck. I could not find anyone with a direct memory; one man said that Minister Ni was very tall, as tall as I was. All these meetings were very evocative, telling me of Grandfather's presence and legacy in the town more than forty years after his departure.

Another unforgettable experience during our short stay in Faku was meeting its children. They had never seen a "big-nose" in their lives and could not hide their curiosity at this strange creature; dozens of them followed me around the streets. I felt like the Pied Piper of Hamelin. One morning I walked up the side of one of the hills overlooking the town, with more than thirty children in tow. If I had asked them to climb to the top of the nearby trees and jump off, they would have done it! I asked them about their lives in Faku and they asked questions about being a "big-nose": "How do you breathe with such a large nose? How do you eat? Are people in your country tall and do they all have such big feet? Does everyone in your country speak Chinese?" To make them happy, I said that yes, everyone in the world spoke Chinese. The children gave us a big smile in return.

Mr Xiu Haizhou was the manager of the guest house where we stayed. He was a friendly man with a broad smile. One morning he asked me to sit down and provide advice on the possible arrival of more "big-noses". "What kind of food do they like to eat? I hear that they have a very sweet tooth, which would mean the preparation of special food." He took out a pencil and notepad and I started with breakfast. People in Faku had a breakfast of rice soup, with vegetables, meat, noodles and buns; so how about the Westerners? I started with toast, butter and jam. Mr Xiu was fine with toast but butter was hard to explain – in Chinese, it is "yellow oil" or "cow oil". He was writing everything down but could not quite visualise it. I said that jam was processed fruit with sugar; curious, he thought, why add the sugar? Breakfast cereals with milk were also hard to explain. "In films, I have seen Westerners taking a drink by themselves when they get home from work," he said. "I find this very strange. They take alcohol just by itself alone? In China, we drink with family and friends and together with food." I was impressed by his eagerness to learn and agreed with his view that the Chinese diet is healthier than the Western one.

So ended our brief but intense visit to Faku. I saw for the first time the evidence of Grandfather's long stay in China – the physical legacy in the church, the school and the house and

Children of Faku in spring 1986

the spiritual legacy in the Protestant congregation and the memories he had left behind in the minds of the people.

What we saw was on the surface; it would take much more time and effort to understand his life and work there. The visit left me more full of wonder and admiration for him and eager to learn more about his life. In the China of 1986, Faku was a remote place, with a standard of living below that of the major cities where most foreign residents of China lived.

Go back ninety years to 1897, the year Grandfather arrived in China; then most foreigners lived in Beijing, Shanghai and Tianjin where many had a style of life not so different to what they had back home. But the Faku of that time had no electricity, running water, paved roads, telephone, railway or modern medicine; the gap between it and China's big cities was even wider than today. What made Grandfather exchange his comfortable life in Belfast for the remoteness and danger of Faku? How did he adapt to such a harsh and difficult climate, living on his own for the first five years? How did the people and officials of Faku react to the arrival of this first "big-nose" who had come to live in their midst? It is these questions that this book will attempt to answer.

History and Culture of Faku

Tracing Grandfather's story made me curious about the area of Faku as a new territory for missionaries. Few outside Liaoning province had ever heard of the town. For most Chinese, Manchuria is an area that came late to Han culture and civilisation; it appears little in literature and history.

"Faku" is a word from the Manchurian language and literally means "a weir to catch fish", a reference to a river in the south of the district that had a plentiful supply of fish.

The area has been inhabited since the Warring States period (475-221 BC). It was for centuries a border area between land under the Chinese emperor and that controlled by non-Han nomadic tribes such as the Xiongnu, Donghu, Nuzhen and Qidan. There were conflicts between them. During the Jin Dynasty (1115-1234 AD), the Nuzhen regained control of what is now Faku district. It then became part of the empire again under the Yuan Dynasty (1271-1368 AD). During the Ming Dynasty (1368-1644 AD), a battle broke out between the Ming army and Mongolian nomads. In 1442, the district was divided into an eastern section under Liaodong province and a western section dominated by Mongolian nomads. At the end of the Ming period, the area fell again under the control of the Nuzhen, the ancestors of the Manchus; they established their first capital in Shenyang before conquering the whole of China and setting up the Qing Dynasty in 1644, with their capital in Beijing.

The new regime divided Faku district into two areas, one under the command of a Manchu army and the other by a Mongolian battalion; both were loyal to the new emperor. In order to prevent an influx of Han and Mongols eager for new land, the emperor built a fortification around the district, manned by soldiers; it was aimed at maintaining the "ethnic purity" of the area. In 1662, the Kangxi Emperor established a fort in Faku; it became an important military garrison. In the last century of the Qing Dynasty, which ended in 1911, these controls on immigration relaxed, in part because of the decline of the regime and in part because it needed more Chinese to combat the rise of Russian and Japanese military power in Manchuria. Han, Mongol and Manchu settlers moved into the district. They were attracted by the good quality of the land, on which they were able to grow corn, sorghum, wheat, soyabean, rice, fruit and vegetables and to raise animals. The land is flat or gentle slopes. The region is well endowed with rivers and forests.

So, when Frederick arrived in Faku, he found a diverse population of Han, Manchu and Mongol people; the parents and grandparents of many of them had come from other parts of China. This was why they spoke the common language of Mandarin which they had to use to communicate with one another. In many parts of China of which the respective population did not migrate, people spoke dialects that were unintelligible to people from other areas. In many provinces, a missionary had to learn one or more dialects as well as Mandarin.

In 1906, the Qing government established a district government in Faku, under the province of Fengtian (Shenyang). In 1913, this became Faku county. After the Japanese occupation of Manchuria in 1931, the county passed under the control of the Manchukuo government and was put under the Fengtian province. After the Japanese surrendered in August 1945, the Communist Party established a government there in November of the same year. In June the next year, the KMT re-established control; but it was unable to withstand the Communist army, which re-took the area in February 1948 and set up a "people's government". Faku was part of Liaoxi (west of the Liao river) province until August 1954, when the Liaoxi and Liaodong provinces were merged to form Liaoning. Since January 1, 1993, Faku has been administratively under the jurisdiction of Shenyang city.

In June 1998, the county opened a cultural museum, with 2,000 square metres of space on five and a half storeys, to present its history and culture.

Today Faku covers an area of 2,290 square kilometers with a population of 450,000, of which 350,000 depend on agriculture and 100,000 live in the urban area. 57 per cent of the land is available for cultivation, thanks to a geography of plains and low hills. It is well watered with four major rivers and seven reservoirs. It is served by expressways to Shenyang, 90 kilometres away, and Tieling, 45 kilometres away, and a railway line in the northeast of the county. It has an average temperature of 6.7 degrees Celsius and one hundred fifty days a year without frost, with the four seasons well defined. This climate means that Faku has one harvest a year, with an annual output of 750,000 tonnes of corn, rice, soyabean, sorghum, wheat and other grains. It is also one of the biggest production bases in North Liaoning for fruit and vegetables. Farmers in the county raise 270,000 cattle and sheep, which feeds an important dairy industry. Forestry is another significant activity, with trees covering about 23 per cent of the county area.

The most important industry is production of porcelain, with an annual output of 350 million square metres of material worth more than 14 billion yuan for the building industry. The factories use the abundant raw materials found in the county, which includes twenty-six different kinds of minerals. It has

59 million tonnes of reserve of porcelain clay and 39 million tonnes of reserve of zeolite. It also has 11 million tonnes of coal reserves. Its reservoirs and attractive scenery make the area a popular site for visitors. They also come to see its rich cultural history, including its many temples, tombs and relics. The most famous – classified as a national cultural treasure – is the Ye Maotai tombs of the Liao Dynasty (916-1125 AD).

Starting from the 1950s, more than twenty were discovered, many in excellent condition and contained historical remains of great importance for the study of this period; there are wall paintings inside the tombs. The Liao was a dynasty established by the Qidan, a nomadic people who ruled over parts of Manchuria, Mongolia and Northern China. The burial customs of the Qidan reflected their belief in reincarnation. The burial chambers have paintings on the ceiling and pictures hanged from the wall. The bodies are wrapped with shirts with tight sleeves and long robes with belts – clothing that enabled them to shoot rapidly; they reflect the Qidan's dependence on hunting and fishing, their main forms of subsistence. In one of the tombs were found chisels for breaking ice, fishing rods and hooks and other iron tools for fishing.

Faku is a small town, but it attracted a group of noble missionaries. It was there they began their special journey of life...

The church that Grandfather built

Chapter 1

From Belfast to Manchuria

The life of Frederick O'Neill from his birth in 1870 until
his departure in 1897

Childhood and Education

Frederick William Scott O' Neill was born in Belfast on August 26, 1870 to a family that lived in 13 Fitzroy Avenue, a modest two-storey home in a terrace of red-brick houses close to Queen's University. It was a pleasant, middle-class area, with tree-lined avenues and convenient access to the city centre. His father was Edward O' Neill; we know little about him or the rest of the family.

In 1870, Belfast was the biggest industrial centre in Ireland and one of the most important cities of the British Empire. Its major industries were linen, rope – making, tobacco, heavy engineering and shipbuilding. In 1861, a company named Harland and Wolff was established; it grew into one of the biggest shipbuilders in the world, employing 35,000 people. In 1870, the company launched five vessels with a combined tonnage of 15,571; in 1913, it completed sixteen vessels with a combined tonnage of 147,000 and, between 1909 and 1914, three giant passenger liners, one of them the ill – fated *Titanic*, which sank on its maiden voyage when it hit an iceberg in fog in the Atlantic on April 15, 1912.

When it was launched in 1911, it was the largest passenger ship in the world, with a displacement of 52,000 tonnes.

The world's largest passenger ship, built in Belfast.

During the twenty-seven years in which Frederick lived in Belfast before going to China, it was a boom town – people flocked there to work in its shipyards, factories and textile mills. Its population more than doubled from 175,000 in 1870 to 385,000 in 1911. The city built a large public library in 1890 and the Grand Opera House in 1895: most imposing of all was a giant city hall, completed in 1906 at a cost of 369,000 pounds, an enormous sum at that time. It has towers at each of the four corners and, in the centre, a copper dome 53 metres high; it was built in the Baroque Revival style, with the exterior in Portland stone. On June 5, 1905, the Presbyterian Church opened an imposing new headquarters in the city centre, costing 74,000 pounds and built in the Scottish Baronial style. These four buildings symbolized Belfast's wealth and self-confidence.

The city in which Frederick grew up was among the most modern in Europe. It had gas light from 1823, its first railway in 1839 and horse-drawn trams from 1872. A major commercial and industrial centre, it boasted large and well-equipped public buildings, a good educational system, modern hospitals, post and telegraph networks, a tramway system and railways to other parts of Ireland. The fifty years before the start of World War One in 1914 were the zenith of the British Empire; Belfast and its inhabitants were part of this empire, in terms of economy, culture and outlook. Its factories and shipyards exported most of their products to other parts of Britain and the wider world beyond. So, while the city was on the far western corner of Europe, it belonged to an economic system and culture that spread around the globe. As a result, Frederick and his classmates could consider a future not only in their native Ireland and Britain, but also overseas, in colonies and countries where British companies and institutions operated. Many of them would go on to live and work overseas, in law, business, banking, medicine or as civilian and military officers in the British empire.

Frederick was born into a middle class family and grew up in the prosperous half of Belfast. It was a different world in the poor half. The unskilled workers who flooded into the city to take jobs in the shipyards, mills and factories lived in crowded, unsanitary brick terrace homes and earned survival wages. The streets had open sewers; infectious diseases like typhoid, small pox, diphtheria and typhus killed thousands of children. The poor had large families and their children slept together in damp and dirty beds. To earn a living, the wives and children had to work, often twelve hours a day or more. Thousands of children did not attend school; many turned to begging and hawked flowers and newspapers on the streets. The poor had limited access to education and health and relied on charity. It was as if they lived on a different planet to Frederick and his well-dressed and well-educated classmates. The poor were divided not only from the rich and middle class but also from each other.

Because of the history of Ireland, Protestant/Unionists and Catholic/Nationalists lived apart from each other, a division especially sharp among the poor. A Catholic/Nationalist farm worker and his family who went to Belfast in search of a factory job would move into a poor Catholic neighbourhood – while a Protestant/Unionist worker from the same town would move into a Protestant district. It was a sectarian division that led to regular and often fatal conflict and has continued until the present day. The Catholics were descendants of the original descendants of the island of Ireland. The Protestants were descendants of the settlers from the seventeenth century, mainly from Scotland. They were part of a colonisation organised by the government to stabilise a country that regularly rebelled against British rule. The government confiscated half a million acres from native Irish chieftains and distributed them to the new settlers, both Presbyterian and Anglican.

This colonisation was concentrated in the North, the area of Ireland that had been the most resistant to British rule during the previous century. The new settlers were required to be Protestant and English-speaking; the native Irish spoke their own language, Gaelic, and were Catholic. This division, between descendants of these Protestant settlers and those of the native Irish Catholics, has determined Ireland's politics ever since. The first group wished and wish to remain part of the United Kingdom of England, Scotland, Wales and Northern Ireland, while the second wished to set up an independent state. They partially achieved this in 1922, but the six of Ireland's thirty-two counties in the Northeast voted to remain within the United Kingdom as Northern Ireland. Belfast became the capital of Northern Ireland.

Frederick went to a local primary school and, in September 1884, to the Royal Belfast Academical Institution, a grammar school established in 1814 and one of the best known secondary schools in the north of Ireland. It had been set up by wealthy city merchants and professionals who wanted a "complete, uniform and extensive system of education". It offered a wide curriculum, including Classics, Science, Mathematics and foreign languages and excellent facilities for sports, including rugby, hockey, cricket and swimming. In Frederick's time, students gained admission through examination; their parents did not need to be rich for them to go. Its curriculum was similar to that of major schools in the British Isles; its graduates were qualified to work all over the country and in Britain's colonies.

During Frederick's time, it had less than 200 students. The school has produced many of the most prominent people in Northern Ireland, including judges, industrialists, soldiers, scholars, sportsmen and Thomas Andrews, architect of the famous *Titanic* and chief designer at the shipyard that built it; he went down on the maiden voyage. It was a school which gave Frederick the knowledge and connections to join the elite of society in Northern Ireland. The school remains on its impressive campus, which he attended, in the city centre; now with 1,000 students, it is preparing to celebrate its 200th anniversary. Frederick was an outstanding student, playing as a three quarter in the school rugby team and becoming head boy. After graduation, he chose to continue his studies at the nearby Queen's University, Belfast, where he graduated with first – class honours in Mental and Moral Science in 1892. The following year he obtained an M.A. in the same subject.

Royal Belfast Academical Institutic

After completing his studies at the university, he decided to become a minister in the Presbyterian Church of Ireland, the institution to which his family belonged and to which he would devote the rest of his life. It was a momentous decision, which would lead to his leaving Ireland four years

later and spending most of his adult life in China, a world away from his family, friends and classmates and the comfort and familiarity of home.

Presbyterian Church of Ireland

The Presbyterian Church was the third largest church in Ireland and the second largest Protestant denomination after the Church of Ireland, part of the worldwide Anglican Communion, which was the official church.

At that time, the Presbyterian Church accounted for 9 per cent of Ireland's population of 5.3 million and the Church of Ireland 12 per cent. The largest church in Ireland was the Roman Catholic Church, which accounted for 77 per cent. The Presbyterian Church was established in the seventeenth century, when thousands of Presbyterians moved from Scotland and settled in the northeast of Ireland.

Presbyterianism is one of the main branches of Protestantism, named after Martin Luther (1483-1546 AD), a German monk who protested against the Roman Catholic Church, which had been the dominant form of Christianity in Europe for one thousand five hundred years from the birth of Jesus. Luther attacked the corruption and malpractices that had become widespread in the Church; he declared that a person could have a direct relation with God and did not have to rely on the Catholic Church as an intermediary. His ideas were developed by a French theologian named John Calvin (1509-1564 AD), who was the founder of Presbyterianism.

"Presbyterian" comes from a Greek word meaning "elder". Calvin established a church that is run by elders – long-standing members – and not controlled by professional clergy who followed the instructions of a single authority in Rome, as is the case with the Catholic Church. So, while the Catholic Church is hierarchical and obedient to the Pope in Rome, the Presbyterian Church is the opposite – locally democratic and participatory. One of Calvin's followers, John Knox, established the Presbyterian Church in Scotland. During the seventeenth century, thousands of Scottish Presbyterians moved to the north of Ireland and the first Presbytery was established there in 1642. "In the Presbyterian Church, everything is openly debated," said the Reverend John Dunlop, 71, a leading figure in the church today and, from 1992 to 1993, its Moderator, the position of principal public representative which a minister holds only for one year. "It is very chaotic, no-one decides anything alone. All is decided by committee. It is hard to get consensus; if there is no agreement, a vote is taken and everyone must follow the decision." Each year, in June, it holds a General Assembly at its Victorian headquarters in Belfast, like the Parliament of the Church, at which all the ministers and representative elders from every congregation come together to debate and take major decisions.

This was the church to which Frederick's family belonged and in which he chose to become a minister. It was a momentous decision. At that time, when membership of the church was substantially higher than it is today and the church was the centre of social and community life, ministers of religion enjoyed a high standing in society. But they had a modest salary – far lower than his classmates from school and university who entered the law, banking, business or civil service. Ministers live in a manse, a house owned by the church in which they have been called to serve by the congregation. Frederick was choosing a life of frugality and self-discipline; devout ministers did not smoke, drink alcohol or dance and ate modestly. He would be judged by higher moral standards than his peers and would be subject to constant scrutiny by his fellow ministers and the congregation he was serving. More than a job, it was a vocation driven by an intense religious faith.

To become a minister, he went to study theology at the Presbyterian Assembly's College, now Union Theological College, a majestic Victorian structure built in 1853 and designed by Charles Lanyon, one of the best-known architects of his day in Ireland; he also designed the main building for the nearby Queen's University. It was the college at which the Presbyterian Church trained and trains its ministers. Frederick was an outstanding student, earning prizes for his

work. After completing his theological studies, he served for a year as the first theological travelling secretary for the Student Christian Movement. In 1900, the Presbyterian Church had 444,000 members.

Missionary work

Go into all the world and proclaim the good news to the whole creation. The one who believes and is baptised will be saved; but the one who does not believe will be condemned. (Mark 16.15-16)

I have been given all authority in heaven and on earth. Go therefore and teach all nations, baptizing them in the name of the Father, of the Son and the Holy Ghost... teach them to observe everything that I have commanded you. I am with you always, even unto the end of the world. (Matthew 28.18-20)

It was this missionary spirit that has driven the Christian church from the day of its foundation. Christianity became the dominant religion in the Roman Empire and then in Europe and, through migration and missionary work, spreaded to the Americas, Africa, Asia and Australia. It now has more than 2 billion members, making it the world's largest religion and accounting for more than 30 per cent of the global population. A major reason for this growth has been the work of Christian churches in sending missionaries to seek new members, at home and abroad. They consider missionary work – preaching and establishing hospitals, schools and colleges – an essential part of their duty to God.

Like other churches, the Presbyterians in Ireland were very conscious of this mission. The Presbyterian Church in which Frederick was raised was set up in 1840 by a union of two branches of the Church. At the first meeting of its General Assembly, it decided to send two missionaries to Gujarat, in Northwest India; this came to be known as the foreign mission. Sending missionaries abroad was expensive. The church at home had to cover all their expenses, such as travel, accommodation, living expenses and their salaries. It also had to pay for the building of churches, hospitals, schools and homes for the missionaries, until such time that they had established a congregation abroad that could support them. This was likely to take several years. The church had limited assets and relied mainly on the generosity of its members to pay the salaries and pensions of its ministers, to maintain its churches and run its operations at home and abroad. Over the next 160 years, its foreign mission regularly ran out of money. It often had to reject those who applied to do missionary work abroad because it did not have the funds to support them; they had to ask churches elsewhere to sponsor them.

The sending of 2 ministers to India was the start of its foreign mission. From 1842, it started to send missionaries to convert the Jews in Damascus, the capital of Syria, and those in Hamburg, Germany. From 1846, it began a Colonial Mission, for migrants in British colonies overseas, countries that later became the British Commonwealth. In 1856, it began the Continental Mission, to help Protestant communities in Europe, especially Italy and Spain, countries which were and are predominantly Roman Catholic. The start of the mission to Manchuria in 1869 was the natural extension of these efforts.

An issue of the *Presbyterian Herald* in March 1971 summarised succinctly the importance of missionary work:

> Mission is such a fundamental and pervasive work of the church... There is no body on Earth today that can offer a hope of preserving the world from self-destruction except the Church. This hope is dependent on the Church being faithful to the Gospel of Reconciliation. So we must insist that the Church has no option but to tell of the healing and redeeming love of God in Christ and continue to witness to Him as Lord to the end of the earth and to the end of the age.

China as new land for missionaries

For Christian churches around the world, China was a natural target. In 1800, it had a population of 345 million, 38 per cent of that of the entire world and more than double the 150 million people who lived in Europe. It was the largest country in the world in terms of population and the biggest outside Christendom. The number of Christians there was negligible – less than 1 million, mostly converted by Catholic missionaries, of whom the first was Matteo Ricci (1522-1619 AD). If Christian churches were to follow Jesus' order to "go into all the world and preach the gospel to every creature", how could they not go to the world's most populous nation?

But no country in the world presented such obstacles to missionary work as China. It had a highly sophisticated civilisation, with a written language, culture and recorded history far longer than that of the "advanced" countries in Europe. In 1800, China had the largest economy in the world, followed by India and France; in 1820, it accounted for 33 per cent of global GDP, more than all the European countries put together. It had a highly centralized government that strictly regulated the movement of its citizens within and without the country. In 1793, Great Britain sent to Beijing a mission led by Lord George Macartney, its first envoy to China, to ask for an embassy there and an easing of restrictions on bilateral trade.

In the eighteenth century, Britain and France were the two most powerful countries in Europe. Macartney brought gifts of the latest European art and technologies which he thought would impress the Qianlong Emperor. The Emperor accepted the gifts, entertained the envoy and his deputy to a banquet and gave many presents to them and the 600 naval officers and men who had brought them. But, in a letter to King George III, he declined the request to send an ambassador. "In the service of the Dynasty, Europeans have been permitted to live in Peking (Beijing) but they are compelled to adopt Chinese dress, are strictly confined to their own quarters and never permitted to return home," he wrote. "Your proposed envoy to my Court could not be allowed freedom of movement and the privilege of corresponding with his own country; so that you would gain nothing by his residence in our midst." On his request for greater freedom over trade, the Emperor wrote: "Your nationals have had full liberty to trade at Canton for many years and have received the greatest consideration at our hands. Why should foreign nations advance this utterly unreasonable request to be represented at my Court? Peking is nearly 2,000 miles from Canton and, at such a distance, what possible control could any British representative exercise?... We possess all things and have no use for your country's manufactures." This encounter symbolized Beijing's view of the outside world: Britain had nothing to offer and had no right to demand improved access – China was a self-sufficient empire that had no need of anything from abroad. How could missionaries work in such a country?

THE BRITISH & CHINESE EMPs:

(POPULATION)

CHINA'S MILLIONS
FOR CHRIST? OR <u>AGAINST</u>?

The world's two biggest empires at the start of the twentieth century, from the *Missionary Herald*.

The first Protestant missionary to try was Robert Morrison, an English Presbyterian minister who arrived in Macau on September 4, 1807. Before leaving Britain, he started an intensive study of written and spoken Chinese. When he arrived, he discovered that Chinese were forbidden to teach their language to foreigners and no-one could remain in China except for the purpose of trade. With difficulty, he eked out a living in Guangzhou and Macau, hiding his Chinese books for fear that someone would report him. In February 1809, he was appointed translator of the East India Company, the most important British trading firm in Guangzhou, for the princely salary of 500 pounds a year. This enabled him to improve his Chinese rapidly and legally; the post gave him a prestige and a measure of protection. He completed an English-Chinese dictionary and the first Chinese translation of the Bible by a Protestant evangelist-two extraordinary achievements, given the conditions of the time and the scarcity of resources he worked with. His aim was a translation into the common language of the time, to make the book accessible to as many people as possible.

When the government found out, it was enraged and published an edict that made it a capital crime to publish Christian books in Chinese. So Morrison had to find a place to print his Bible and to train missionaries; he chose Malacca on the Malay Peninsula, which was under British protection and had a British governor. The East India Company undertook the considerable cost of bringing a printer and printing press from Britain and helped Morrison with the cost of printing a pocket edition of the New Testament. It was this edition which Morrison gave to Chinese in Guangzhou; it was easy for them to hide. In addition to his official duties, he did evangelising work and baptised his first convert on May 1814, seven years after his arrival. The converts he made had to practice their religion in secret. In 1817, he accompanied a British ambassadorial mission to Beijing; the mission failed, as Macartney's had, but it gave Morrison a rare opportunity to visit different urban and rural areas of China. He discovered that, along the entire route, there was not a single missionary station.

Morrison's life showed two things: one was his extraordinary dedication in the face of enormous obstacles; the other was

Robert Morrison's dedication and perseverance were instrumental to the mission's success.

the hostility of the government, which, like the governments of Korea and Japan at that time, regarded missionaries as a greater threat than foreign merchants with whom they allowed to trade. The merchants were useful in facilitating the import and export of Chinese goods and providing access to foreign markets which Chinese firms did not have access to; these merchants were severely limited in what they could do and where they could live. Beijing regarded the missionaries as more dangerous because the doctrine they were preaching challenged the imperial and social order, proclaiming a God who was higher and more powerful than the Emperor and a set of beliefs different to Confucianism; they sought to take from the government the right to set moral standards. Many Chinese people, especially those in the gentry class, supported the official position. They saw the missionaries as a threat to Chinese culture, traditions and way of life, people who were seeking to impose their beliefs on Chinese and would use foreign military power to enforce their will.

The missionaries did not obtain the freedoms they needed to operate until the Convention of Peking in 1860 that brought an end to the Second Opium War. Under this convention, the Qing Dynasty agreed to freedom of religion in China and to full civil rights for Christians, including the right to own property and to evangelise. The Treaty of Tianjin, signed two years before, gave foreigners, including missionaries, the right to travel for the first time in the interior of China. These two treaties laid the legal foundation for the flood of foreign evangelical activity of the following ninety years, including the mission of the Presbyterian Church in Manchuria.

The treaties were a poisoned chalice for the foreign churches. They had gained the right to proselytise only after a war that had forced China to legalise the opium trade, allow greater export of unskilled labour, open more ports to foreign traders and exempt foreign imports from internal transit duties. During the war, British and French troops killed tens of thousands of Chinese, military and civilian, and, on the orders of their commander, looted and destroyed the Yuan Ming Yuan, or Imperial Gardens, in Beijing. In the decisive battle in September 1860, almost 10,000 Chinese soldiers, the elite of the imperial army, were killed when they charged on horseback against British and French soldiers who mowed them down with artillery and rapid-fire guns. This left a bitter legacy. For many Chinese, missionaries had gained entry into their country through military slaughter and the opium trade: "Opium in one hand, the Bible in the other" would be an accusation made against them for decades to come. In the mind of many Chinese, missionaries were associated with the foreign soldiers and opium traders who had made their entry possible. What kind of morality were they preaching when their countrymen poisoned millions of Chinese with opium and forced the country to accept unequal treaties through the use of force?

The famous British missionary in the nineteenth century was James Hudson Taylor (1832-1905 AD) who founded the China Inland Mission in 1865 and spent more than forty years in China. He declared:

> It was formed under a deep sense of China's pressing need and with an earnest desire, constrained by the love of Christ and the hope of His coming, to obey His command to preach the gospel to every creature. Its aim is, by the help of God, to bring the Chinese to a saving knowledge of the love of God in Christ, by means of itinerant and localized work throughout the whole of the interior of China.

This mission brought over one thousand missionaries from Britain, the U.S., New Zealand, Australia and other Western countries; they started 125 schools, converted 18,000 Chinese and set up 300 stations of work with 500 local helpers in eighteen provinces. Taylor was able to preach in Mandarin and the dialects of Chaozhou, Shanghai and Ningpo. He arrived Shanghai in March 1854 and made preaching tours in the city's outskirts; he dressed in Chinese clothing, shaved his forehead and grew a pigtail in order to blend more easily among ordinary people. He spent his life evangelising in China and working abroad to raise support for the China mission. During the Boxer Rebellion of 1900, 58 missionaries of the China Inland Mission were killed, along with 21 of their children. On his eleventh visit to China, he died on June 3, 1905 at his home in Changsha and was buried next to his wife in Zhenjiang, Jiangsu Province. His example inspired many people to follow him as foreign missionaries, to China and other countries. He is regarded one of most influential foreigners to go to China in the nineteenth century. Curiously, he was not a minister, but a lay person; he and his mission were supported by individual Christians and not by denominations.

Presbyterian Mission in Manchuria

The mission of the Presbyterian Church in China began in April 1867 when four ministers organised a conference on "The Friends of a Mission to China". This was part of a renewed interest in worldwide mission emphasised in the eighteenth century. In June 1867, the General Assembly asked the Foreign Mission to consider establishing a mission to China; in 1868, two candidates put their names forward for this, Hugh Waddell, a minister, and Joseph Hunter, a medical doctor. They chose as their base Yingkou in Liaoning Province, Northeast China, where a Scottish Presbyterian minister named William Burns had settled in August 1867; he had first arrived as a missionary in China in 1847. Unfortunately, Burns died on April 4, 1868 at the age of fifty-three. The three northeast provinces of China were known as Manchuria, taking the name from the Manchus, the tribe that established the Qing Dynasty in 1644.

To maintain the racial balance in their homeland, the Manchus banned migration to central and northern Manchuria by the Han, the race that accounts for over 90 per cent of China's population. They knew that, if they did not, the Han would soon outnumber the small number of Manchu and the region would lose its separate identity and language. In 1850, the region had a population of just 3 million, a fraction of that of the whole country. But, in the late 1860s, as the dynasty became increasingly weak, the ban became unenforceable; landless Han farmers began to migrate to the empty areas of Manchuria, mainly from the eastern province of Shandong. The Qing Dynasty realised that both Japan and Russia wished to exploit or even occupy Manchuria, so it encouraged Han emigration; at the same time, growth in population in Shandong, Hebei and other provinces of North China meant that there were thousands of farmers who had no land and were willing to move. The quality of the soil in most of Manchuria was good and the rainfall sufficient. By 1900, the population had grown to 9 million.

From the Presbyterian Church's point of view, Manchuria had much to recommend it. The population was mostly migrants who had been uprooted from their native places. They had lost the ties with their villages and the ancestors buried there; they needed spiritual support and guidance. They were more open to conversion by this "foreign" religion. Another positive factor was that few other Christian missionaries – Catholic or Protestant – had gone there. Dr Lars Peter Laamann, a lecturer in History at the School of Oriental and African Studies at London University and a specialist on the missionary movement in China, remarked:

> It was virgin land... There was infighting and turf battles among the Protestant missionary societies, on the basis of nationality and doctrine. They did not like to share bases. The English societies focused on southern China, after Robert Morrison. The China Inland Mission included many free thinkers and many factions, some of whom fell out with their governments. The Irish and Scottish Presbyterians in Manchuria worked well together with the other missionaries there.

On February 20, 1869, the new missionaries sailed on a ship from Southampton, in the south of England, and arrived in Yingkou on April 29. This was the start of the Presbyterian Church's mission to Manchuria, which then had a population of 8.5 million. On May 3, the two men started learning Chinese, which became a priority. Within a year, Waddell was able to preach in Chinese; by June 1870, he was preaching three or four times a week to groups of 50 to 60 people. In April 1870, Dr Hunter opened his dispensary and, by the end of the month, had treated 667 patients.

Then, on June 21, 1870, an angry mob stormed a Roman Catholic mission in Tianjin, killing 18 foreigners, including 10 nuns and the French consul. France demanded severe punishment; 20 Chinese were executed and the Emperor issued an official apology. In the aftermath, anti-Western feelings ran high throughout China; from July, the two Presbyterian missionaries were forced to suspend their activities for several months. Worse was to follow. During the harsh Manchurian winter, Dr Hunter's wife contracted tuberculosis and died on February 2, 1871, leaving a young son. In early summer of 1871, the health of the Reverend Waddell also deteriorated and he was forced to return to Ireland on medical grounds; he took Dr Hunter's young son back to Ireland. He later worked as a missionary in Cordova, Spain and in Japan, where he lectured at the Imperial University of Japan.

Dr Hunter overcame the death of his wife and continued his two jobs as a doctor and a preacher; by June 1874, he and his two Chinese workers had sold 10,534 Christian books in Yingkou port and the surrounding area. He founded five small schools and gave sermons at a chapel on most afternoons. He found that opium was widespread in the port, and wrote:

> It is affirmed with certainty that 80 per cent of the population are opium smokers... I am told that boys in this place now take the pipe of opium and it is well known that women, as well as men, are opium smokers. In a house very near mine, a mother smokes opium, so do her two sons and a nephew and a niece – mere children they are. Out of a household of eight, only one little girl does not smoke opium.

Sunday, November 11, 1877 was a landmark day for the church in Yingkou – the day the first two Chinese were baptised as Christians through the witness of Presbyterian missionaries. They were a man named Djin Dsoa Young, 28, and his twenty-year-old wife. Djin went on to become an accomplished preacher. The next conversion came in January 1881, when a man named Leo, who worked on a cargo boat in the harbour, was baptised. He then opened a school in his native village, for which he paid the rent. In May, 1882, eight more people were baptised. In the first fifteen years of the mission, the ministers made only 15 conversions, a poor return. Dr Hunter refused to take a holiday in Ireland, as it was his right. But his health began to fail. He was finally convinced that he should return to Ireland to recuperate. He left Yingkou on April 1, 1884 and died on board ship on May 8; he was buried at sea.

Over the next thirteen years before Frederick's arrival in 1897, the Presbyterian mission grew steadily, with the arrival of more ministers and medical doctors, who were regarded as an essential part of the work. It took an important step in 1889, when a missionary named Thomas Fulton and his wife moved to Mukden, the capital of Liaoning Province and the most important city in the region. It is now called Shenyang, the name we will use in this book. It would become the centre of the mission's work for the next sixty years. The first medical missionary opened a centre in Changchun in May 1890. By the end of 1890, the Presbyterian Church had six centres in Manchuria, with 6 missionaries, two of them doctors, 12 local assistants and a total church membership of 76. Between 1890 and 1900, 22 more missionaries arrived from Ireland, 14 men and 8 women; 9 were ministers and seven were doctors, three of them women. The doctors were very effective in attracting people; their good results in treating people who came to see them, especially successful cataract operations, overcame superstition and opposition to Western medicine. The missionaries aimed to build a church, a hospital and a school in each centre which they established, with out-stations which the missionary and local evangelists visited. This was the good news for the church at home, which Frederick followed with great interest.

The bad news was the heavy human cost. Two of the first eight Presbyterian missionaries died of illnesses contracted in Manchuria and a third was forced to leave because of ill health. One lady doctor arrived in December 1896 to join her minister brother in Jilin city but died of dysentery only eight months later. One man arrived in Yingkou in September, 1890, one day after his twenty-sixth birthday. Three months later, after giving two sermons in English, he died there of typhus. Many children of missionaries died in infancy. They also faced threats to their personal safety. On the evening of August 7, 1891, a medical missionary, Dr James Greig, was attacked in a village 24 kilometres from Jilin city. He was dragged from his bed during the night, suspended by his arms and severely beaten by 23 men for over four hours; he was threatened several times with decapitation. The men believed that he was kidnapping children to steal their eyes and hearts for his medicines. They left him unconscious. Another missionary found Greig; he had to return home to Scotland to recuperate for a year.

Another unexpected hazard was the risk of offending the cultural norms of Chinese people. In late 1891, three young missionaries, one man and two women, were forced to resign and return home because local members of the church were deeply offended by their being too familiar with each other. The church at home investigated the case and found that, although the three had done nothing improper by Western standards, they had upset the sensitivities of Chinese people, which permitted no social exchanges between the sexes.

Why did Frederick go?

Back in Belfast, Frederick heard and eagerly digested all the news and information. He understood that working in China involved a significant, possibly fatal, risk to his health and that of a future family, with medical facilities there decades behind what was available at home. At that time the medical care available in Belfast was among the best in Europe. In addition, as in other parts of China, many people in Manchuria opposed the arrival of foreigners, especially missionaries. So he would face not only possible attack and robbery by bandits and criminals but also hostility from those who objected to his presence in China at all. In 1892, about 700 people were beheaded in the city of Jilin alone for robbery.

Despite all these risks, why was Frederick so determined to go? While he was growing up, the enthusiasm for missionary work was growing among religious young people in the Christian nations of Europe and North America. In 1886, a Student Volunteer movement was established in Mount Hermon School in Northfield, Massachusetts in the United States; 100 people volunteered to become missionaries. In subsequent years, several thousand new members signed the following pledge every year: "It is my purpose, if God permit, to become a foreign missionary." The objective of the movement was "the evangelisation of the world in this generation." The Student Volunteers Missionary Union was established in Edinburgh, Scotland in 1891, with students from Belfast in attendance. Frederick shared this fervour: driving it was his deep religious conviction that a minister had the responsibility to spread Christianity around the world.

It was also a reflection of the world that existed in the 1890s. The European powers – Britain, France, Belgium and Germany – controlled colonies all over the globe. The biggest and most powerful of these was the British Empire on which, as the popular saying went, "the sun never set". It was possible for a British person to visit, work and settle in dozens of countries without a visa; a British passport was sufficient. The British government began to issue standard passports in about 1855; it was a simple, single-sheet document, issued solely to British nationals. It was the opposite for a Chinese, who could scarcely imagine a life outside his own village and community, except for the tiny proportion of those who were rich or well educated and joined the civil service or went into business. Even for them, going abroad was almost out of the question, because of restrictions imposed by their own government and the countries which they wished to visit. In the late 19th century, the only Chinese who left the mainland for abroad were labourers recruited for manual work in Southeast Asia, Hawaii or the Americas and a very small number left to study in Hong Kong, Japan, Europe or the United States. As a native of Belfast and citizen of Britain, Frederick had the opportunity to consider a life in many places around the world. This was a privilege enjoyed by people in only a few countries.

During his years at Queen's University and the theological college, Frederick developed this conviction to become a missionary abroad. He was inspired by his own inner calling and the evangelical ferment around him, among the students in his class and those he met and read about from other universities. So it was that, in May 1895, Frederick and four other students at the theological college wrote a letter to the Presbyterian Church's mission board: "Having completed our theological studies, we wish to offer ourselves to the board to serve with the foreign mission on whatever terms the board might decide." The request was referred to the General Assembly, which received it with great enthusiasm. It accepted the offer; it promised to pay them 200 pounds a year for five years, two thirds of the starting salary of a normal missionary. This amount would be enough for a person to live but not to marry and raise a family. After five years, the five would receive the normal salary.

The church decided to send three to India and two to China – Frederick and John Omelvena; the latter would stay there until 1929. The church then had to appeal to its members to raise enough money to support these new recruits. Frederick was fortunate to receive the support of six Presbyterian churches in Londonderry, the second largest city in Northern Ireland; they decided to pool their resources to support him as a missionary in China, because they were impressed with the enthusiasm and dedication of the five young men. Frederick went to thank them in person and asked for signed photographs of them so that, when he was in China, he could remember those who were praying for him. He promised to send them his signed picture. They felt that his mission was their mission; so they were happy to support him. Even today, members of the Presbyterian Church refer proudly to these students as "the famous five". Between them, they spent a total of 169 years in India and China and were models for foreign missionaries.

This is how Frederick himself described the process of how he became a missionary, in *The Quest for God in China*, one of three books he wrote about his life there.

Speaking for myself, it is to the Student Movement, under

God, that I owe the happiness of missionary life. The immediate occasion for signing the declaration (with the four other fellow students) was a remark made in 1893 by the travelling secretary of the Student Volunteer Missionary Union. In reply to the question, "If we volunteer and our church is unable to send us, what are we to do?" he said: "You must find your own way out somehow." That unexpected dart must have been barbed for me. The decisive consideration was this: there being opportunities at home for everyone to hear the Gospel, our Saviour's last command meant that, in my case, I must give a reason for not going abroad. I could think of no valid excuse for staying at home. If that sounds like unwilling surrender, at least I was not disobedient to the heavenly vision.

In other words, he believed that, while people in Ireland had many opportunities to learn about Christianity, those in China did not and he should go there and tell them about it.

He described his feelings of this period in a more poetic way in another one of his books, *The Call of the East*:

Down deep in our hearts, in early youth, we hear the whisper of the immense Unknown. The desire for adventure is in our blood. The mysterious world lies at our feet. Then, over the restless tumult of our life, comes the gentle voice, unmistakable and clear. Jesus calls. No King is listened to so gladly. No commander is obeyed with such devotion. "Stay" is his His command to some. "Go" is His command to others. And, if to us His word is "Go", then with a thrill we follow Him away to the Front, into the thick of the battle of the Kingdom, the highest and happiest service known to man.

Over a hundred years later, Frederick is well remembered by the Presbyterian Church as an outstanding missionary, preacher and model. It considers its mission in Manchuria, from 1869 to 1951, as one of the proudest pages in its history and Frederick as part of that history. The Reverend John Dunlop said that Frederick had a profound sense of vocation and calling. "He could have gone to Australia or Canada. Why go to Faku? In those days, it was a lifetime vocation. You did not come back other than for periodic leave, then known as 'furlough'. He was inspired by the global missionary movement." The first Presbyterian missionary in Yingkou,

William Burns, died only eight months after settling there. "The conditions of life described by the early missionaries were difficult and primitive. Presbyterian missionaries followed him," Dunlop said. "We should evangelise the world. The world belongs to God. We should spread the word."

Frederick's ordination as a minister was delayed for a year, while he served as the first theological travelling secretary of the Student Christian Movement. He was ordained for service in Manchuria by the Belfast Presbytery on August 31, 1897 and left for China a few days later. He had just celebrated his twenty-seventh birthday.

Wife or no wife?

Frederick left for China alone. The salary he would receive for the first five years would be enough to support himself, but not a family. Did he expect to spend the rest of his life as a bachelor? According to the customs of that time, missionaries did not marry Chinese men or women, except in rare cases – such marriages were opposed by the mother churches, which considered that missionaries should keep a distance between themselves and the communities they lived among. They considered the missionary to be a teacher who should be different to his students and sex between the missionary and a Chinese a taboo. This custom was in part to protect the women who played such an important role in the Presbyterian mission in Manchuria; of its 91 missionaries between 1869 and 1951, 48 were women, most of them single. These women lived and worked in cities and towns, many of which had poor law and order; their safety was often at risk. Their status as foreign women and missionaries gave them a level of protection from bandits and robbers.

At that time, Chinese society did not welcome marriage with foreigners either; most marriages were arranged by the parents who regarded them as the union not only of two individuals but of two families and were vital for continuing the family name and lineage. Marriage with a foreigner meant children of mixed blood and a disruption of this lineage. So this social separation suited both the Chinese and the foreign sides. In China at that time, most marriages were arranged by members of the two families. The gentry and the rich kept concubines in addition to their official wives and often had a large number of children. As long as they could support them, this was socially accepted. This class did not want any change to the status quo and the privileges they enjoyed.

The missionaries' attitude toward marriage was similar to that of the wider foreign community in China. While many expatriate businessmen and other residents had Chinese mistresses or girlfriends, they – and their families – chose women from their own countries when it came to the question of marriage. One example was Sir Robert Hart (1835-1911 AD), one of the most respected foreigners to work in China in the nineteenth century. Like Frederick, he was a native of Northern Ireland, a graduate of Queen's University, Belfast and came from a devout Protestant family. From 1863 until 1907, he was Inspector-General of the Chinese Maritime Customs Service; he was credited with modernising the customs system and earned a huge amount of money for the government, which showered him with honours. As a young man in Ningbo and Guangzhou in the 1850s, he kept a Chinese mistress who bore him three children. "It was common practice for unmarried Englishmen resident in China to keep a Chinese girl," he later wrote in a legal deposition. "I did as others did." But, when it became time for him to marry, he chose a woman from a good British family; he paid off the Chinese woman with 3,000 dollars and sent the children to Britain so that they would not embarrass him in Shanghai with their presence.

For a missionary, it was not easy to find a wife. She would have to accept the harsh conditions of his posting, far from her family and friends, in a land where living conditions and medical standards were far lower than those at home; missionary couples usually sent their children home for education, meaning that they would be separated from their parents for much of their childhood. It took a woman of unusual strength and dedication to become the wife of a missionary in a foreign land. Missionaries usually found their partners among members of the same religious community or remained unmarried.

When Frederick left Ireland, he had a long-time girlfriend named Annie Wilson; she would later become his wife. She was the daughter of a prominent Belfast Presbyterian minister, the Reverend Andrew Wilson. From 1883 until 1912, he was the minister of Malone church in one of the city's most prosperous district, and a well-known figure in the Presbyterian Church. He had eleven children, of whom Annie was the fifth and the second daughter. All eleven received a good education; it was a warm, secure family that lived comfortably, if modestly. They lived in the manse, a home of the minister that came with the church; it was a spacious home with grounds, a stable for horses and a fine view of the mountains to the south of the city.

The Reverend Andrew Wilson was a gregarious and popular man. He decided to replace the Malone church with a larger and more modern one; he successfully raised 865 pounds for this in 1898-1899, from members of his congregation and business people in the area. The church he built remains today; it is a majestic grey stone structure whose steeple towers over the neighbourhood. It has stained glass windows in memory of the Reverend Wilson and his wife. It is a strong statement of the faith of the donors and the strength of the Presbyterian Church at the end of the nineteenth century. He also raised money to build a primary school attached to the church.

The Malone church – a symbol of when the Church was at its most influential

In a booklet that the church published to celebrate its centenary, the Reverend Wilson's first daughter, Ada, recalled her childhood life: "Looking back on the early days in Malone, when my father and mother arrived with their big family of young children, we like to recall the overflowing personal generosity and kindness of members of the congregation. The gifts that used to flow into the manse brought joy to a home where means were small and needs many." Her mother developed acute heart trouble and became an invalid for the rest of her life. Ada

described her father as a "generous, kind, gentle and unselfish man. His children can scarcely recall a harsh word spoken by him. His life was a full and happy one. When he passed away (in October 1920), he left behind him a well-equipped church and school, a congregation noted for its generosity and friendly spirit and the loving remembrance of all those who ever knew him."

Of his eleven children, two sons became ministers of the Presbyterian Church, including one who was a missionary to India, where he was awarded the Kaisar-i-Hind medal; India became his adopted home and he remained there until his death in 1959. One son became a Lieutenant-Colonel in the British Army, another a famous artist and cartoonist in Fleet Street and a third went into business in South Africa. So Annie Wilson grew up in a deeply religious family, in which all the children were educated and the idea of missionary work was encouraged. Her father was a strong supporter of the Presbyterian Church's missionary work. Five of her brothers attended the same secondary school in Belfast as Frederick and three the same university; the two who became ministers attended the same theological college. So she and Frederick belonged to the same religious and missionary world; she would have well understood the kind of life he was going to lead in China.

Chapter 2

Manchuria

The Boxer Rebellion and the Plague

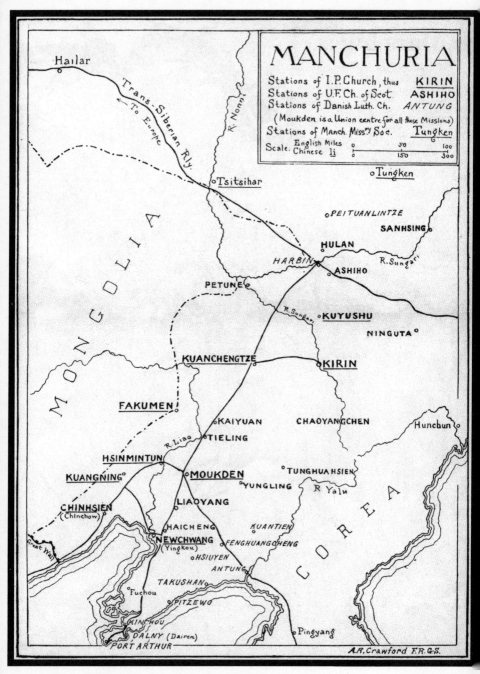

Church map of Manchuria, showing mission stations of Irish, Scottish and Danish churches.

Arrival in Manchuria

In early September 1897, Frederick left England on the passenger boat *Victoria*, which carried him to Colombo, capital of what was then Ceylon and is now Sri Lanka. He described meeting other missionaries, including twelve who belonged to the China Inland Mission, with whom he shared each day a Bible reading and thirty-minute prayer meeting. The voyage was calm until outside the Gulf of Aden, when they were hit by a monsoon and many people were seasick. At Colombo, they transferred to another ship, which took them to Singapore and then to Hong Kong. Just before they reached Hong Kong, they were delayed by a hurricane. "It was so severe that all the life boats were lost, some cabins wrecked and the ship badly damaged," Frederick wrote. "One of the engineers said that it was touch and go. Most of us were very sick. My cabin was at one time several inches deep in water; trunks, boots and collars were floating about merrily."

Since the boat was damaged, they had to switch to a cargo vessel that took them to Shanghai and then another ship for the final leg of the journey to Yingkou. He arrived there on Saturday, October 30; it had been a journey of 11,000 miles and taken two months. He recorded the first impressions of his new home: "The port did not look inviting on a cold, windy day. The roads around the mission house were covered in mud after rain." He stayed in the home of a fellow missionary and, five days later, left with others in four horse-carts for Shenyang. It was a form of transport he would often use in the years ahead in a vast region with few paved roads. "The best part of cart-travelling is walk, of which I did a good deal," he wrote.

The Missionary Herald
Of the Presbyterian Church in Ireland

DECEMBER, 1937   Price One Penny

The Church's monthly magazine on its missionary work.

On November 12, he arrived in Shenyang, where he went to stay in the house of one of the leading Presbyterian missionaries in Manchuria, the Reverend Thomas Fulton, who had arrived there in 1884 and would remain until 1941. For him and for the other missionaries, the first priority was learning Chinese. "It seemed better to start at once on the language, as one is quite helpless along the road or anywhere among the people, looking on quite from the outside," he wrote in one of many reports for the *Missionary Herald*, a monthly magazine published by the Presbyterian Church about its missionary work around the world. Material from magazines is the most important source of material for this book.

Staying in the house of an experienced minister was a good way for Frederick to acclimatise himself to his new country. He had never travelled outside Britain, let alone Europe. Everything was different – the climate, the landscape, the language, the culture, the way of dressing, the etiquette, the food, the way of eating and the organisation of society. To become a successful missionary, he would have to understand all these things. To sell a bicycle, radio or sewing machine, you only have to persuade people of the usefulness of your product; to convert them to your religion, you have to persuade them of the truth of Christianity and change their way of thinking and how they see the world.

Frederick would have to touch them in a profound way that was only possible if he could speak their language. For a young man of twenty-seven dropped into this strange country, this was an enormous challenge, like a person thrown from a boat into a surging ocean. Staying with the Reverend Fulton, he saw at first hand the life that awaited him; he had the support of a man who had been through the same experience.

He read in the church report for 1897 that 1,473 people had been baptised in Manchuria during 1897, taking its total membership to 3,234 by the end of the year. That was a lean return for twenty-eight years of missionary effort – 116 converts a year. But missionaries were patient people; they saw themselves as part of a long-term plan, agents of a project directed by God.

Frederick also read the annual report of the Presbyterian Mission Hospital in Jilin city – 2,711 patients, of whom 536 were women, 78 major and 158 minor operations. Introducing hospitals that provided Western medicine was a very important contribution by the missionaries to China and one of the best ways to reach out to the Chinese. Jilin was one of the oldest cities in northeast China. The Qing government established a fort city there in 1673; it was one of the major cities of Manchuria in the eighteenth and nineteenth centuries and a logical choice for the Presbyterians to set up a missionary station and hospital.

Shenyang was the most modern city in Manchuria and the most comfortable one for foreigners. It was untypical of the region as a whole, one of the most remote and least populated areas of China. It was the native place of the Manchus and the last imperial dynasty known as the Qing. It was in the 1580s that a local chieftain named Nurhaci started to unify the Manchurian tribes; in 1616, he declared himself Emperor and founded what in 1636 became the Qing Dynasty. In 1644, the Manchu armies conquered Beijing, overthrowing the Ming Dynasty and establishing the rule of the Qing over all of China. It would last until the revolution of 1911. During most of this period, the Manchu restricted the migration of Han Chinese to their homeland; they knew that, if they did not, the number of Han would soon outnumber the small number of Manchu and the region would lose its separate identity and language. But, by the late nineteenth century, the government had relaxed this policy and Manchuria empty land and good soil had attracted many Han Chinese migrants.

It has the coldest winter in China, with temperatures as low as minus 30 degrees Celsius in the North, and a hot summer, with a maximum of 31 degrees Celsius in the South. These conditions mean that the ground can be cultivated for only six months during the year. The Manchu and other tribes in the region were nomads who lived off hunting and raised sheep, goats and livestock; the Han Chinese who inhabited the rest of the country were mainly settled farmers who cultivated the same plot of land. By 1850, the population of Manchuria was just 3 million, a fraction of that of the whole country.

The Presbyterian Church came late to missionary work in China. By 1869, other Protestant churches had established missions in the major cities of the East and the South and many provinces in the interior. The Presbyterian Church went to a region that had not been evangelised; Manchuria was remote and far from the main centres of population. It posed special challenges to missionary work. One was that, away from major cities like Shenyang, Dalian, Changchun, Jilin and Harbin, the population was scattered in villages hundreds of kilometers apart. This meant that, like other missionaries, Frederick would spend a great deal of his life travelling across the country to visit different Christian communities. Away from the few railway lines, this meant travel by horse-and mule-cart across earth roads and country paths. Since the carts had no springs and the roads were rutted, not smooth, riding in the cart was very bumpy, so Frederick often walked most of the way, leaving his baggage in the cart. On these long journeys, he and the other missionaries would rise in the early morning while it was still dark, and walk hours before breakfast. It was a severe test of physical as well as spiritual endurance.

Another challenge was that Manchuria was a lawless region. Most of its population were new immigrants who did not have the settled communities and social networks that existed elsewhere in China. The rule of the central government in Beijing was weak; it declined sharply in the last fifty years of the Qing Dynasty. Control passed into the hands of local warlords, bandit gangs and, increasingly, the Russian and Japanese militaries. For example, of the three main railway lines in the region, the Russian controlled one, the Japanese another and only one was controlled by the Chinese authorities. The missionaries had to work with whoever controlled their city or area; it was a time-consuming and sometimes dangerous task. As outsiders, they could be suspected of disloyalty to the ruler and of helping his enemies. The third challenge was the poor quality of medical care; it was non-existent outside a small number of hospitals in the major cities. Diseases that were cured at home took the lives of missionaries and their children.

Frederick stayed in the Reverend Fulton's house in Shenyang for six months until the end of April 1898, when he had to give up his room to a lady missionary who had just arrived; he moved into a Chinese house near the city centre. He was gradually introduced to the work of a minister. In May, he was called to baptise an old man on his death bed; all the mourners were dressed head to toe in white. The following is what he wrote home, after eight months in Manchuria:

> I must say that I am thankful to God for sending me here. I like the country, the people, the language and the work. We younger missionaries are reaping the fruits of the toil and suffering of our honoured predecessors, so much so that it is difficult to imagine what bitter opposition means. The weird-looking face and hat and trousers of the foreigner still excite audible laughter from men who are scantly covered. It has been a blessing to me that the Chinese I have immediately to deal with are trustworthy and likeable.

He wrote that one missionary had cholera and then dysentery and had to leave; another had malaria and there was a constant need for more people from Ireland.

Shenyang, the largest city in Manchuria, was also the centre of the Presbyterian mission to the region. In 1896, it ordained its first Chinese minister, Liu Chuen-yao. In 1898, together with the Scottish Presbyterian Church, with which it worked in Manchuria, it set up a theological college in the city, with a

The theological college in Shenyang

four-year course running from October to April. The aim of this college was to train Chinese ministers; they were essential to the long-term growth of the Church, which could not solely rely on missionaries sent from the other side of the world. This college – without foreign teachers since the 1940s – still exists in Shenyang, in a new building close to its original location, and continues to train ministers for the Protestant Church in the Northeast. During the summer of 1898, the Reverend Fulton told Frederick of the posting where Frederick would spend the next forty years of his life – Faku, a busy market town 100 kilometres northwest of Shenyang, and four areas around it. It was part of the Reverend Fulton's district, which was far too large for one minister to handle. The Reverend Fulton was a mentor to Frederick.

Frederick was responsible for a district of 13,000 square miles with a population of 500,000. It was 48 kilometres or one day's journey by cart from Tieling, the nearest station on the South Manchuria Railway, which ran the length of the region from Harbin in the North to Dalian in the South. Set amid rolling hills, it was an agricultural district whose inhabitants made a modest living from growing millet, fruit, vegetables, grain and timber and raising sheep and cattle. A Presbyterian missionary had established the Faku Protestant Association in 1890; a small number of believers met in a dilapidated room which they rented.

The community developed thanks to an outstanding preacher named Xu Guangming, whose eloquence and good character attracted many people. Frederick's role was to move into the town and develop this community, following the model of missionaries in other parts of Manchuria. In March 1900, he found a house there and paid a mortgage of 30 pounds for two and a half years. Moving to Faku was the real test; he would be living on his own, without ministers around him as in Shenyang. The only other foreigner there was a French priest, a missionary of the Roman Catholic Church. It was a poor and backward town, without paved roads, running water or electricity; it had no street lights, no telephones and not even a post office. Letters to and from home had to be delivered by messengers. The sewage system was primitive. Frederick often found on the streets the bodies of infants – dead or ill – who had been cast out by their families and became food for stray dogs. This custom continued until the Japanese banned it after 1905.

In his first book, *The Call of the East*, which he finished in 1919, he described vividly his feeling of strangeness:

> Our appearances, our clothing and our ways are so very peculiar to Chinese people. But the strangest thing of all is that we should wish to teach the people of the Middle Kingdom. A farmer rode by and saw a missionary teaching: 'The impudence! Coming here pretending to teach us,' he said and rode away. No wonder they are astonished at our impudence. A thousand years before Rome was founded, the Chinese were civilised and prosperous. Five hundred years before Caxton taught Europe the art of printing, they already had printed books. Their great sage Confucius lived five centuries before our Lord came to earth. Naturally, they are surprised at the barbarians from the outer fringes of the world trying to instruct them.

Boxer Rebellion

Frederick had been living in his new house for only three months when posters appeared in several places in Faku saying that, by order of the Emperor, he and other Christians were to be killed and the Protestant and Catholic churches to be burnt on July 8. This was the Boxer Rebellion, the most violent anti-Christian movement in China's history. His first mention of the rebellion was in a letter to his mother on June 26, 1900, telling her not to worry about his safety. "I do not wish to leave my work and the Christians here. My duty lies here at present."

The Boxers, or Society of Righteous and Harmonious Fists, was a secret society founded in the eastern coastal province of Shandong in 1898. Its members were peasants and workers who were angry over drought and widespread opium addiction and wished to rid China of foreigners. They believed that, through martial arts training and other disciplines, they would be invulnerable to the swords and bullets used by foreign soldiers. They believed that foreigners were attempting to destroy China through the promotion of opium, propagation of Christianity and seizure of land and economic privileges.

In 1899, for example, the Roman Catholic Church had obtained from the government official rank for its priests, enabling them to support their converts in legal disputes or family feuds and go over the heads of local officials. The Boxers declared missionaries to be "foreign devils" and their Chinese believers "secondary devils". Initially, the government suppressed the Boxers as a form of rebellion. But, in early 1900, the Empress Dowager changed sides and threw the support of her government and army behind them. They began to attack foreign and missionary compounds across north China. "Take away your missionaries and your opium and you will be welcome," was how one official summarised the government's position.

The most famous battle was the siege of the foreign compound in Beijing from June 20 until August 14, 1900 – 473 foreign civilians, 409 soldiers from eight countries and 3,000 Chinese Christians took refuge in the city's Legation Quarter. The siege was lifted by an international army from eight nations. The foreigners and Christians in the legation were well defended by soldiers – but not those in mission stations around China who had no such protection. The largest massacres occurred in Shanxi Province, where the Boxers killed 5,700 Chinese Catholics and several thousand Protestants. On July 9, 1900, in front of a government building in the capital Taiyuan, they killed 46 foreigners, including 12 priests and nuns and 34 Protestant missionaries and their children. They went from house to house, checking the religious beliefs of the residents and targeting Christians but not those who followed other religions.

The Legation Quarter was the area of Beijing that was home to diplomatic homes and offices. Before 1860, the area had hostels that were built for diplomats from tributary countries like Vietnam, Mongolia, Korea and Burma. After the Second Opium War, it became a district for embassies from Western countries.

The Boxers also came to Manchuria. In June, the missionaries in the south and centre of the region fled to the port of Yingkou, where they had the protection of foreign soldiers; in August, these soldiers repelled several attacks by the Boxers. Reluctant to leave so soon after his arrival, Frederick delayed his departure. He gave the following vivid description of the Boxers in Faku:

> One of the elders of the church was walking along a rural road far from the town when he was challenged by a group of Boxers. One pointed his long sword at the elder's face and then said: 'He has no cross on his forehead.' The Boxers believed that they could see a cross on a person's forehead – meaning that he was a Christian – which others could not.

The man walked through the night and came to Frederick's house. He informed him that the Boxers had set fire to the churches in Shenyang; the Chinese army had used artillery to blow a hole in the wall of the Catholic cathedral. Then they had set it alight, burning to death or shooting the French bishops, priests and nuns and all the Chinese Christians inside. He said that the Boxers would soon be in Faku. "You must leave us," he said. "If you do not go, we Christians cannot scatter but will feel bound to remain here with you. If we do not flee, nothing is left for us but torture and death." Frederick did not want to leave but realised that he had no choice. He did not want to defend the compound with arms. Dressed like a Chinese – in a light blue robe and a coolie hat – he and his cook sadly left his friends. One of them, the most valuable member of the Faku Christian community, Elder Xu Guangming, asked him: "Will you take me with you?" Not knowing what would happen or what to do, Frederick declined; he would never see Xu again.

The two men reached Tieling, the nearest town on the South Manchuria Railway. His cook went to buy something to eat, was arrested and put into prison; since he had not been baptised, his relatives were able to buy him out. Frederick joined a party of Russian engineers and other railway workers led by a Polish engineer; they decided to try to reach Shenyang. Fortunately for the missionaries in Manchuria, the Russian military chose to protect them and other foreigners. The train that the party rode on was blocked and attacked by

Boxers; the Russians put seat cushions against the windows and backed the train to Tieling. From there, with the addition of Catholic women and children, Frederick's party took large carts to escape northwards towards Harbin and the Russian border.

It was a difficult and dangerous journey, taking nine days, at the height of summer, with heavy rains; Boxers lining the hills above the route fired at them. Frederick and the others lay down in the hollows between the rows of ploughed fields. They had to carry the sick and wounded and bury those who died or were shot. Finally, they reached Harbin, from where they took a steamer on the Sungari and Amur rivers and reached Khabarovsk; the government there ordered all the civilians to leave, so they went by train to the far eastern port of Vladivostok, whose Chinese name is "overlord of the East"; they reached there in September and found PCI missionaries who had escaped from Jilin city. They were delighted and astonished to see Frederick; they had received no news from him for two months and feared the worst.

Sanitary conditions in Vladivostok were primitive and the port was crowded with refugees. Before he could arrange his departure, Frederick contracted typhoid fever; he was fortunate to be treated by a missionary doctor, Dr James Greig, who called in an eminent Russian specialist to help. Greig had lost his wife to disease shortly before; he arrived in China in 1889 and worked as a medical missionary in Jilin city until he left China in 1926. Frederick made a good recovery. In a letter on September 2, he wrote that he planned to stay there for about a month and then go to Yingkou. "We have our duty to the native Christians; they may be subject to heavy persecution and great trouble. The sooner we can get near them, the better. Besides, we want to know how our property stands or rather what is left, if any." He reached Yingkou via Japan and Tianjin.

As time passed, Frederick came to realise the extent of the damage the Boxers had done in Manchuria during a six-week reign of terror that ended through intervention by the Russian army. The Boxers killed 332 Chinese Christians in Manchuria but no foreign missionaries: all were given the opportunity to renounce their faith but refused. About one third of the Christians did renounce it and were spared. The Boxers destroyed most mission property – churches, schools, homes and hospitals. There were many atrocities – the Boxers smeared one believer in Changchun with oil and set him alight. In Kuangning, they brought one restaurant owner to the town centre, cut off his arms and legs and then beheaded him. In Shenyang, they killed 20 Christians and raped girl students from the church school; they cut off the ears of an evangelist, gouged out his eyes, cut off his lips and killed him.

When he returned to Faku, Frederick learnt of the death of its most important Christian, Elder Xu Guangming, and his son; it was Xu who had asked Frederick whether he should escape with him and Frederick advised him to stay where he was. Father and son went into hiding in the town but were betrayed by members of the family who wanted to seize their property – which they did.

The Boxers took the two men to the gate of the city for examination. The chief merchants of Faku, who had known and respected Xu for many years for his honesty and integrity, begged for mercy. "No, he is one of the worst Number Two Devils, he must die," said the Boxers. Two men who had been expelled from the local church five years before demanded death. Xu's son offered to die should they set his father free, but the offer was refused. At the side of a river, father and son were bound, knelt and beheaded, in front of Mrs Xu and her other children. All the Christians in the town had fled but local merchants paid for two coffins, so that the two received a decent burial, and hired labourers to sew the heads onto the bleeding bodies, so that they would go to the next world in one piece. This was a terrible blow. "No one was a greater loss to the church than Elder Xu," said Frederick. "A man of piety and learning, he would soon have been one of the leading pastors of the church."

The Reverend Fulton later wrote a long essay in praise of Elder Xu and his thirteen years of work with the mission; he was to be appointed a minister for the western district of Shenyang that autumn.

He has been of untold service to me both as a personal friend and as a missionary. He did far more for me than I ever did for him. In all our sixteen years' experience, he was the only really intimate Chinese friend I have ever had. He was a good preacher... his discourses were racy, full of dramatic power and alive with references to local incidents and apt quotations from ancient records. The whole tone of his life was pure, strong and spiritual.

The Boxers in Faku also sought a blind man named Chang, who had become a very successful preacher . He surrendered to them of his own free will...

In all of China, the Boxers killed 241 foreigners, including 53 Catholic missionaries and 135 Protestant missionaries and 53 of their children; they killed about 23,000 Chinese Christians, of whom 18,000 were Catholic and 5,000 Protestant. In Manchuria, the number of Chinese Christians killed was 332.

The rebellion ended with terrible punishment for China. A foreign army with 55,000 troops from eight countries defeated the Qing troops and the Boxers in battles between Tianjin and Beijing. In revenge, the foreign troops engaged in looting and murder similar to that of the Boxers. According to Chinese accounts, the violence lasted more than three months from the end of July 1900, with foreign soldiers and civilians looting gold, silver and precious items from Beijing palaces, temples and shops and killing and raping Chinese – some women took their own lives to save themselves from this disgrace. In September 1901, the Qing government signed the Boxer Protocol, which ordered the execution of officials linked to the violence and war reparations of 450 million taels of silver, equal to 335 million U.S. dollars, to 11 countries. That was equal to almost two entire years of government income. From 1901 to 1939, China paid, including interest, a total of 669 million taels of silver. One terrible injustice was followed by another.

Despite this terrifying display of anti-foreign anger by some of the Chinese people, it never crossed Frederick's mind to abandon his mission and go back to Ireland or to another country; his life's work was with the Christian community in Manchuria. At the end of January, he went to Changtu, a town controlled by Russian troops; there he wrote to the Chinese general who controlled Faku and received his permission to return. En route, he was met by three horsemen sent by the merchants' guild of Faku and was given an official reception at an inn, where he met the Chinese general who

The church in Kuangning, built in honour of the martyrs of the Boxer Rebellion.

assured him of his protection. He reached Faku on February 5, 1901, seven months after he had been forced to escape. He found that the thatch of the roof of his house and the paper on the ceiling had been removed but otherwise it was habitable. But he found the church and all it contained had been burnt down.

The widow of Elder Xu came to see him to demand justice for those who had killed her husband and son. "How can I live if their blood is not avenged? If the murderers are allowed to go unpunished, how can I be faithful to my dead?" she pleaded, kneeling at his feet. But he refused. "It was heartbreaking to refuse her. It was like spurning the poor widow in her grief." He said that the church did not ask for punishment for any of the murders. "The church would allow nothing that savoured of revenge on the prosecutors. The matter was left in the hands of God. This quality of mercy made an abiding impression on people." This attitude of the church was in stark contrast to that of the western countries from which they had come: no wonder that Chinese were confused – did the West stand for compassion or vengeance imposed by force?

Aftermath of the Boxer Rebellion

The rebellion was a terrible blow to the Manchurian community. It inflicted enormous damage to its churches, schools and other property. The number of members fell from 7,920 in 1899 to 4,000 in 1900, because of those who renounced it, on pain of death. It was not until June 1901 that all the mission stations were operational again. Christians claimed compensation for their losses totalling 250,000 pounds; the church finally settled on 70,000 pounds, to be paid in ten instalments over three years. The church had to decide whether or not to re-admit those who had recanted. Frederick saw the persecution as a test; the believers who remained showed the quality of their faith. "The church of Manchuria, smaller and purer, came out of the furnace with the proud seal of martyrdom upon its brow," he wrote.

There was also the larger question of whether the church had a future in China at all. Did the bitter hostility shown by some Chinese and the government's support of the Boxers mean that the missionaries should pack their bags and go home? What lessons should they learn from this terrible experience?

Given the intense emotions and anti-Chinese feeling common among foreigners at that time, Frederick had a surprising viewpoint: the cause of the uprising was the immoral behaviour of the European powers – Germany, Russia, France and Britain – towards China and their demands for land and economic privileges. "Without a strong army and navy, with no friend except Right on their side, what could the heathen Empire do but submit to the mailed fist of Christian Europe? They were very angry." He said that, unwittingly or not, the Church had become identified with the interests and privileges of the countries from which they had come. "Our followers were regarded as unpatriotic and disaffected citizens for their own private ends, siding with the strangers, whose purpose, though announced to be exhortation to virtue, was not so at all. I cannot say that we Protestant missionaries have done nothing to deserve such a reputation."

He gave examples of where the church had written a letter to a magistrate on behalf of a member who was being wronged. "We have, as it were, put the whole power of England and her gunboats at the disposal of our Chinese fellow-Christians. On the other hand, we have unwittingly given this native friend and all others a mistaken conception of the kingdom of God." He said that the Church must explain to members and potential members that their connections with the Church were not meant to help them in problems with the law or to reduce payments to the authorities. "The strength of our religion lies in weakness, sacrifice, actual loss and the negation of force," he wrote. The church must distance itself from the European powers who had won it the right to evangelise in China and whose greed and privileges had aroused such anger among the Chinese. Only in this way could it show them that it was a Chinese church for Chinese people and not a foreign implant that could not take root in local soil. These were not opinions that were easy to express in the months after the rebellion.

Like the other missionaries, Frederick had to rebuild the community, which the Boxers had nearly destroyed. In 1902, he founded a primary school, to which was later added a middle school. Then he built a church, a hospital and a school for girls, with four classes and seven to eight teachers; the aim was to provide girls with an education equal to that of boys and abolish the centuries-old habit of foot-binding among the Han Chinese. This was a breakthrough in China, where girls were not educated, except those from wealthy families who received private tuition at home; the education of women would prove to be one of the biggest contributions of missionaries to the country.

In 1909, the Faku church built a hospital offering Western medicine, called the Christian Women's Hospital; it employed people who had been trained in Western medicine. This was the model for all Presbyterian mission stations – to have schools and a hospital, as well as a church. All aimed to provide people with services they needed and to bring them into the Christian community. In November 1905, a lady doctor from Belfast who graduated from Glasgow University, named Ida Mitchell, arrived in Faku to become the resident doctor at the hospital.

To spread the Gospel, Frederick had to travel widely. One letter describes a six-week journey in February – the depth of winter – between Jilin city and Shenyang, during which he baptised 102 people. Another missionary, Andrew Weir, described a journey with Frederick on which they stayed in an inn. It was a long room, in which everyone slept on kangs, brick beds with pipes underneath that were heated during

Manchuria Christian College

the freezing winter. Weir said that people crowded around them and asked them questions: "What is your name? Where do you come from? How old are you? Are you married? How much do your clothes cost? After a little conversation, O'Neill often took the opportunity to tell them something of the gospel and got a good many to listen." They went to sleep at about seven or eight o'clock and rose at about two or three the next morning. To make an early start; they travelled for five or six hours before stopping for the first meal, in order to cover the vast distances over poor roads. At that time or even today, few foreigners in China had or wanted to have this kind of close contact with local people; most did not speak the language, were not accustomed to the food, smells and customs and feared for their safety. But, for missionaries, such contact was essential if they were to bring people into the Church.

In November 1902, the church opened in Shenyang the Manchuria Christian College, to teach subjects such as Bible Study, Mathematics, Biology, History, Geography and English. It was opened by the Viceroy of Manchuria, at the head of a procession of dignitaries, while the students wore khaki uniforms. The government provided cheap land, some of it free for twenty years: foreign churches provided the 4,000 pounds to build it. On completing their second year, most students took a year out to teach as volunteers in a mission school. Many graduates went on to the theological college to become ministers. In 1907, the Presbyterian Church ordained its first local minister, named Chen, from Chinchiatun. In 1910, the college moved into an impressive new building in the south of Shenyang. In March 1912, the church opened a medical college, also in Shenyang. These two imposing colleges aimed to provide graduates and doctors for all of Manchuria, especially to work in the church's schools and hospitals.

In addition, the church built YMCAs in Shenyang and Jilin, to reach young people through the teaching of English and Science, sports and other healthy amusements. The building of these institutions showed the rapid development of the mission and a normalisation after the terror of the Boxer years from 1898 to 1901.

Marriage

By 1902, Frederick had completed his first five years in Manchuria and, according to his contract, his salary would increase from 200 to 300 pounds. He felt conditions were ripe and the security situation sufficiently stable to invite his long-time lady friend, Annie Wilson, to come to China to marry him. He first met her when he was seventeen and she was twelve; they had known each other for twelve years. She wrote to him in Faku, urging him to make a decision. He wrote back to her a long letter, saying that missionaries should be celibate and devote themselves to their work. He believed that, as with a Catholic priest, his vocation left no space for family life. Later, however, he reflected on whether he wanted to spend the rest of his life as a bachelor in this cold and forbidding place; he changed his mind and sent Annie a telegram, asking her to come to China to marry him.

In those days, a letter took two to three months to reach Ireland from Manchuria. According to one version of the story that has been circulating within the family, Annie received the letter early one morning and was digesting its contents, when the doorbell sounded again and the postman returned with the telegram, asking her to be Frederick's wife.

At that time a teacher in the Royal School Raphoe in Donegal in the northwest of Ireland, Annie accepted the offer. She came from a deeply religious family; her father was the minister of the Crumlin Road Presbyterian Church in Belfast and one of her brothers was a missionary in India. She herself had applied to work as a missionary abroad but was refused on health grounds. So she understood well the kind of life she was going to have.

She left the family home in Belfast on August 23, 1903 and took a North German Lloyd steamer to Shanghai, where

she and Frederick married in the city's cathedral on October
7. They had a brief honeymoon in Zhejiang, including
Hangzhou, and then took a boat to Manchuria. It met a
gale and was marooned for one day before it took shelter in
Yantai. "As I lay in my bunk, I was taught to count 1 to 300 in
Chinese," she wrote in a letter home.

She spent her first two weeks in Manchuria in the homes of
other missionaries, while Frederick attended meetings. They
finally reached Faku on November 26. His cook had come to
meet them in Shenyang. This is how she described her arrival
in the town where she would spend nearly forty years:

> When we reached the city gate, Fred left the cart and set off
> to light the lamps in the manse. The cook walked beside the
> cart in the dark. No lights visible from the houses – no street
> lamps. And such uneven streets. It seemed hours before we
> turned into a gateway. The Russian stove had been going
> for some days – there was a minimum of furniture. The first
> thing my husband did was to lead me to his study and there
> on the wall was a telegram, with one word 'Coming', dated
> November 26, 1902.

This was her telegram saying that she would accept his offer
of marriage. It had taken 12 months to the day from her
sending the telegram to reach her new home. They had the
weekend together. On Monday morning, Annie found herself
at a table facing a nineteen-year-old teacher from the girls'
school for her first Chinese lesson.

> It lasted three hours and neither of us could understand a
> word the other said! Frederick told me to keep out of the
> kitchen and study Chinese as I was of no use until I learnt
> to speak it. I was supposed to do three hours in the morning
> with my teacher and three hours by myself in the evening.

She was thrown into the deep end at once. Learning Chinese
was one part; another was involvement in the work of the
mission – the school, services at the church and visiting the
members of the congregation. The wife of the minister was an
integral part of the life of a mission, taking part in everything
that her husband did. Annie was surprised to see a curtain

dividing men and women during religious services, something unheard of in Ireland but introduced in Manchuria at the request of local people.

She accompanied Frederick on his tour of out-stations: visiting the small Christian communities, to conduct services, lead the singing of hymns and examine those who wanted to be baptised. Especially during winter, these were gruelling journeys, with long hours of travelling by cart and foot over poor roads and sleeping in large inns or the houses that were used as churches. The two carried with them sheets, curtains, hammers and nails, to make a little privacy for themselves at night in those large public places. She described leaving an inn early one morning: We walked down the rows of sleeping carters and, to my astonishment, saw the heads and the pigtails which hung on the edge of the kang." Foreign women were even rarer than foreign men, so she aroused much interest. "Of course, they were full of curiosity about me – did I make my own boots? Why did I not wear padded clothes? My knitted stockings?

Russo-Japanese war

Manchuria was still recovering from the aftermath of the Boxer Rebellion when it became the scene of another armed conflict – the Russo-Japanese War of 1904-1905, which was fought in neither Russia nor Japan, but on the land and sea of a third country – China. Both Russia and Japan wanted to take advantage of China's weaknesses to exploit the vast region of Manchuria for their own benefit. Since the port of Vladivostok was frozen during the winter, the Russians wanted a port they could use all the year round for military and trading purposes; this was Dalian. In 1898, they leased the port from China and, the next year, began building a new railway from Harbin to Dalian, via Shenyang. Russia was one of the major contributors to the international army that occupied Beijing in 1900 and, in the aftermath of the Boxer Rebellion, had 177,000 soldiers in Manchuria.

For its part, Japan wanted to maintain control over Korea and limit Russian influence in Manchuria. Tokyo and

Moscow held negotiations in 1903 and in early 1904 but could not reach agreement. On February 8, 1904, the Imperial Japanese Navy attacked the Russian Far East Fleet in Dalian. It badly damaged 3 major Russian ships but did not capture the port. The Japanese army then landed in Seoul and occupied the whole of Korea. After more naval engagements, Japan began a long siege of Dalian, which costs thousands of Japanese casualties; on January 2, 1905, the Russian commander surrendered. In January and February, the two sides fought ferocious land battles south of Shenyang; in March, the Russian general decided to withdraw north of the city.

All the capital ships of the Russian Pacific Fleet had been destroyed. So the Tsar sent to the Far East the Baltic Fleet, which sailed 29,000 kilometres round the Cape of Good Hope, with a total of 38 ships. On May 27-28, 1905, the Japanese fleet inflicted a crushing defeat on the Russians in the Battle of Tsushima Strait; the Russians lost 8 battleships and more than 5,000 sailors, while the Japanese lost only 3 torpedo boats and 116 men. It was a historic battle – the first victory by an Asian country against a major European power. Under the Treaty of Portsmouth signed in September that year, Russia agreed to leave Manchuria and recognise Korea as part of the Japanese sphere of influence. During the war, the Japanese lost 15,892 dead and 59,612 wounded and the Russians over 40,000 killed, missing or captured and over 49,000 wounded; such a high death toll shocked the world. It was a precursor to the terrible loss of lives in World War One.

The Russo-Japanese War would have a profound impact on Frederick, although it was not immediately evident to him. Since his arrival in Manchuria, Russia had been its dominant military force; without the help of its soldiers, he probably would not have survived the Boxer Rebellion. After the war, Japan became the dominant foreign power in Manchuria; twenty-six years later, it would annex the entire region and, in 1941, would intern him and the other missionaries and, finally, expel them from China. For the rest of his life in Manchuria, Frederick had to deal on a regular basis with Japanese officials – civil and military, good men and barbarians. The war also devastated areas of Manchuria in which it was fought; scholars estimate the losses at about 69 million taels of silver – about 51 million gold dollars – with 20,000 Chinese killed.

News of the war first appeared in a report written by Frederick to the church in Belfast in July 1904. A party of 20 Cossacks (Russian troops), together with 11 Chinese soldiers from the local garrison, arrived in Faku and went to search for Japanese-led troops. Shortly after, a robber band of 100 armed Mongolian and 170 Chinese men, led by 6 Japanese, arrived. The Russians just succeeded in escaping in time. In November, three Russian officers and a doctor arrived at Frederick's house one Friday evening; they conversed in French – the *lingua franca* of the intellectual class of Europe at that time – and exchanged news of the war. One Russian officer presented Annie with a small revolver. "I was scared to take it in my hand. He said that he carried one, not to shoot anyone but to fire into the air, to frighten away robbers or their kind," she wrote. Sometimes the Russians detained the missionaries, including Frederick, for several days at a time; they were suspicious of these foreigners and wanted to know if they were helping the enemy. In the spring of 1905, after the surrender of Dalian, the Russians left the region and Faku awaited the arrival of the Japanese.

Before the Japanese came, a Chinese magistrate arrived at the house; he spoke some English. He informed Frederick that he had left two wives in South China and now had a third one, aged nineteen and with bound feet. He said that, if the Japanese came, they would cut off his head; could he leave his wife and a heavy wooden box in the house? Frederick agreed and the box was carried by two men and placed in his bedroom; it was full of Mexican silver dollars. The Japanese then came and occupied the wife's house, so she moved to Frederick's house; she stayed for three weeks, playing cards and occupying herself with their son Patrick, who was born in January 1905.

It was during the Sino-Japanese War that Frederick became for two years the county chief of Faku. This improbable situation arose because the elders feared that their town would be devastated by the soldiers of the two armies, neither of whom had any allegiance or loyalty to Faku. So they picked him – a foreigner – to provide a measure of protection; Japanese and Russian soldiers would think twice before attacking a citizen of what was then the world's most powerful empire. In this diplomacy, Frederick was successful.

"Being active on many fronts, he used his status as a British citizen and his personal reputation to save Faku county from misery and affliction," reads a record later published by the official Faku Protestant Association. In the interregnum of several months before the arrival of the Japanese army, Frederick also invited leading citizens of the town to his house, where they established a "Peace and Order Society", which levied taxes and managed the town.

One day in June 1905, Frederick found two Japanese officers at his home; they informed him that 34,000 troops would be stationed in Faku and that they would commandeer houses to live in, including those in the compound of the church's girls' school. Frederick spoke to one of them, named Hirota, using German. He persuaded him to exclude the boys' and girls' schools and their compounds from the homes to be occupied by the soldiers. Annie found them quite different to the Russians.

> They were so correct, how different from the happy-go-lucky Russians. Britain and Japan were on good terms then. If we invited them for a meal, they would arrive punctually and leave when the meal ended. Conversation was difficult. They asked us if we had met any Russians (We heard from outside that Fred was a Russian spy!). If soldiers were billeted in a house or carts and animals hired, money was paid down – this pleased the Chinese.

The Japanese opened a dispensary and treated patients free. Frederick and Annie found a friend in a British officer, Colonel Dye, who was an adviser to the General Maresuke Nogi, the commander who captured Dalian; Dye was an elder in the Presbyterian Church in Tokyo.

> Little groups of soldiers came to see us. They would leave their shoes at the back door and walk quietly through the

house, bowing again and again and thanking us. Frederick would show them things – pictures, photos, anything – for we could not talk, unless someone knew a little Chinese.

After the armistice, General Nogi moved his headquarters to Faku, bringing with him foreign military attaches from Britain, France, Germany, the United States and Turkey. They became friends of Frederick and Annie, playing tennis on the rudimentary court next to the house and visiting for dinners. They also became friends with two American war correspondents and a war photographer. One day, at a banquet, they met General Nogi: "He was very slight, the face of an ascetic, making a speech and reciting one of his poems," Annie wrote. He gave them a name-card to use in case of difficulty. When he returned to Japan, General Nogi gave Frederick a ceremonial sword as a gesture of friendship.

Leave

In January 1906, the time came for Frederick and Annie to return home for a holiday or furlough, the term used by the Church. For him, it would be the first visit to Ireland for more than eight years and, for her, the first since her arrival in China two years and four months before. In those days without Boeings and Airbuses, these journeys were major undertakings, by rail, ship and road, especially with young children; this was one reason why missionaries only took such holidays every seven to eight years. Other reasons were the cost to the Church and a shortage of manpower: during their absence, they passed the responsibility for their respective districts to other missionaries, greatly increasing their workload. In addition, some missionaries chose to remain in their adopted countries and returned home very rarely. Faku and Belfast were at the opposite ends of the earth. Should Frederick and Anne go by train across Russia and Europe? Or across the Pacific Ocean, North America and the Atlantic? Frederick applied to travel home via the Trans-Siberian Railway but the Japanese refused permission; they controlled the southern part of the railway and passenger trains were not running so soon after the war. So Frederick and his family had to go the long sea route via Japan and Canada.

All their trunks and suitcases were covered with official documents in Japanese, which enabled them to pass through all the border controls. It was only due to the help of their friends in the Japanese military that they were able to go home at all. So soon after the war, passenger trains were not running in Manchuria; they would travel on military trains and boats. They set out at the end of January, the height of winter, boarding a train in Tieling en route for Dalian. They took with them Patrick, their first child, who had been born in Faku a year before. The train was freezing cold, with heavy snow falling; they nailed blankets on the side of the carriage and huddled round a charcoal brazier. They arrived at Dalian station early one morning and were met by a large group of Christians and a senior Japanese colonel, a friend of Colonel Dye whom they had known in Faku. The colonel took them by rickshaws to a large government building, where they were given a comfortable bedroom, a hot bath and a banquet with English food and a military band.

Two days later they sailed from Dalian and, on arrival in Japan, had to have a disinfectant bath to protect them from an epidemic which had hit the country. They went to Hiroshima, intending to stay with a young missionary. "When we reached his house, it was still early and a young man opened the door, very slightly," Annie wrote. "I can never forget this. He explained he could not invite us in. His little child had died of diphtheria and he had just returned from the crematorium. We felt so sorry for him." They boarded a vessel in Yokohama and crossed the Pacific to Canada. On arrival, they learnt that some of the Chinese servants on board had caught small pox. All the passengers had to be vaccinated and their luggage and bedding fumigated. On land, they had to stay in a quarantine building. After two weeks, they were allowed to leave. They went by train to Toronto, visited Niagara Falls and went to New York, from where they caught the boat home. They arrived in Ireland in the spring of 1906 and remained at home for the rest of the year. They stayed in Malone Manse, the home of Annie's parents, and with her sister, who lived in a small country town 50 kilometres away. Frederick spent his time fulfilling the responsibility of a missionary: deputation work, explaining what he was doing in China and encouraging support for the Church's missionary work.

They left Ireland early in 1907, spending several weeks in India. Annie had a brother working as a missionary there; India became his adopted home and he would remain there until his death in 1959. In addition, Frederick had a younger brother in the Indian medical service; he visited many mission stations and recorded the differences between them and the work in Manchuria. First, he wrote, the intense heat in India absorbed a good deal of the energy of the British missionaries who were not used to it. Second was the caste system: "The principal cause of difficulty is the social-religious system of the Hindu," he said. This caste system divides people at birth into different classes in which they remain their entire lives. Because of this, Indians who converted to Christianity had to leave their families and native places and move into separate Christian villages. "The missionaries have been compelled to form what amounts to a Christian caste, separate from the world around them." This caste system also greatly restricted social contact; Christians could not go for a meal at the home of a Hindu. In Manchuria, by comparison, the social structure was more flexible. Converts could continue to live in the family home and meet socially whoever they chose.

In May, they reached Shanghai, where Frederick attended a conference of Protestant missionaries, before returning to Manchuria. These conferences were important for missionaries like Frederick who lived in remote towns, largely cut off from the outside world. It enabled them to meet fellow ministers, exchange information, pray and discuss together and encourage each other. By the time he and Annie arrived in Faku, they had been away for sixteen months.

Religious Revival

In 1908 there occurred what the Church called the Great Manchurian Revival. This was an upsurge in religious fervour as a result of preaching, especially by three individuals, a Canadian missionary named Jonathan Goforth and two preachers from Manchuria. The three men went to Pyongyang in Korea to visit the Presbyterian churches there and attend its services. It was the fastest growing Protestant community in Asia; the believers in the city supported a total of 400 preachers. When they returned to Shenyang, Goforth preached at a church on Sundays. He chose to speak in a very emotional way, talking of the evils and sins within the Christian community and calling on members of the congregation to confess their sins openly.

This was unusual in the Chinese context, because Chinese are sensitive to the loss of face. But his audience reacted positively and persuaded him to come to spend six months in the city, which meant leaving the province of Henan in Central China where he was stationed. Frederick said that his sermons had an electrifying effect: one elder got to his feet and told an astonished congregation that he had committed a great sin – perhaps sleeping with another woman – his wife had found out and criticized him often for it.

> "At last I made up my mind to get rid of her," he said. "Three times I mixed poison with her food, each time without effect. All the while I was a member of the church and often preached from that pulpit there." He threw himself upon the ground in a very agony of weeping. Immediately, the whole congregation broke into loud lamentation. Scores of men and women rushed forward to the platform, fell on their knees and made abject confession of sin. There was not a dry eye in the building.

One of the most remarkable conversions was that of an evangelist who was the nephew of the blind Elder Chang beheaded by the Boxers in Faku eight years before. After they had killed him, they threw away their weapons and fled in terror, believing that they had executed a good man. Since then, Chang's nephew had been planning to kill those who murdered his uncle, men who were the leading citizens of his village. At one of the revival meetings, Chang was asked if he had forgiven his enemies. He remained silent; loyalty to his uncle and a sense of justice demanded that he take revenge. Then he was overcome by faith:

> I forgive them. Pray for these men, all of you, that they may be saved. And pray for me that I may be given the victory over myself and them. I shall first write to them and tell them of my forgiveness and hopes and then, at the earliest

opportunity, visit them and plead with them to repent and be saved.

Another man, a doctor of Chinese medicine, became unconscious; when he came round, his face the colour of ashes, he admitted that, before becoming a Christian, he had committed five murders.

For Frederick and the other missionaries, these confessions were evidence that the Holy Spirit had overcome the natural modesty of people and their desire to save face and their public reputation and forced them to say things about themselves that they never wanted others to know. Those who heard these confessions would never look at them in the same way. It was a cleansing of the soul. The revival led to a sharp increase in the membership of the Irish missions; it reached 10,203 in 1910 from 6,443 in 1904 and 4,000 in 1900, in the immediate aftermath of the Boxer Rebellion. It also led to an outpouring of donations to the church, in the form of money, jewellery, silk, ornaments, grain and cattle and time given by people to preach the gospel. The revival helped to fill the new church in Faku, seating 500 people, which officially opened on October 17, 1907. It is still standing today. This is how Frederick poetically described the Revival of 1908: "It was a time of wonder and of joy. The black cloud of sin was swept away and the sun of righteousness shone forth. Depths of sorrow gave place to gladsome songs of praise."

Frederick had become a missionary in part because of his involvement in the global student movement in the 1890s; it had inspired hundreds of young people to become missionaries abroad. In 1913, Dr John Mott, an American who was head of the

From one of Grandfather's books.

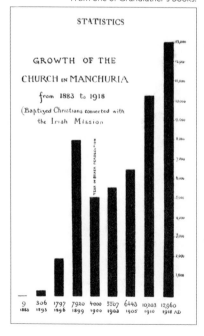

STATISTICS

GROWTH OF THE

CHURCH ɪɴ MANCHURIA

from 1883 to 1918

(Baptized Christians connected with the Irish Mission)

9	306	1797	7920	4000	5507	6443	10203	12960	
1883	1893	1896	1899	1900	1903	1905	1910	1918 AD

Student Movement of the World and one of the most famous evangelists of his day, came from the United States to preach in Shenyang. More than 5,000 people came to hear him; it was the biggest such event ever held in China.

Tragedy in the family

In 1908, the family experienced a terrible tragedy – the death of their first-born son Patrick, at the age of three; he had pneumonia and bronchitis in both lungs and died after a two-day illness – Frederick was three days' journey away. He was buried in the compound of the new church. He had been born there in January 1905, with the aid of two missionary doctors. "We have all been wonderfully upheld but no-one knows what those days and nights were," wrote Dr Isabel Mitchell. "When the little coffin was carried out, the compound was lined with all the Christians. Such a long procession of people walked the road he had raced along a week before on the little dancing feet." The choice of the burial place for Patrick would later become a point of contention with members of Frederick's congregation; some said that a tomb so close to the church defiled it and that he was giving a privilege to his own son that he would not extend to a Chinese.

Their second son, Denis, was born in 1908 and a third, Terence, in 1910. Their fourth son, Dermot, was born in April 1914 but died in Faku of dysentery at the age of sixteen months on August 2, 1915. When he fell ill, his mother was in Shenyang, nursing Frederick who had caught a fever. A telegram was sent to the parents who came back but found their son dying. Their fifth and final son, Desmond – my father – was born on September 12, 1916. Sadly, such deaths were common among children of missionary families – and, of course, the population among which they lived. The level of preventive health and medical care was far below what they would have received at home in Belfast. This was one price they paid for choosing a missionary life in a poor country abroad.

The Plague of 1911

The winter of 1910-1911 saw a human catastrophe that no-one could have imagined – an epidemic of pneumonic plague that killed 60,000 people in Manchuria over a period of four months; it was the most serious epidemic of its kind since the Black Death in Europe in the fourteenth century. The plague came from marmots, a rodent the size of a cat that was hunted for its pelt; some were infected with plague. Local hunters knew how to avoid catching infected animals; but, when the price of a pelt soared from 12 U.S. cents to 72 U.S. cents, thousands of inexperienced hunters came from Central China to Manchuria to trap the animals; they captured ones that were sick and infected. As the deep cold of winter approached, thousands of trappers and migrant farm workers took trains south to spend the Chinese New Year with their families.

The epidemic followed the railways – overcrowded carriages and inns where the workers stayed were perfect breeding grounds to spread the virus. The men died, often a few days after contracting it. Nearly everyone who was infected died from the disease. In some villages, nearly entire populations were killed. The plague brought life in Manchuria to a standstill. Towns and villages barricaded themselves against

The first disinfection station in Harbin, with Dr Wu's laboratory marked on the left with a cross. (credit: Dr Wu Yu-lin)

strangers. In towns, people left their homes as little as possible; if they did, they walked down the deserted streets with a mask covering their mouth. Through fear of contagion, Christian services in churches had to be suspended. Corpses lay in the streets, some in coffins stacked on the ground. Outside the city of Harbin, 2,000 frozen corpses lay unburied because no-one dared to touch them. The epidemic overwhelmed the poorly equipped Manchurian health system; it had no experience of such an epidemic, no medicines to treat it, few trained personnel and no safe way to handle patients or corpses. The risk to doctors and nurses treating patients was extremely high; they had to wear gowns, goggles, gloves and special masks. The Qing government closed the border between Manchuria and the rest of China, in an effort to stop the epidemic spreading.

Faced with this unprecedented emergency and without an organization to deal with it, the government in Beijing sent in December a three-year-old Malaysian Chinese doctor, Wu Lien-teh, a specialist in bacteriology and infectious diseases, to Harbin. A native of Penang, Wu was the first ethnic Chinese to earn a Ph.D. in medicine from Cambridge University. He had moved to China in 1907 as deputy director of a hospital in Tianjin. He set up a research centre in Harbin to find the cause. While others locked themselves up at home, he and his team went to the infected areas. "Everywhere I saw people suffering from a high fever, coughing blood and dying suddenly," he wrote later in his autobiography. "As far as the eye could see, the roads were covered with corpses."

On December 27, he secretly conducted an autopsy on the Japanese wife of a Chinese resident and found the plague bacillus. He concluded that it was spread not from marmots to people but from people to people through coughing and the spreading of fluids and then infected the lung. On January 2, a senior French doctor from a Beijing hospital arrived in Harbin; he wanted to take over management of the epidemic. He did not believe Wu's diagnosis and thought it should be treated like a gland disease. Believing this, he examined 4 infected people without the proper protective equipment; he contracted the plague and died.

This death of a leading western specialist and the mis-diagnosis stunned the authorities and persuaded them to accept Wu's proposals to combat the disease. He quarantined the victims in 120 railway carriages and student dormitories, to prevent them having contact with others, and organised mass cremations of the corpses – despite widespread public opposition to disposing of bodies in this way.

The city of Shenyang also turned to its only source of Western expertise – the Church's medical mission. It appointed a Presbyterian missionary doctor, Dr Dugald Christie, as its honorary medical advisor and implemented his proposals, similar to those of Wu. The best method was to isolate those infected and those suspected of carrying the disease. Shenyang played a critical role; it was the largest city and biggest railway junction in Manchuria. Nearly all the thousands of workers going south passed through its railway station. The first case in Shenyang occurred on January 2, 1911, when a patient arriving from Harbin was found ill on the street. In January 1911, a train carrying nearly 500 passengers was stopped at the Great Wall, on its way to Beijing, and sent back to Shenyang; some had the disease, others did not.

It was imperative that the spread of the infection be controlled at the city's railway station and an area was set aside for this purpose. But who was to examine the travellers and separate the healthy from the sick? Who dared to take on the job which involved putting his or her own life at risk? A missionary doctor named Arthur Jackson, a graduate of Cambridge University who had been in China for only two months, volunteered for the assignment. Wearing a white smock, hood and face-mask soaked with disinfectant, he examined the passengers carefully, mindful of the risk to himself and his

ain in Harbin with patients in quarantine
dit: Dr Wu Yu-lin)

assistants. Despite his efforts, he was unable to save a single patient; all he could do was alleviate their pain. The first week passed safely but, on the tenth day, he contracted a fever and his body temperature rose. A visiting doctor saw on his lips the froth of blood, which meant that he had contracted the disease. He died the next day, January 25; he was just twenty-six. Two students from a medical college in Beijing who were attending the passengers from the train also died. This is how Frederick described Dr Jackson's death:

> Shenyang was stunned. Of all the 46,000 deaths from the plague, no other death made such an impact on the Chinese, near and far. The British Consulate held a memorial service for him at which Xi Liang, the viceroy of Manchuria, gave this remarkable speech: "He went out to help us in our daily fight, where the pest lay thickest. Among the groans of the dying, he struggled to cure the sick and find medicine to slow the evil. Worn out by his efforts, he was seized by the plague who took him long before his time. Our sorrow is beyond measure and our grief too deep for words. O Spirit of Dr Jackson, we pray you to intercede for the 20 million people of Manchuria and ask the Lord of Heaven to take away this pestilence, so that we may once more lay our heads in peace upon our pillows. In life you were brave, now you are an exalted spirit. Noble Spirit, who sacrificed your life for us, help us still and look down in kindness upon us all."

The viceroy of Manchuria sent 10,000 dollars to Jackson's mother as an expression of sympathy; she sent the money to the Shenyang Medical College, where he was to have been a teacher. The college was the idea of Dr Christie, the man whom the city had made its honorary advisor. After arriving in Manchuria in 1881, he set up a large mission hospital in Shenyang, where he gave medical training to his local assistants. In 1909, he proposed a Christian Medical College in Shenyang, to train doctors in Western medicine that the region desperately needed. By the end of 1910, he had raised nearly 5,000 pounds in donations from churches in Scotland and Ireland and 1,380 pounds in China,

Shenyang Medical Co

as well as 3,000 taels from the Viceregal government, which strongly supported the idea. The money given by Jackson's mother went to build the west wing of the college and was named after him.

Jackson was among 297 doctors, nurses, soldiers and police who perished during the prevention effort; the government mobilised nearly 3,000 of them. By March, the methods advocated by Dr Wu and Dr Christie had succeeded in controlling the epidemic.

In April, Wu chaired the International Plague Conference in Shenyang, attended by 33 specialists from eleven countries, over twenty-six days. It was the first international scientific meeting in China, with twenty-four sessions on the nature and course of the epidemic. Wu presented to the delegates his analysis and control methods. It presented forty-five resolutions on its prevention and control of future outbreaks to the Imperial Commissioner.

Like other towns in Manchuria, Faku was paralysed by the epidemic; it had no resident doctor at that time. This was how Frederick described it:

> Faku was placed in quarantine: the streets were almost empty, business nearly at an end, schools closed and a sense of terror pervaded the countryside. Public meetings were stopped. Our women's hospital then had no resident doctor but the young Chinese nurses fought the scourge with all the resources at their disposal.

Among those on the front line was a church elder named Shang, who was assistant chief of the city's Sanitary Board and in charge of fighting the plague. He had the unpopular job of burning and burying dead bodies. The government prepared a rough isolation hospital on the outskirts of the town, to accept patients who had caught the plague; those taken there would not recover, since there was no cure. To stay there meant almost certain death. But who would run this hospital? No-one could be ordered to go and no-one was willing. Officials, doctors and landowners all refused.

Finally, it was Elder Shang who volunteered; he was Fredericks's closest Chinese friend. "There were tears in his eyes as we parted. Was the leader of our Christian congregation leaving me for the last time? For no reward, he went forth readily to offer his life on behalf of his heedless fellow townsmen." Shang was a wealthy farmer with fields outside the town gate. He collected the plague patients and housed them in field shelters on his land, where he fed and cared for them. He remained at the post for the four-month duration of the epidemic. Unlike Jackson, he survived and came back alive in the spring. For Frederick and the other missionaries, Dr Jackson and Elder Shang embodied the highest ideals of the Christian spirit: willing to sacrifice their lives on behalf of their fellow citizens and, by so doing, to serve God. Frederick and his family were fortunate; they survived the epidemic unscathed.

By the early spring of 1911, administrative measures succeeded in controlling the outbreak. These included plague hospitals – like the one in Faku – and quarantine and isolation units: military cordons around and within towns: travel restrictions and cremation of the dead. From this terrible evil came something good. Most important was the recognition, in the government and among the general public, of the importance of Western medicine and the need to train doctors and nurses in it. Practices that had been controversial before, like autopsies, dissection and cremation, became acceptable. This recognition gave a status and prestige to the new medical college and the hospitals which the church had built at its mission stations in Manchuria. Over the next thirty – seven years, before the Communist government took over the medical college in 1948, it trained more than 1,300 Chinese doctors who made great contributions to developing the medical profession in Manchuria. Another positive outcome was the formation of the Manchurian Plague Prevention Service, the first public health service in China.

Wu Lien-teh went on to a distinguished career as a public health doctor in Manchuria and Shanghai before returning to his native Penang after the outbreak of the Sino-Japanese War in 1937. In 1935, he was nominated for the Nobel Prizes in Medicine, the first ethnic Chinese to be put forward for a Nobel Prize.

Manchuria

89

Chapter 3

Death of a Missionary Doctor

(1911-1921)

The end of Imperial China

On October 10, 1911, an uprising by rebel soldiers overthrew the Qing Dynasty, bringing to an end more than two thousand years of imperial rule in China. The revolutionaries proclaimed the Republic of China in the central city of Nanjing, with Sun Yat-sen as Provisional President. The next fifteen years were a period of political instability, with a weak central government and power in the hands of local and regional warlords. For the new government, the most important regions were the major cities from Beijing in the north to Guangzhou in the south, the industrial centre of Shanghai and the provinces with the largest populations and most developed economies. Remote and sparsely populated, Manchuria was not a priority. So the revolution of 1911 changed little for Frederick and the other missionaries – even though Sun himself was a Protestant. The most important change was the disappearance of Qing officials and their replacement by soldiers loyal to a warlord named Zhang Zuolin. He and his son, Zhang Xueliang, would control Manchuria for the next twenty years. The rule of these two warlords, father and son, and the region's isolation from the rest of the country turned out to be a blessing; it largely protected the area from the social and political upheavals that convulsed China over this period and gave ministers like Frederick a freedom and stability to develop their mission.

Zhang Zuolin was born in 1875 in the south of Liaoning Province to a poor family; he had little or no formal education. As a young man, he hunted hares to help feed his family. According to one story, during a hunting trip, he spotted a wounded bandit, killed him and took his horse. By his late twenties, he had formed a small personal army, which served the Japanese as mercenaries in the Russo-Japanese War. When fighting broke out in China in late 1911, he ordered 3,500 of his men to occupy Shenyang. The Republican government appointed a new military commander in Manchuria, but the troops remained loyal to Zhang. In 1915, he ignored orders to move his army elsewhere. By 1918, he had gained control of the whole of Manchuria, after troops in Jilin followed those in Heilongjiang in pledging loyalty to him. So following the establishment of the Republic of China, Zhang and his army became the most powerful force in Manchuria, followed by the Japanese army, which controlled a 560-square-kilometre area in the far south of Liaoning Province around Dalian and the South Manchuria Railway, which ran from Dalian via Shenyang to Harbin; this army controlled land on either side of the railway line and maintained 7,000 to 14,000 troops there.

Hospital

The status of the mission in Faku was greatly improved by the opening in October 1907 and October 1909 of a large church and hospital. The hospital was the brainchild of the town's missionary doctor, Isabel Mitchell. She was born in Belfast in 1879, the daughter of a Presbyterian minister and one of five children; three became missionaries. When she was eighteen, she heard a talk in Belfast by a veteran missionary doctor named James Greig. He had arrived in China in 1889, worked in Jilin city, lost his wife to disease and treated Frederick in Vladivostok after he had escaped from the Boxers. He would leave China in 1926, after thirty-seven years of service. On leave in Belfast, Greig spoke of China's desperate need for women doctors, so she decided to study medicine and become a missionary. At that time, few women in Britain were able to go into this profession. Undeterred, she completed her medical degree at Glasgow University, one of the few universities in Britain to accept women as students of medicine; she graduated there in July 1903.

Because of the Russo-Japanese War, she was unable to travel to Manchuria and went to work at a surgery in Manchester, England. She left for China in October 1905. At her farewell meeting, she told the audience:

I feel you are doing me an honour of which I am utterly unworthy... It is my own earnest prayer that God in His great goodness may use even such an unworthy instrument to help in some small measure in His great plan for the Evangelisation of the World.

She arrived in Shanghai on October 14, 1905 and took the boat for Yingkou. From there, she left in two carts, pulled by two mules. "There was absolutely no road, only deep cart ruts through the ploughed fields," she wrote in a letter to her family. "We stayed in an inn, a big dark place with uneven mud floor and one end piled with millet stalks. We were awoken at 02:15 A.M. and travelled for many hours before it was light. I saw 164 camels." She arrived in Faku on November 12 and became its first Western doctor. It was a daunting assignment for a young woman of twenty-six; in this small and remote town, she had no clinic, assistants, dispensary nor medicines. The only treatment was provided by practitioners of traditional medicines; some were hostile to the arrival to this challenge to their authority. She had to start from zero.

In June 1906, she opened a dispensary in two small attic rooms in the compound of the girls' school. It was soon full of patients who brought many kinds of illnesses, at all hours of the day or night. Once an old woman covered with sores was

Dr Mitchell treating a patient with 3 Chinese dispensers (from left: Miss Shang, Miss Ki, Miss Jang).

brought in on a plank. It was a hot day and the flies swarmed in after her. When Dr Mitchell opened the sores, the stench was unbearable; she wrapped her in ointment and newspapers and then had to hurry away to change her clothes. She trained young Chinese women to work as dispensers. In January 1907, the first operation was performed in the dispensary, by a visiting missionary doctor named Emma Crooks; without chloroform, they used cocaine. Grateful patients gave presents, such as a live sheep, pheasants, fish and eggs.

In May 1907, Dr Mitchell asked the Church for approval to build a woman's hospital in Faku. Her aim was to provide for the first time western medical care to the people of the town and its surrounding area free or at a low cost. Previously, such care was only available in a few large cities, a far distance from Faku; a seriously ill person might die during the journey. Otherwise, the residents had to rely on Chinese medicine and traditional remedies, which were ineffective in treating many serious conditions. The project came to fruition in October 1909, at a cost of 600 pounds, raised from members of the church in Ireland, local merchants and donations from patients and other individuals, in money and in kind. It consisted of two one-storey blocks, one for out-patients and one for 40 in-patients and a large operating room. The walls were covered in Chinese calligraphy and gospel pictures. Its opening, on October 16, 1909, was a milestone in the mission's history; the prefect of Faku, the town's most senior official, and his wife attended the opening, with firecrackers and a local band. When it opened its doors, the hospital was debt-free.

Isabel M. Mitchell

From that day, Dr Mitchell devoted herself to the hospital. It received up to 100 patients a day. Her records for 1916 showed 156 in-patients, 111 major operations and 7,865 treatments. She started each morning at eight o'clock with prayers with her staff and then went over the schedule for the day, including the necessary medical instruction. She trained six Chinese women dispensers, opened a branch dispensary in a nearby town and planned more. She selected a lady student to go to Beijing and train to become a Western doctor; but, in early 1917, the student caught typhoid and died.

In addition, she went to visit patients outside the hospital, either as part of a scheduled visit to a town or village or when called out in an emergency, at any hour of the day or night. This meant a journey by horse cart over rough and dirty roads, sometimes in the snow and driving wind and rain. She would combine these visits with preaching, talking to the patients and their families after the treatment. It was a vocation more than a job; she had no time to herself, except on Sundays, the day of worship. For the missionaries, in Manchuria as elsewhere in the world, this medical service was one of the most important ways to bring their Christian message to the population. People who would not go to a church would seek the help of a doctor if they or their family members fell ill.

Doubt and loneliness

In letters home to her family published after her death, Dr Mitchell left a rare insight into the complex emotions of a young person who left her beloved family at home to work in a poor, dirty town on the other side of the world. Frederick published these letters in a book entitled *Dr Isabel Mitchell of Manchuria*, which came out in 1918. Having just spent six gruelling years to learn medicine and pass the university examinations, she found that she had another mountain to climb – learning Chinese. Without it, she could not practise her profession. She must treat patients on her own after just one year of experience at home, without the aid of colleagues or advanced equipment. She discovered the fierce winter climate of Manchuria: "The winds are howling through the dark night and heaping the snow in great drifts at my window."

Since Faku had no railway or proper roads, a visit to patients outside the dispensary or hospital involved a ride in a horse-

or mule-cart or walking next to it – fine during the warm days of spring or summer but dangerous and uncomfortable during the long winter, snowfalls and rainstorms. A month after her arrival, she went shopping with two foreign lady friends; the strangeness of these "big noses" was too much and a large crowd of men and boys formed to stare at them. They had to fight their way through the crowd: "One could have walked on their heads for the length of the street." Worst was the loneliness. She lived with another young lady missionary, Sara McWilliams, who was often away on long preaching trips in the countryside.

The only other foreigners in Faku were my grandparents and their little son Patrick; but they departed on leave in January 1906 and did not return for sixteen months. Looking after the Christian community in their absence was an Irish missionary based elsewhere who came periodically. Dr Mitchell had no newspapers, radio or television; for news of what was happening in the world outside Faku, she relied on visitors and letters from home. In November 1907, a girl was brought to her with a foot heavily swollen; she had been unable to walk for eight months and had been carried for three days through the snow and the mud. Dr Mitchell decided that she must amputate the foot. "You cannot think what it was like to come home that night to a little lonely house and not be able to say to anyone 'I have to amputate a foot tomorrow.'"

In another letter, she wrote:

> It is dark night and I have been coming home alone under the quiet stars. Perhaps I am lonely. Certainly I am homesick... I am not really lonely as you seem to be afraid, except sometimes, especially when my work does not seem to go on very well and I cannot understand my patients. I think that, if I had stayed at home, I could at least have understood what was wrong. But then the people at home have somebody else to look after them and there are so many here with nobody to look after them... Do you realise that I am quite alone, alone medically I mean? I would be ashamed to tell you how frightened I have been. Sometimes I just clench my hands and wish I could rush away anywhere and leave it all.

Once she described Faku as "the place of squalor and ugliness, of poverty, mud houses and dirt." She was delighted to receive letters from home:

> Never think your letters are too long. Remember your news is all that keeps me in touch with the outside world and the sheets are soon read, though I read them over and over until the next comes.

She was happiest at the opening of the hospital, something she conceived of and brought to fruition; it gave her for the first time an environment in which she could work in conditions approaching those at home. She was very proud of the hospital and the quality of treatment it provided. She also took great pleasure in her missionary work and the children she trained for Sunday school; the religious aspect of life was very important to her. In 1910, she was very excited at the approach of October, where she could take a year's holiday – "the golden year, the year I am to be home".

The letters read like a struggle between her heart and her head. Her heart wants the warmth, companionship and familiarity of her family, her friends – and possibly a husband; her head tells her that her duty was to be in Faku and provide an invaluable, often life-saving service that no-one else could and bring the message of Christianity to people who have never heard it. "Sometimes I think I like it better than anything else in the world; and sometimes I am so tired and things are so hard that I want to go home to the quiet room and the hyacinths." Finally, in October 1910, after five exhausting years, she returned home and the gates of the hospital were shut; there was no doctor to replace her. After her return to Ireland, she fell seriously ill, although doctors could not diagnose the cause. She remained sick throughout 1911. In early 1912 she had an operation in Glasgow and stayed for months in a nursing home. Was part of her trying to protest, to say she did not want to return and preferred a more normal life in Ireland?

Finally, after two years' absence, the doctors approved her return to Manchuria in the autumn of 1912; she took the Trans-Siberian Railway and reached the city of Jinzhou, where she went to work in a mission hospital with another doctor. After she returned to Faku in October 1913, she resumed her gruelling schedule, with close to a hundred patients a day; she badly wanted another doctor. One evening in September 1915, she returned to Faku through a terrible rainstorm in which she nearly drowned. She thought of how Patrick and Dermot, the sons of Frederick and Annie, had died as young children in the town: "I sometimes wish I could leave Faku and the scene of all these disasters. But I know that is weak and I try to be more conscientious in my study and reading, to save more lives and not lose them." In January 1916, she wrote: "My hopes of going home on war service are fading. Ah well, I am needed here." The next month, Frederick and Annie returned to Ireland on leave, taking their two sons with them; Dr Mitchell did not expect to see the boys in Faku again.

In mid-March 1917, she was examining the throat of a lady patient, who coughed in her face. On the afternoon of March 12, she complained of feeling tired and the next morning had a sore throat. The only other qualified doctor in Faku came to see her and said that it was serious. They called the nearest mission doctor from Tieling who gave her two serums of anti-diphtheria. She seemed to be recovering but, while being nursed, her heart stopped beating at 03:00 A.M. on March 23. She had died from diphtheria. Her death shook the whole town; it took from them one of their only two doctors trained in Western medicine. More than 700 people, including hundreds of patients, attended the funeral. A church elder named Shang said in his eulogy:

> Our doctor has given her life for us. For twelve years, she has been at the call of anyone who suffered and rose at any hour of night or day to help us. Her name is known and revered through all this country. Her skill was most wonderful to us. We have lost what no words can express and our sorrows cannot be counted.

On March 28, she was buried near the home of her sister, also a missionary, in Jilin city, in the Russian cemetery, close to the grave of another missionary doctor who died young. Later the citizens of Faku built a memorial to her outside the hospital.

In her last letter to her family, dated February 25, 1917, she wrote:

There are times when it is good to be alive and life is very sweet. And one time is when you come in from three days in an out-station, in a crowded stuffy room and Chinese food and a three days' headache – and here is clean, sweet home and a bath and a bed and a big letter from Mother.

She was called to a branch dispensary 20 miles away to see a woman in great danger.

Mrs Pan and I started at 09:00 P.M., a wonderful journey under the stars. We got in long before cockcrow, probably about 03:00 A.M., but my watch had stopped. By daylight, the mother and little son were both flourishing. Then they fed us with hot rice and pickled cabbage and maybe it was not a tired trio who lay down to sleep at seven o'clock on the kang.

By "trio", she meant herself, Mrs Pan and the mother.

One missionary from Manchuria wrote:

No other brought so much sunshine into our annual gatherings at Shenyang and so much sane, cheerful, quiet, high-toned counsel and inspiration. How they are to carry on at Faku without her I find it difficult to imagine. But they will not be "without her"; she must remain immortal there, inspiring everyone to the highest devotion in service for others and for Christ.

After her death, there was no doctor at the hospital. Frederick's book is extremely moving; it was perhaps an attempt to understand the mystery of how and why such a dedicated person was taken away at the height of her powers, when she had overcome the early obstacles of her mission, mastered Chinese and had the hospital and staff she needed to utilize her skills to the full. He saw her remarkable qualities in medical practice.

Medical College

The missionaries realised early that they could not continue to rely on ministers, teachers and doctors sent from Britain, like Dr Mitchell, and had to localise, to train Chinese people for these roles. So, in Shenyang, they established a theological college to train local ministers in 1899 and an arts college in 1902. It was the same spirit that persuaded them to set up the medical college in Shenyang. The idea was first proposed in autumn 1909 by Dr Dugald Christie, a Scottish Presbyterian medical missionary, who had arrived in Yingkou in the summer of 1882 and went to Shenyang. Since he could find no Chinese willing to rent him a house, he returned to Yingkou, where he spent a year learning Chinese. In 1883, he returned to Shenyang and persuaded someone to rent him a property next to the Wanchuan River.

He opened a clinic which provided free care and was soon looking after many of the city's leading officials and their wives. The introduction of Western medicine aroused fierce opposition, because of ignorance of its benefits and suspicion of what the foreigners were doing with their knives, needles and instruments. But, by 1886, Christie's clinic received 10,000 patient visits and performed 251 operations. In 1885, he started teaching and offering practical instruction to his Chinese assistants. On November 8, 1887, he opened a large hospital, with wards for 50 patients, a dispensary and a house for female patients – the first women's hospital in Manchuria. During the Boxer Rebellion, he and his wife had to flee to Yingkou and Japan and the hospital was burnt down. He returned to Shenyang in 1902 and rented space for a dispensary with room for a few in-patients. During the Russo-Japanese War, he and his colleagues looked after tens of thousands of refugees, spread over seventeen buildings in Shenyang, treating Chinese, Japanese and Russians alike. He raised money for a new hospital that opened on March 5, 1907, with room for 110 in-patients, with funds from Scotland, the Governor of Manchuria, local business people and grateful patients.

With the new hospital working again, Christie turned to the idea of a medical college, which would be the first

in Manchuria to teach medicine in the Chinese language. He returned to Edinburgh to raise funds and recruit doctors. His church at home supported the idea of the college but declined to provide the money. Christie was very successful, raising 5,000 pounds, including 1,000 from the family of a woman whom he had treated in Shenyang fifteen years earlier for a badly broken arm as well as from other individuals and institutions. During the Plague of 1911, he became a household name in Shenyang; for his work fighting the epidemic, he received the Imperial Order of the Precious Star from the Chinese government and the Order of St Michael and St George from the British government.

This work and the death of missionary doctor Arthur Jackson so moved the people of Shenyang that they gave generously, enabling him to complete the college. The plague caused everyone to realise the urgent need for modern medicine and doctors trained to administer it. By the end of 1911, a large block of buildings had been completed next to the mission hospital. The college opened its doors on March 29, 1912 with 50 students out of the 142 candidates who had applied for the entrance examination in thirteen different centres. It was the birth of modern medicine in Manchuria. While English was included as a subject, the medium of teaching was Chinese. Initially, the eight professors were foreigners; but Christie's vision was that Chinese would not only staff and manage the hospital but also control it financially. He wanted to create a Chinese medical profession in Manchuria imbued with the Christian spirit. During World War One (1914-1918), several lecturers had to return home to do military service, leaving a heavy burden on those who remained. Several graduates of the college served with the Chinese Labour Corps in France during World War One. The last section of this chapter contains a detailed description of this corps and the church's involvement with it.

The Biblewoman instructing patients in the waiting room of a hospital.

On June 30, 1917, it held its first graduation ceremony for 20 Chinese doctors. The event was attended by over 200 people, Chinese, western and Japanese. Among them was China's Commissioner for Education who said that he considered the medical college one of the best in the whole country. It was one of several medical colleges in China established by missionary and other organizations, including in Beijing, Changsha, Jinan, Chengdu and Hong Kong. The commissioner said that the government made an annual grant of 3,000 taels to the college and hoped that this might be increased. The ceremony concluded with prayers and the singing of the Chinese national anthem. Dr James Greig, the missionary doctor from Jilin, said that the church's medical work had been utterly inadequate to meet the tremendous needs of Manchuria's millions. "It needs not tens but hundreds of skilled Christian doctors. It was an urgent necessity that led to the establishment of this medical college in 1912. It was with peculiar gratitude that we witnessed the graduates receive their diplomas on that bright June morning."

The college was affiliated with the largest hospital in North China. In 1919, it secured the services of two European nursing sisters. The college also received a donation of 10,000 pounds from Sir Joseph Maclay, a Scottish businessman and public servant who was the British Minister of Shipping between 1916 and 1922. This substantial donation enabled the college to inaugurate the training of nurses, including women. By 1921, the hospital had one hundred forty beds in comfortable, airy and heated wards and 57,000 out-patient visits a year. It had 24 nurses under a British matron, six

Chinese surgeons and physicians and five consulting rooms – medical, surgery, eye, ear, nose and throat and skin diseases. It had an out-patient operating theatre, a dispensary and drug store.

In 1922, it celebrated its tenth anniversary and third graduation ceremony, bringing the total number of graduates to 75. The college had a faculty of 16, of whom 4 were Chinese. Christie insisted that classes be taught in Chinese, while other medical schools in China used English or Japanese. "The foreign physicians have no desire to make these institutions permanently foreign," he wrote in 1913. "We aim to hand them over ultimately to the Chinese themselves." A few weeks after the 10th anniversary, Christie retired with his wife to Scotland, at the age of sixty-eight. In 1926, people from the three provinces of Manchuria unveiled a statue in his honour in front of the gate of the medical college as the founder of the first western hospital in Manchuria; Zhang Xueliang, the son of the ruler of the region, attended the ceremony. Christie died at home in 1936. This was a tribute written to the Christies in 1940 by Dr Lechmore Taylor in a paper to the *Edinburgh Medical Mission Society Quarterly*:

> By their devoted service, inspired by the highest ideals, warmed by the kindliest human feelings and guided by the wisest common sense, they had given a contribution of supreme value to the land and people they loved and gained an affection and respect which it can have fallen to the lot of few to command.

The Manchurian Christian College was another part of this effort to train local people. It was founded shortly after the Boxer rising and was the first institution of higher education in Manchuria to offer a bachelor's degree similar to that available in Britain. Initially, classes were conducted in a disused pawnshop in a southern suburb of Shenyang. Then the church acquired a large site outside the city's western wall; the governor general presided at a ceremony to open a new building, which included classrooms and dormitories. "You ought to be thankful to the churches in Ireland and Scotland for their goodness," he told the students. "The principal has done so much for you that you ought to be grateful."

After World War One, it added a new science block, with classrooms and laboratory, which permitted the teaching of physics, chemistry and biology. By 1924, it had graduated 120 young men, most of whom went to work in the church. Its example helped to persuade the Chinese and Japanese governments to build schools and universities in Manchuria.

The rationale for these institutions was set out in an article in the *Missionary Herald* in November 1924:

> No mission field can be evangelised by foreigners. Without the aid of native evangelists and teachers, no country can be won for Christ. The most vital part of a missionary's task is the training of workers who shall carry the gospel to their own people. All missions have recognised this and the two Presbyterian churches in Manchuria have not lagged behind in this matter.

Some of these local missionaries went to Heilongjiang, the most northerly of the three provinces of Manchuria which borders Russia and where the PCI had no mission station.

This need to train Chinese evangelists was understood by foreign missionaries in as early as the 1840s, with George Smith, the first Anglican bishop of Hong Kong one of the earliest advocates. A member of the Church Missionary Society, he arrived in Hong Kong in September 1844 as one of the first Church of England missionaries to China.

Church

In Faku, the opening of Dr Mitchell's hospital was one landmark in the life of Frederick's mission. Another was the opening of a new church, which could seat 500 people, on October 17, 1907. It was a symbol of the recovery of the church after the Boxer Rebellion and became the centre of Frederick's life and work. It was built of grey adobe brick, with a corrugated iron roof surmounted at one end by a cross. It had an oblong shape, with two entrances, one for women and one for men. The sexes sat separately, on benches with backs. The floor was of wood and the aisles were covered with thick, plaited straw matting. Shoes were made of cloth or felt, so there was a quietness as people walked in and out.

In the early days, men and women were separated by a curtain running the whole length of the church; it would have offended public opinion and social customs for men and women who were not related to sit together. In the early days, too, Communion* service had to be conducted with great discretion and with reliable witnesses from outside as spectators; rumour had it that a human sacrifice was offered up and flesh and blood eaten and drunk. Every Sunday Frederick led the service and preached; he supervised the singing and the Sunday school. His main responsibility was to build up the size of the Protestant community in Faku; like other missionaries, he measured his success by the numbers of people he was able to attract and turn into regular members of that community. At the end of every year, each mission station reported on the growth of its membership during that year.

To help him, Frederick had the services of Sara McWilliams, the lady missionary who shared the house with Dr Mitchell, and Chinese pastors and evangelists. They worked in the main church in Faku and in small communities around it. The town had a population of 30,000 and the region surrounding it 500,000; this was the area for which Frederick was responsible – to use a church term, his diocese. He spent a good deal of time visiting these small communities; because the roads were so poor, this often meant journeys lasting days or weeks by horse-cart. Like most missionaries, Frederick enjoyed walking; so he did almost as much walking as the horse or mule carrying the luggage in the cart. Frederick stayed in the houses of believers or in local inns, rising early in the morning to have time to reach the next village. He welcomed the opportunity to mix with ordinary Chinese and to preach to them. Non-missionary foreigners in China – or wealthy Chinese – would not travel in this way; most foreigners did not speak Chinese and did not want to be close to ordinary people. For them, travelling meant trains and cars and staying in Western hotels with privacy, servants, bathrooms and Western food.

*Communion is a Christian rite, in which believers remember the last supper of Jesus. It involves the giving of consecrated bread and wine or grape juice to the believers in the church. While the Catholic Church teaches that the bread and wine become the body and blood of Christ, the Presbyterian Church see them as symbols for God's spiritual presence.

Elder Teng

Another regular part of Frederick's annual schedule was meeting other ministers, foreign and Chinese, to discuss the developments in the church and plan the future; these meetings were not held in a small town like Faku but in large cities like Shenyang, Yingkou or Jilin. This meant another long journey, by horse cart to Tieling, the nearest town on the South Manchuria Railway, and then by train. In the winter, when temperatures fell below freezing, these journeys had to be carefully planned, with sufficient clothing, food and heating en route and warm places to stay; Frederick also had to plan for contingencies like a snowstorm or a railway breakdown. This frequent travelling called for a strong physical constitution and the need to adapt to different settings, from a high-class Japanese hotel to an inn crowded with dozens of Chinese sleeping on kangs next to each other.

This travelling was typical of the missionaries. In a lecture given on October 21, 1999 to the Presbyterian Historical Society, the Reverend Ivor Smith of the Claggan Presbyterian Church described the journeys of Andrew Weir, who served in Manchuria from 1899 to 1933.

He travelled with a Chinese assistant, as far as and even over the Russian and Korean borders, prospecting the country, journey on foot and by mule cart, over periods of two to three months. The pattern was soon set of preaching and engaging in personal conversation, striking up discussions in inns or market places, making friends and encouraging any who showed interest, dispensing simple medicines, selling Bibles and distributing tracts... On Friday the 10th, he was off with O'Neill (Frederick) by mule cart and foot on a 400-mile journey to Changchun, which took two weeks. Over the next eight years or so, he would travel over 13,000 miles over the rugged countryside by this means.

In one period of eighteen months from 1907, he covered 4,320 miles, with one tour of nearly 900 miles lasting forty-two days, during which he baptised 96 adults and 8 infants.

In his first book, *Call of the East*, Frederick described Chinese members of his congregation. One was a man in his forties named Teng, a former opium addict; one day, he heard an Irish missionary preach in the open air near his shoe shop. He decided that he must quit opium.

> "I am over 40 and my life is a ruin," he said. Giving up opium nearly cost him his life. For three days, lying in excruciating pain, he ate nothing. Then he rose up, weak and worn, but free from the galling chain that had bound him. "When no man cared for my soul, the Gospel came with power and wrought a great change in my life," he said.

He was baptised in 1884 and entered the church in the town of Jinzhou, where he served as an elder for twenty years.

> Many a poor Chinese boy owes whatever education he received to the Elder's gifts, often unknown to others. While still paying attention to his boot shop, he never tired of preaching on the streets and in the villages. His last illness was brought on by over-exerting himself in Christian work. He died in 1916 at the age of seventy-three, with 34 descendants to mourn his loss.

Another lay preacher was Mrs Martha Chang, a teacher at a government girls school in Faku who was very active in training children at the church how to sing. She organised a branch of the World Women's Temperance Union, to encourage people to give up alcohol. With other volunteers, she visited the homes of families to explain the principles of good health. At that time, it was unusual for a woman to take such an initiative. She also tried to persuade her colleagues at school to give up smoking, for reasons for health and cost. "The lives of the women are so empty, empty of interest, of beauty, of love. Their homes are to us so un-homelike," Frederick commented. He said that Chang was the best speaker among the 30 trained preachers and two ordained pastors in Faku. Sadly, she died in 1918 at the age of thirty-four and was buried on a hillside overlooking the town. He also described outstanding Chinese ministers. "It is one of the peculiar privileges of missionary life to come into close contact with the present-day saints of other lands," he said.

The church in Faku had 1,269 believers, with Frederick the only foreign male missionary and 2 foreign female missionaries. It had two ordained Chinese pastors, eighteen out-stations and fourteen Sunday schools. It had 455 pupils in twenty primary schools. At that time, Faku had a town population of 30,000 and a mission district of 5,000 square miles.

Was that a good return on twenty years of missionary endeavour in Faku that had cost the lives of Dr Mitchell and two of Frederick's children? Missionaries took the long view; they saw themselves as instruments in God's plan to evangelise the world, a plan not drawn up in months or years but decades and even centuries. Presbyterian missionaries like Frederick knew full well the dangers of their profession. They and their families knew that they could die during the journey to the foreign land, of diseases they contracted there or at the hands of bandits, opponents or hostile governments. Similarly, families who sent their children to foreign missions knew that they might not see them again. They believed in life after death, that their loved one would leave this earth and go to heaven where they would be united with God. It was God who decided the length of their child's life, long or short. This was in the minds of the family members of Arthur Jackson, Isabel Mitchell and others who died in the field, as they dealt with their loss.

Heresy charge

In the autumn of 1914, Frederick received an unpleasant surprise: a fellow Presbyterian minister at home in Belfast named James Hunter had filed a complaint that an article Frederick had written in a church magazine contained material that was heretical – against church doctrine. This was a very serious accusation; if it were accepted, Frederick would have to resign as a minister and a missionary in

China and return home. The Church considered its doctrine as the basis of its faith in the same way as doctors regard their medical knowledge; should a minister stray from this doctrine, he was no longer qualified to exercise his profession. The Church wanted to avoid Hunter taking the issue through its courts; such a public dispute could greatly damage the reputation of its foreign missions.

Frederick's colleagues praised him as an evangelist but considered him an independent personality who was ready to debate issues and often ignore what was said to him. The Mission Board asked him to draft a careful reply:

> The great cause, in which your interest is just as great as ours, would seriously suffer from any suspicion of heresy in the teaching of the missionaries. The committee (of the foreign missions) is persuaded that they all preach the pure gospel of Jesus Christ, but it appears that some expressions used in your paper have been regarded with grave suspicion by some who have the interests of the Foreign Mission at heart. We believe, however, that your answer will cut away all ground for any suspicion.

Frederick carefully drafted his reply to the accusations and sent them to Belfast. Hunter was not satisfied with his answers but refrained from taking the issue further. At a meeting of the Belfast Presbytery in October 1915, Hunter withdrew his complaint. This was not because he had changed his view but out of sympathy for Frederick over the passing of his fourth son, Dermot, who died on August 2, at the age of sixteen months.

The Reverend William Addley, a Presbyterian minister in Belfast and a historian of the church, said that Frederick liked to challenge people and cause a stir. "He was less circumspect than the average missionary. He had a good analytical mind which made him think about Christianity and culture and what validity there was in Chinese culture. He liked to challenge people to think things through." While other missionaries kept to themselves opinions that would upset people at home, Frederick was willing to express them and risk controversy. "The China experience changed him, as it changed other missionaries," Addley said. "These changes got him into trouble at home. The Foreign Mission Board was embarrassed by Frederick but stood by him." For the missionaries, this support from home was critical; they relied on the home church for their income right until the end, for moral support and the continued opportunity to serve.

Later Hunter continued to attack what he considered deviations from correct doctrine. He criticised individual professors at the church's theological college in Belfast, including Ernest Davey, the Professor of Biblical Criticism, whom he charged with heresy in 1926, in connections with books he had written. Davey was a brilliant scholar and speaker; he defended his position in front of his fellow ministers and persuaded them by a large majority to acquit him of the charges. This decision persuaded Hunter and his associates to leave the church and set up a rival one, which they called the Evangelical Presbyterian Church. The fact that Hunter was able to bring these charges is evidence of the democratic nature of the Church; each minister has an equal status and the right to speak out. It was this church organisation which the missionaries were seeking to recreate in Manchuria.

In 1916, Frederick went on leave and was diagnosed as being in poor health. On medical advice, he spent several months living an outdoor life among pinewoods beside a lake in Vancouver Island, British Columbia, in western Canada. The records we have do not say if he went alone or with his family.

Chinese Labour Corps

In 1917, Frederick received an unusual assignment. He was asked to accompany Chinese workers sent to Belgium and France to help the Allied war effort against Germany in World War One. The workers were sent to areas in the north of France and Belgium close to the front line, to support the troops there. The job of Frederick and the other missionaries would be to minister to the workers, console those who were wounded and conduct funerals for the dead; they would look after their spiritual needs. The workers were required because of the terrible losses of manpower by the Allied countries in the war, which led to a severe shortage of male labour; Britain and France recruited workers from their colonies. In 1915, China offered them 300,000 workers for non-combatant duties. Then neutral in the war, it believed that the workers would learn skills useful for the country's modernisation and give it a stronger hand at the negotiating table at the end of the war. The French government was the first to take up the offer. Initially, Britain rejected it but changed its mind because of the enormous losses on the battlefield.

At the request of the British government, missionaries helped to spread the news of the recruitment, offering each worker a three-year contract, free food, clothing and accommodation and a voyage home at the end of his or her service; Britain offered 1 French franc a day – equivalent to 1 British shilling and 4 pence, a third of the amount it paid to a private, the lowest rank in the British army. Part of the money would be given to the worker himself and the rest sent to his family at home. Those employed by the British would be given work to support the troops on the front line, including loading and unloading cargoes, laying railway lines, building huts and aerodromes, digging trenches and filling sandbags, repairing roads, tanks, trucks and motor cycles and maintaining artillery. We do not know if Frederick helped to recruit the workers; it seems unlikely, since they come from provinces other than Liaoning. He did not write down his opinion of the project; as a loyal servant of the church, he followed the instructions he was given and went to France to carry out the mission assigned to him. Annie did not go with him; she is likely to have returned to Ireland during his period in France.

In May 1916, France signed a contract to hire 50,000 labourers and the first group left the port of Tianjin in July 1916; the journey to France took three months. They were accompanied by missionaries and Chinese-speaking officers. The workers came from Tianjin, Shandong, Hebei, Guangdong and Zhejiang and left from the ports of Tianjin, Weihaiwei, Qingdao, Shanghai and Hong Kong. Most were illiterate and believed that they would be able to earn a good salary in Europe which they could bring home; few realised the perils of a three-month journey across the Pacific,

Atlantic and Indian Oceans and a job close to one of the most calamitous wars in human history.

The British government followed the French example and set up what it called the Chinese Labour Corps (CLC). Opposition from trade unions at home was so intense that these workers could not be brought to the British Isles; they would support British and other Allied troops in France and Belgium. Recruiting began in the autumn of 1916. The first transport ship with 1,088 workers left the port of Weihaiwei in Shandong on January 18, 1917. They were considered contract labourers and were subject to military law for discipline. The fastest route was via the Suez Canal and through the Mediterranean. But, on February 17, 1917, a German submarine sank the *Athos*, a French transport ship, 200 nautical miles off the coast of Malta; 543 Chinese workers aboard drowned. This persuaded the British to change the route and carry them across the Pacific, Canada and the Atlantic, a journey of two to three months. The corps also included interpreters recruited in China to accompany the workers; they received a higher level of pay and better quality food than most of the workers.

By the end of 1917, the corps had 54,000 members and, by the armistice on November 11, 1918, nearly 96,000; in addition, 40,000 were working for the French, of whom 10,000 were lent to the Americans. Six months later, 80,000 members of the corps were still at work. After the armistice, they cleared battlefields, levelled shell holes, searched for and unearthed unexploded ammunition, rolled up barbed wire and collected the remains of bodies and buried them in graves they had dug. The corps formed the largest contingent of foreign workers employed by the Allies during the war, outnumbering the Indians, black South Africans, Egyptians and West Indians.

The workers lived in enclosed camps which the British army built behind the front lines, in the French cities of Boulogne, Calais and Dunkirk. The corps headquarters was at Noyelles-sur-Mer in the French region of Picardy and 100 kilometres from the site of the Battle of the Somme, the most devastating engagement of the war, between July and November 1916, in which 1.5 million soldiers from the two sides were killed.

The town also had a hospital and a detention centre for the Chinese workers. The hospital had two thousand beds, making it the largest Chinese hospital in the world. It was well-equipped and staffed by British Mandarin-speaking doctors and nurses, many of them recruited from China. Of the doctors, many were medical missionaries.

It had an isolation wing for those with infectious diseases and an asylum for those who lost their minds under the stress of war. The workers lived in camps guarded by soldiers; they worked ten hours a day, six and a half days a week, except on traditional Chinese holidays. They needed a pass to leave the camps after work and were not allowed to mix socially with Allied soldiers, other foreign workers or French people. They could not use the same toilets as the British soldiers, largely to prevent the spread of trachoma, an eye disease, which was rampant among the Chinese. Outside the camp, they wore a uniform and a cap, to be easily recognizable as civilians and not soldiers. They could write a maximum of two letters a month; like all letters, these were read by military censors, in France and in Weihaiwei. They were under the command of British officers, who worked through Chinese chosen as leaders of each work team. They had two meals a day, prepared by Chinese cooks. A typical company had 500 people, of whom 25 were British officers and the rest Chinese workers.

Overwhelmed by this enormous number of people under their control, the British army asked the Young Men Christian Association (YMCA) to help with the welfare of the workers. Most had not left China before and found themselves thousands of kilometers from home, in camps in a strange land, close to the most terrible war in human history. How did they adjust to this environment? Before they came, did they know what they had signed up for? How could they face sickness, injury and the stress of being bombed?

The YMCA asked churches with missions in China, including the PCI, to provide Putonghua-speaking volunteers; they agreed to send 40. The PCI missionaries worked with the YMCA. They could provide a level of familiarity and intimacy; many saw this as a golden opportunity to spread the Gospel; far from home, friends and family, the workers had few opportunities for relaxation and entertainment in the large huts in which they lived. Gambling was a serious problem, which sometimes led to disputes and even the killing of individuals who could not pay his or her debts. A church service, with singing and a sermon in Mandarin, provided a welcome relief from the monotony of camp life. The YMCA also recruited Chinese Christians studying in the United States to come and help with the welfare of their countrymen in the camps.

Frederick was assigned to the large Chinese general hospital in Noyelles-sur-Mer. There he comforted the sick and dying, wrote letters for them, held services and conducted burials. He also managed a facility of the YMCA which sent men and women to the camps to provide recreation, talks, rest facilities and entertainment, including cinemas; they helped the workers – most of them illiterate – write letters home and post them. In a report published on December 1, 1917, Frederick described holding the first religious meeting for Chinese, at 05:00 P.M. on a Sunday.

> A big hall, with 250 or more in it, closely attending. At times you could almost have heard a pin drop – all eyes and ears. I taught them the first two clauses of the Lord's Prayer, which was chalked on a blackboard... On the platform were two rows of officers in uniform, many of them missionaries, doctors and others. All were delighted with the meeting. This hall can easily be filled from hospital people alone. In the adjoining depot are hundreds more, or thousands, here for a few days and then going on to their locations.

He conducted a funeral for one of the Chinese workers, with a coffin draped in a British flag. He led the procession to the graveyard: "A neat grave and white wooden cross, with name and number painted on; already a long line of crosses not far from this hut, beside a turnip field, where women are working today." In the camps, he met members of the Manchurian church, including three students from the Shenyang Medical College, who were working in the hospital. He and the other missionaries lived together with the workers.

In another dispatch, published on May 1, 1918, he described the camps close to the headquarters of the Tank Corps. The workers were employed in large numbers in the tank workshops:

> Far spread to right and left, the tarred huts and wide workshops of our long camp dotted the road. Overhead a flight of aeroplanes sped away to the north. The steady booming of the distant guns made no impression on the solitary cow gazing mildly up at the stranger in her field... in our hut, in this barbed wire compound, nearly one half of the 23 occupants are Christians. Others wish to join their number (become Christian).

That day he visited another compound:

> At present, it is occupied by a section of the company recently returned from the battle-front. At the beginning of the recent great attack, they had not been not many miles behind one of the hottest centres. Bombs scattered a hundred of them working on the roads. They ran. The company was ordered to retire, leaving their kit behind. Stragglers were picked up. No transport was available. By night and day, they trudged along, sleeping anywhere. The nearest they came to danger was when a shell burst on the road, 50 yards ahead. No-one was hurt. An American camp gave them food. On foot, and later by train, they reached the Chinese depot in a week. A few days of rapid refitting with new clothing and equipment and the refugee company, with not one Chinese missing, was ready again for service. Most of the company is now wood-cutting in our neighbourhood.

They came to hear Frederick preach.

> I praised them for their good behaviour in the battle. They beamed with pleasure. Then, as I talked in a simple way about the true meaning of our religion, about God and Christ and Love, about danger and fear and death and immortality, they listened with rapt attention. It is almost painful to be watched so intently. One could not help feeling that the foundations of their faith and of their life had been ploughed up. By the experience of war, God had broken up their fallow ground. Now is the time and here is the place to sow the seed.

The YMCA provided a valuable service. They organised performances of Beijing Opera, using actors and musicians from among the workers. One show in the open air on Christmas Day enthralled a large crowd for many hours. They organised free theatrical shows – subject to censorship by the British side – musical performances, football games, classes in English and letter-writing and visits to patients in the hospital. Frederick wrote the following in April 1919, just before his return to China:

> When one attempts to consider the results on the visit of 100,000 Chinese to the West, one's impressions are necessarily mixed... It can be confidently said that the YMCA has shown the Chinese the spirit of brotherhood. By means of lectures, cinema, literature and religious addresses, thousands of the strangers have received more instruction than ever before in their lives. The outlook of the travelled peasants and artisans will have been widened and the hold of superstition upon them probably lessened. They will have seen Christianity as active service.

The armistice that ended World War One was signed in a forest in Northern France on November 11, 1918; Frederick was in Noyelles-sur-Mer. France still needed thousands of labourers; the Chinese stayed on to work in factories, hospitals and building sites. Some were sent to the front line, to collect the corpses and clear the battlefields. Compared to those working for the British, those who worked for the French government enjoyed more freedom. They had the same rights as French citizens and were free to go where they wanted after work. An estimated 3,000 settled in France and a small number married local women; the war had killed nearly 2 million French people, most of them men of marriageable age, and led to a great imbalance between the sexes. The Chinese usually met their wives in the factories where the two worked, making machinery, tanks or other weapons. They enjoyed access to French society unavailable to those who worked for the British. The British forbade the labourers under their control to remain in Europe and repatriated all of them. Those who were injured received a wound gratuity, which could be up to twelve months' pay, but no further care after they returned home.

Not all those who went to France returned home. The attack by the German submarine killed 543; in addition, an unknown number died from disease or by throwing themselves into the sea, because they could not endure the heavy waves, overcrowding and cramped conditions. There are two thousand Chinese Labour Corps graves in France and Belgium; they died as a result of tuberculosis, bombs, accidents or were killed by unexploded shells and grenades which they were clearing after the war. Many died from the Spanish Influenza Pandemic, one of the deadliest natural disasters in human history, which killed an estimated 50 million people between March 1918 and June 1920. It killed more than 400,000 people in France. There were four cemeteries specially created for the Chinese dead; the rest were buried in regular military cemeteries. A group of 60 workers stayed behind until late 1920 to carve the names of each victim on his tombstone. It was a tragic end to their lives, so far from home and family, where no-one would come to mourn them.

The corps made an important contribution to the Allied war effort; Chinese labour built the ferry ports of Calais and Boulogne and they were praised for their discipline, hard work and perseverance, in difficult and dangerous conditions. "Their emigration from the shores of Shandong will take its place certainly as one of the most important aspects of the Great European War," said Manico Gull, the British commander of the second group of corps workers, in 1918. All who served were eligible for the British War Medal, five received the Meritorious Service Medal and two the Royal Humane Society Bronze Medal, for bravery. Of the missionaries, three were killed – one aboard the *Athos* trying to save the life of a Chinese worker, another killed by a German shell and the third who died in France of pneumonia.

But, after the war, China did not receive the reward it had hoped for, as recognition for the contribution of its workers. It had also offered soldiers to the Allied side but this was rejected. At the negotiating table, it was not treated as a victorious power. Its priority was recovery of German concessions in Shandong, the province which had provided the largest number of workers. But Article 156 of the Versailles

Wen-Hu medal given to Frederick by Chinese Government in 1920.

Peace Treaty transferred these concessions to Japan rather than to China. Outraged at this provision, the Chinese delegation refused to sign the document; its government signed a separate treaty with Germany in 1921. This transfer to Japan reflected both the military and diplomatic balance of power and also the widespread prejudice against China and Chinese as a second-class nation.

While the majority of the workers returned home in 1919 and 1920, a small number remained in Europe, becoming the nucleus of the Chinese community in France and Belgium. About 3,000 came from Qingtian, outside Wenzhou, Zhejiang Province. One was Ye Qingyuan, a native of Qingtian who volunteered at the end of 1917. "My home village was a poor mountain village, a disaster for heaven and man alike, where you could not make a living," he wrote in his diary. "When Germany surrendered in November 1918, the government gave us a bonus. With my cousin, I opened a restaurant near the Gare de Lyons in Paris. The French were very curious and wanted to sample Chinese food. Within six months, we were run off our feet." By the end of 1920, he had enough money to return home, marry a local girl and return to Paris with three brothers. They opened restaurants and shops that sold groceries and carved stone from Qingtian. In 1985, he retired and returned, finally, to live in his ancestral village.

The most famous one was Zhu Guisheng, who came from Danyang in Jiangsu Province. He arrived in France in 1917, at the age of twenty. After the war, he married a French woman and settled in the northern city of Lens; they had one son and two daughters. During World War Two, he served with distinction in the French army. He died in 2002 in the eastern city of La Rochelle, at the age of one hundred and six, the last surviving Chinese worker from World War One; the city's mayor praised him as a model of integration into French society and the pride of the citizens of La Rochelle.

Frederick and Annie left France in mid-May 1919, travelling by ship to Canada, then by rail across North America and then across the Pacific. He and another Presbyterian missionary in Manchuria, William Cargin, were decorated by the Chinese government with the Order of Wen-Hu[*] for their work with the Chinese Labour Corps. By the time Frederick reached Faku in the autumn of 1919, he had been away for three years; such a long absence was another good reason, if one were needed, to train Chinese ministers and create a strong local organisation.

[*]The Order of Wen-Hu, was awarded by the Chinese government – mostly in February 1920 – to many British officers and civilians who served with the Chinese Labour Corps. In English, it means Order of the Striped Tiger. The Order was issued in five classes, with the first going to someone with the rank of General or Field Marshall. The one Frederick received was of the fifth class, for the rank of Lieutenant or below.

Chapter 4

The Missionary Community Takes Root

(1921-1931)

Growth of the
Presbyterian Church

Manchuria was relatively peaceful during the late 1920s, providing conditions for the Presbyterian Church to grow. Its congregations experienced a revival and a renewed spirit of enthusiasm. Features of this revival were short-term Bible schools and the prominence of Chinese preachers, in contrast to the 1908 revival, in which foreign missionaries had played a major role. In 1924, 10 new missionaries arrived from the Presbyterian Church in Ireland. In 1930, the church recorded over 2,000 baptisms.

As the Presbyterian Church grew, the role of Chinese ministers and lay people increased and the importance of foreign missionaries diminished. China's Protestant church now included many educated in church schools and those who had returned home after studying abroad; some belonged to the country's intellectual and political elite. Sun Yat-sen, the leader of the 1911 Revolution who became National President, had been educated in Hawaii and was a Protestant; so was his successor Chiang Kai-shek, who converted so that he could marry Song Mei-ling. Song and her two sisters were educated in the United States; they were children of a Methodist minister from Hainan in southern China and formed the most powerful political family in the first thirty years of the Chinese Republic. These people, educated and self-confident, wanted to play a full role in the management of the church and would not accept a secondary status.

Frederick described one of this new generation at a Student Conference in Manchester, England which he attended in 1925; it attracted 1,600 young people from all over the world. One of the most popular speakers was T.Z. Koo, Vice Chairman and Oriental Travelling Secretary of the World Student Christian Federation. Educated at St John's College in Shanghai, he had held important positions in the Chinese railways and represented the Chinese National Anti-Opium Association at an International Opium Conference in Geneva. He gave an excellent speech, which was warmly applauded by the audience. In its news report, *The Manchester Guardian* described him as "possessing an extraordinary mastery of English, a keen sense of humour and an earnestness and eloquence which aroused the enthusiasm of his large audience". An artistic scroll hung from the desk at the centre of the platform with the words in Chinese "Knights of the Kingdom", presented by Chinese students. People like Koo were able to operate comfortably and confidently in the foreigners' world.

One factor in this rising self-confidence was the foundation of the Chinese Republic in 1911, which ended two millennia of imperial rule. Millions were inspired by the ideals of the republic, that China finally was becoming a modern nation and taking back its rightful place in the world after a century of decay and humiliation. In 1820, China had produced 29 per cent of global GDP; it was the largest economy in the world. But, after the Industrial Revolution in Europe and North America, China's share of global GDP dropped sharply and the country fell into industrial and military decline. People were inspired by Sun Yat-sen's Three Principles of the People – nationalism, democracy and livelihood. They considered China a sovereign nation, equal to those of Europe and the Americas, and could not accept the unequal treaties signed by the Qing Dynasty that gave preferential treatment to foreign companies and individuals, including missionaries, on their territory. All the political parties in China were united in calling for the abrogation of these treaties. Similarly, Chinese Christians no longer accepted unequal treatment in their churches and demanded an equal role with the missionaries.

As we described earlier, the Presbyterian Church was from the beginning a strong advocate of localisation. "No mission field can be evangelised by foreigners," wrote the Reverend

Professor James Haire, the Church's Foreign Mission Convenor, in 1924. "Without the aid of native evangelists and teachers, no country can be won for Christ. The most vital part of a missionary's task is the training of workers who shall carry the Gospel to their own people." It was for this purpose that the church established the theological college in Shenyang in 1899 and its medical and Christian college there in the following years. It knew that it could not rely on missionaries, doctors and teachers sent from Ireland.

Medical missionaries were a good example. The Church sent no male medical missionaries between 1905 and 1927. In 1926, after thirty-seven years of service, Dr James Greig was compelled by ill-health to resign his position as a doctor in Jilin city and no-one was appointed to take his place. Filling the place of Dr Greig and those like him were graduates of the Shenyang Medical College, set up in 1912. As of 1925, it had 84 students in residence and 12 professors, of whom 2 were Chinese, 2 Danish and 8 British; it had produced 109 Chinese doctors. Of the 34 graduates in 1924, four took up short-term medical/evangelistic work in different parts of Manchuria, before filling permanent posts.

In 1907, the Presbyterian Church of China was formed as a national organisation; the Presbyterian Church in Manchuria joined it. In the summer of 1922, three senior ministers from the Presbyterian Church in Scotland and the Rev Professor James Haire from Ireland visited Manchuria with the purpose of discussing how to accelerate this localisation and devolve more power to the Chinese Presbyterian Church. At the meeting of the Manchurian synod in July that year, Chinese members outnumbered missionaries by more than two to one. As a result of these discussions and after consultations with the mother churches, the Manchurian synod set up a policy committee which became the most important executive organ of the Presbyterian Church. It had 14 Chinese, 4 Irish and 4 Scottish members.

Its remit included controlling and allocating funds, both from China and abroad, general medical policy in the church hospitals, and coordinate educational standards and policy in church schools. Another change gave the synod the power to decide where missionaries should serve; the individual had the right to appeal to his mother church in Ireland or Scotland, which had the final veto. These changes meant a significant transfer of power from the foreign churches to the Chinese one. They reflected the strong belief of the Presbyterians in self-rule and in local congregations running their own affairs. They also reflected the wider changes in China as a whole, that inequalities between Chinese and foreigners in their own land were increasingly intolerable. But it would still be another decade before there was a Chinese member of the staff of the theological college.

In May 1922, 1,000 Christian leaders from all over China met in Shanghai to form a National Christian Council, to coordinate missionary work through the country. The Protestant church at that time totalled 375,000, including 87,332 Presbyterians. One demand of Chinese Protestants was a single church, not one divided into the many denominations of the west. At that time, there were, astonishingly, 140 different Protestant missionary societies working in China; this reflected the many denominations formed on the basis of doctrine and nationality. For Chinese Christians, these differences were baffling and related to issues in Europe and North America which had no relation to them. Spreading the gospel in China was difficult enough, given all the political, cultural and military obstacles; how could the Protestants be so divided among themselves?

They took a major step in this direction in 1927, when sixteen regional churches – mainly Presbyterian and Congregationalist – formed the first General Assembly of the Church of Christ in China; this included about one third of all Protestants in China, of which the Manchurian church was the largest single member. This would be a church without denominational labels and one which was self-supporting and stood on its own two feet. The era of domination by the foreign missionaries was ending.

At its assembly in 1930, the church declared:

> We desire first of all to take the opportunity of expressing
> our deep sense of gratitude to the older churches of the west
> for the help, both spiritual and material, which has been

afforded by them to the work in China. By the sending of splendid men and women as missionaries and by financial aid, they have earned our sincere and lasting gratitude... We believe that the earlier period during which the missionary bore the burden of leadership was a necessary stage in a God-directed process of development. More clearly still do we see that God has now laid on the church the privilege and burdens of leadership and that the missionary still has a service to render in that church and under its direction... We are conscious that our gratitude can best be showed by our definite endeavour to develop as speedily as possible the spirit of stewardship and self-support in the church in China.

With their knowledge, experience and contacts with the outside world, the missionaries still had an important place and the local churches needed some financial help from the mother churches. But a page of history was turning and the missionaries needed to accept their place in the new order.

Faku – new hope

The 1920s were a time of steady growth of the church in Faku, according to Hu Changyu, a Chinese minister in the town, in a written account of its history.

The period from the early 1920s to the late 1930s were the best time of the Protestant church in Faku and the time when it had the most believers. Each time there was a service, there was not an empty seat in the church, with extra seats added during festival days. As the number of believers increased, so did the number of evangelists.

These included Frederick and Annie, three to four lady Irish missionaries, three Chinese ministers and male and female evangelists. In addition, preachers came from outside to speak in Faku. The church had a board of directors, with Frederick as chairman and head of the district. It had jurisdiction over a dozen local churches, which elected directors to the board. The board supervised the spending of money, approving new ministers and allocating evangelists. In 1929, Frederick reported that, to pay the salaries of 8 evangelists, 108 pounds came from the mother church in Ireland and 36 pounds from the areas they administered; 75 per cent of the money still came from abroad. He also recorded a gift of 56 pounds – an astonishing amount at that time – from an elder in Faku to a pastor in Shenyang to relieve famine in the western province of Gansu.

One of the Irish lady missionaries, Mamie Johnston, who lived in Faku and served in Manchuria from 1923 to 1952, described the church:

> Best of all was singing to old Chinese religious music, with excerpts from the Scriptures. There was a small folding organ; as often as not, the singing was led by a bugle or drum keeping the beat. The sermon lasted at least one hour but it did not seem long. The church was not heated, so people came wrapped to the eyes in padded clothing and felt boot and fur-lined hats.

She said that the church combined the festival of Easter, the resurrection of Jesus, with the Chinese festival of Qing Ming, when people go to sweep the tombs of their loved ones. "White flowers were changed to red ones, for life and joy. We went in procession through the streets to the Christian cemetery on the hill; the men and women went around tidying the graves. We mourned our dead too but we rejoiced, gathering around the memorial stone, to sing our Hallelujahs." This was a

Faku Church today

good example of how the church in Manchuria overcame the cultural obstacles it faced.

In April 1926, an Irish missionary doctor returned to the Faku hospital after an absence of nine years, since the death of Isabel Mitchell. In the interim, a Chinese chemist and her colleagues had worked hard in the hospital to meet the needs of the many patients. The new doctor, Rachel Irwin, had spent two years in Beijing learning Chinese and then worked in a hospital in Shenyang. Her arrival was the occasion for a major celebration, attended by the town's chief magistrate, a nephew of Zhang Zuolin, the warlord who ruled Manchuria, and a representative of the city police.

But, as he reviewed his three decades of work, Frederick was sanguine. In a report in September 1927, he gave a sober assessment of his thirty years of missionary work in Faku, which he described, using church language, as his "diocese", with half a million industrious farmers, shopkeepers and artisans, luxuriant grain crops and sandy steppe.

What can the bishop of Fakumen (himself) do with it? Let us confess the humiliating truth. He does very little with it. He places Christian evangelists here and there, as Christian groups arise in different regions. A few years ago the district had 35 such evangelists on its payroll but now only 15, excluding the two pastors. Several small out-stations have no resident evangelist. The reasons for the drop are the loss of income and weeding out of unsuitable men and extreme difficulty of finding the right kind of Christians to take their places. The chapel is, as it was at the beginning, the main feature of our work in the villages. It is a sort of social club, as well as a place of worship. Although chapel-preaching is not so much relied on now as at first, it is still a ready means of delivering our message.

Very few Chinese wish to join the church, to become full members. On the other hand, the barriers are down. Whether deserved or not, we have gained the respect of people in general, high and low. The beggars come to us. The officials do not scorn our friendship. We are looked up by the leaders in education, not indeed because of the efficiency of our schools but rather on account of the enlightenment of our aims. The community seems to be with us. Why can we not win them over? Many of our own older Church members have fallen away. It is a condition not peculiar to this station or district. In one of our out-stations, Chinchiatun, for instance, we have an earnest, devoted, well-educated, wise, self-sacrificing Chinese Pastor, Chen, the first to be ordained in the Irish mission. Yet, apart from his school boys and girls, he can hardly, in numbers, hold his own. May it be that the old mixed motives for entering the Christian church have ceased to draw the crowd, while the purer spiritual attraction is slow in winning its way?

The women's hospital had had no resident doctor after the death of Dr Mitchell. "There remains a hospital, never full: an operating room, seldom in use, a tall grey stone memorial tablet, with a canopy surrounded by a cross and a spiritual influence that is living and abiding." More positive were the boys' and girls' schools and mission houses and a street chapel on one of the best sites in the town, in the centre of the busy traffic.

> There we have also a flourishing Bible and book depot, selling a variety of students' requirements, besides books. We also have a kindergarten, behind the women's hospital, as well as Sunday schools, football and other games for boys and girls. One church evangelist organised an athletic club for local schools, which is becoming increasingly popular. It is one of the links with the community. Another link is a weekly evening meeting in our Reading Room, for addresses and debates, attended chiefly by government teachers.

In November 1929, an electric power plant opened in the town, which lit up the street at night and transformed the shopfronts. At Chinese New Year, the church had one of its most successful evangelistic campaigns – for several days, the church was packed to overflowing, 500 or more of both sexes listening attentively to the gospel message, helped by choral music and scenes from the parables and *Pilgrim's Progress*. But very few of the listeners followed up by joining a Bible class for further instruction.

> The head boy of the boys' school said that he was close to becoming a Christian but his mother opposed it. "I have lost my son. When I die, you will not burn incense of my behalf," she said. So he said he would not ask for baptism.

In a letter in March 1930, Frederick described a visit to a town of Chanyuxian. He took a small bus crowded with people and luggage that was stopped en route by a police roadblock. The officers asked Frederick if he had a gun. "'No and, if I had, I do not know how to use it.' 'Have you any opium?' I explained to him the Christian attitude to the curse of China. When we had settled down in the bus again, one of the guards made a little speech of apology for putting us to this trouble. It was their duty."

Dr Mitchell's memorial

In August 1927, he described a meeting with a forty-year-old Taoist priest who lived in a temple at the top of a mountain and rarely went down to the valley below. He wore the same cloak throughout the year and washed it once a year during the summer, adding the necessary patches. He ate little, all vegetarian. "40 per cent of the priests in my temple lead moral lives," he told Frederick. "The majority go in for gambling and other forms of immorality. Is it not the same in most religious communities, your own, for instance?" Frederick replied that his religion was different. "We are more strict in supervision and can enforce discipline among the ministers. And we have a Saviour who has the power to save and keep us."

In his written account of the history of the Faku church, Minister Hu Changyu expressed a high esteem for Frederick.

> He spoke excellent Chinese and had a good knowledge of Chinese classics, including Confucius and Mencius. By the 1920s, he was respected by the higher levels of society in Faku and well known in the church and outside as a scholar, humble, well-mannered and approachable.

But he blamed Frederick for causing a split in the church in 1930, which led to a rival one being set up in another part of the town.

He had a difference of opinion over doctrine with two preachers, Wang Shangling and Yao Zhihui; both were very popular and attracted full houses whenever they spoke.

In the interests of maintaining the correct doctrine, Frederick used the excuse of lack of funds to dismiss the two preachers. The board of directors held a discussion on the issue and accepted the shortage of funds; but many said that Wang and Yao, who were very popular, should not be the ones to leave. They proposed two other names. In a dictatorial manner, Frederick ordered the two to leave.

Yao went to the nearby city of Tieling but Wang refused to leave Faku.

Frederick then stopped his wages; Wang went to discuss the issue with him and Frederick expelled him from his house impolitely, causing the anger of many members. In August, Wang and his supporters set up a rival church, the Faku Christian Independent Association, in rented rooms; it received the support of the principals of the church's two schools and more than 30 members of Frederick's church left to join it. Wang was the minister.

The congregation in the breakaway church grew to 50-60 members, who in 1934 contributed money to build a courtyard as their new headquarters; two years later, they demolished some of it to build a new church with five rooms. The number of members rose to more than 150 and they set up branches in two outlying districts. After Frederick's return to Ireland in 1942, the Manchurian church held talks with the breakaway members and agreed that they rejoin the mother church. So, while Hu had a high overall regard for Frederick, he blamed him for causing this split.

China at that time was under colonial occupation and the foreigners in China considered themselves first-class citizens. Minister O'Neill considered that God had sent him on a mission and his behaviour over the split was an example of pure arrogance. He used his control to expel the two preachers, Wang Shangling and Yao Zhihui, who enjoyed the trust of the believers. He was extremely impolite to Wang.

He gave a second example of Frederick's arrogance in Frederick's decision to build a large marble tombstone in memory of his deceased son Patrick close to the church and plant flowers around it, "which aroused great dissatisfaction among the church members." Chinese believe that cemeteries bring bad luck and should be built far from buildings used by people; in the West, on the other hand, cemeteries are built around churches. The members of the Faku church believed that the tomb of one even so loved as Patrick should not be located next to the church; Frederick ignored their views.

Sunshine Chen Xianjun is a minister and teacher at the Northeast Theological Seminary, an eight-storey building in downtown Shenyang. It is the successor to the seminary opened in 1898 by Presbyterian missionaries to train Chinese ministers. Minister Chen said that she appreciated the hard work of Frederick and the other missionaries in bringing the gospel to China. I asked what criticisms she would make of them, to which she replied:

> First, they did not always separate religion from politics... They were too close to the colonial power. They would use it to win a case but, in doing so, lost popular support. Second, they controlled the churches, even though they were in a minority, right up to 1949. There were a few independent churches but they lacked money and power. Third, they went for numbers and not quality. As a result, some bad people came in. They did bad things and the church helped, which was bad for its reputation. I want to attract more intellectuals. This was especially the case before the Boxer Rebellion. After it, the church invested in schools and attracted a better quality of people.

She also said that the foreign missionaries had a sense of Western cultural and moral superiority and believed that Chinese beliefs and culture were backward and inferior.

> This still exists among Chinese ministers and believers. They believed that it was improper to have a picture of a dragon in the house, firecrackers at a wedding or two lions at

the door of the church to keep away demons – they felt that they were like Satan. They felt that Christianity was above other religions and did not integrate it well with Chinese traditions and values. Some did not try to understand Chinese culture at a deep level. Protestantism excluded other religions. I believe in Christianity as a universal religion, which includes other religions.

Shenyang Church

One early missionary who practised localisation was John Ross, a Scottish Presbyterian who established the first church in Shenyang and was one of the founders of Protestantism in Manchuria and Korea. He was the only foreign minister of his Shenyang church; since his retirement in 1910, it has had only Chinese ministers, of whom he trained more than 10. He realised early on that local people made the most effective church leaders because of their understanding of local culture and conditions.

He was born in 1842 in Balintore, north of Inverness, in the north of Scotland. A member of the United Presbyterian Church, he trained in Edinburgh and first worked as an itinerant evangelist in the Scottish Highlands for six years. After marrying, he and his wife set sail for Manchuria and arrived in Yingkou in 1872. Shortly after their arrival, his wife gave birth to a son but died in the severe winter cold. "I have not the shadow of a thought of retreating from this position," he said solemnly. He arrived with the objective of preaching the gospel to Korea. But, since that country was closed to foreigners – including missionaries – he studied Chinese; because he aimed to reach the intellectual class, he learnt the works of Confucius, Mencius and other famous scholars. Within five months, he was able to preach his first twenty-minute sermon in Chinese. He settled in Shenyang, the biggest city

Korean Protestant church in Shen[

1913년 설립 ✛ 제93권 제42호 ✛ 2005년 10월 16일
● 하나님 중심 ● 성경 중심 ● 교회 중심

沈阳市基督教 **서 탑 교 회**
Shenyang Xita jiaohui

담임목사: 오 애 은
担任牧师: 吴 爱 恩

주소: 료녕성 심양시 화평구 시부대로 37호
地址: 辽宁省 沈阳市 和平区 市府大路 37号
☎ 23412254(收发室-8000)

in Manchuria, with the aim of establishing a church there. After arriving, he found no-one willing to rent a room to a minister of this "Western religion". Everywhere he asked, he was refused. He finally found a space of 60 square metres in poor condition, with a leaking roof, that had been vacant for a long time and nobody wanted. In 1873, he opened a school in Shenyang which taught general subjects and enabled children to read the Scriptures in their native language; the teaching and the food was provided free of charge. That same year he baptised his first three converts and trained one as a native evangelist. In 1876, he established the East Gate Church. That year, he married Catherine, a sister of one of his fellow missionaries, who cared for his young son.

Full of suspicion, the local government sent soldiers to follow him wherever he went and stand guard outside the inns where he stayed. When he walked on the street, he was followed by the soldiers and then a large crowd of onlookers curious to see this strange creature with a big nose and round eyes. Once, people threw him into a ditch; he pulled himself up and carried on walking, showing no anger. When he started holding services in his tiny church, the soldiers stood next to him and a large crowd of people came, filling it to capacity. Finally, the government agreed to withdraw the soldiers. Ross used to preach on the street; sometimes, people threw mud and stones at him. But he gradually built a small community. He regarded as a priority the training of Chinese evangelists and ministers; he started month-long training courses and was the first principal of the Shenyang Theological College, which opened in 1898, offering a four-year course. In 1882, with members of the PCI, he opened a free medical dispensary, which became the Shenyang Medical College in 1912.

He did not forget his mission to Korea. Undeterred by its closed-door policy, Ross made friends with four Korean businessmen who lived in a border area and persuaded them to come to Shenyang and teach him Korean. He also met in Shenyang a Korean merchant of herbal medicine who was suffering from a high fever and was cured by a mission doctor. He baptised all five. In 1879, the first Korean Presbyterian Church was formed in Manchuria; the region was home to thousands of ethnic Koreans who had migrated in search of a better life. Between 1882 and 1888, Ross and his five associates translated the Bible into vernacular Korean that could be read easily by ordinary people; he printed 20,000 copies of his Bible and had them taken into the country by Koreans. It was written in the Hangul phonetic script accessible to a majority of the 12-million population rather than the Chinese characters used by the court and the scholarly elite. To escape detection by border guards, the carriers often divided the Bible into different sections which they hid in their clothes; once they had entered Korea, they put the book together again.

In 1885, the Korean king permitted the establishment of an American consulate in Seoul, which included a doctor. When the king was wounded in battle, Korean doctors were unable to cure him; but the American doctor was able to. After this, the king changed his attitude and allowed the entry of foreign missionaries. When they reached there in 1885, they found many Christian communities already established in Seoul and elsewhere. They were mystified and asked where they had come from. In 1887, Ross finally went to Seoul, taking with him 30,000 copies of the Bible and other religious material and formally set up a Christian association. Believers who had been converted by the people Ross had sent insisted on being baptised by him in person. From the beginning, the church in Korea was self-supporting. Ross is regarded as the father of Protestant Christianity in Korea. Today South Korea has one of the largest Christian populations in Asia, with about 8.6 million Protestants and 5.1 million Catholics out of a population of 49 million. Its Protestant churches have sent missionaries to countries around the world. In 2006, the Korean Alumni Association of New College, the main Presbyterian college in Edinburgh, established a John Ross scholarship for a Korean candidate to study at the college's School of Divinity for one year.

After 1887, Ross devoted himself to the church in Manchuria. He opened a larger building for the East Gate Church in October 1889, with eight hundred seats. A minister at the church, Liu Quanyue, was the first Chinese pastor in Manchuria in 1896. In 1900, the Boxers burnt down the East Gate Church, as well as other churches, the mission hospital and homes. In 1907, it was rebuilt with government money.

In 1910, in failing health, Ross retired to Scotland at the age of sixty-eight. During his thirty-nine years of missionary life, he returned home only three times. An outstanding linguist, he could speak eleven languages, including Chinese, Manchu, Korean, German, French, Latin, Greek and Hebrew. He died in 1915 and was buried in Edinburgh. A year later, the East Gate Church erected a monument in his memory. After his departure, the church was run by Chinese ministers and elders, up to the present day. The church's official history lists the names of its ministers; only one was a foreigner, John Ross, from 1875 to 1910.

All those since have been Chinese, including Liu, who served from 1896 to 1919; he retired after a distinguished career, celebrated his eightieth birthday in 1932 and died in 1940, at the age of eighty-eight. From the 1910s, the church became financially self-sufficient and, over the next twenty years, raised enough money to fund five churches in other parts of the city. In 1941, the number of believers reached nearly 1,300 and the church built an extension to accommodate all the people. In 1950, following the establishment of the Communist government, the Chinese Christian Church declared itself to be "self-governing and self-supporting".

Today it prides itself on being the largest church in Manchuria, with 35,000 registered believers and 10,000 people at each of its four services on a Sunday. It has four ministers, two elders and four volunteers. Because of the Cultural Revolution, the church was closed from 1966 to 1978; worship resumed at the end of 1979. In 1998, a new four-storey church was built behind the existing structure. Elder Yu Qingcheng, 69, a third-generation Christian, told me in an interview:

Before 1949, people considered Christianity a Western religion. But I do not think so. It is a religion of love. Churches can run shops, factories, businesses and hospitals. Ministers should be everywhere, as in South Korea, in the prisons, the hospitals, the army and the hospitals. We have plenty of money from the believers and would like to run a hospital; the problem is the equipment and the right doctors and nurses.

Yu said that his mother was baptised in 1925 and lived to the age of ninety-six; my father was baptised in 1932. "I graduated from a missionary school, where the other students were from rich and elite families."

Since 1980, many foreign Christian delegations have visited the church, especially from South Korea; they have a special affection for the Reverend John Ross. The church has material in the Korean language for these visitors.

On May 5, 2011, church leaders from Scotland and Korea gathered in Edinburgh to unveil a memorial stone to the Reverend Ross. His translation was completed in 1911 and millions of copies have since been printed. "We have come to Scotland to celebrate the efforts of John Ross," said the Reverend Jae Min Ho of the Korean Bible Society. It designed the new stone and had it specially made in South Korea before shipping it to Scotland. He said Ross had used the Korean alphabet to publish the Bible, rather than the Chinese characters used at that time for official documents. "This allowed the Korean people to read the Bible much more easily. His decision allowed the spread of Christianity in Korea," he said. Elaine Duncan, chief executive of the Scottish Bible Society, said:

> The Rev John Ross could never have dreamed of the impact his work was to have on the Christian community around the world. The church in Korea grew significantly in the latter part of the twentieth century and today has some of the largest congregations in the world. Missionaries from Korea now serve the church in many nations – so much stemming from the work on a gifted and skilled Scotsman.

In September 2006, the Young Nak Presbyterian Church,

which had 50,000 worshippers and was the largest Presbyterian congregation in the world, received a memorial plaque from Scotland. Made from brass set in wood, the plaque contains words in English and Korean; it was donated by the Mayfield Salisbury Church in Edinburgh, where the Reverend Ross became a church elder after retiring to the city in 1910.

The growth of the Protestant Church in Korea has been the most dramatic success of the missionaries in Asia. As the first translator of the Bible into a Korean which everyone could read, the Reverend Ross was the father of that success.

John Ross is a revered figure in the Korean Christian community.

IN MEMORY OF DR. JOHN ROSS (1841-1915)

A theologian from Great Britain, Dr. John Ross was born in Scotland in 1841. After completing theological training he answered the Lord's call to cross the ocean, traveling long distance to China as a missionary at age 31 years. He was a true pioneer, laboring tirelessly to found churches, establishing many in Fengtian, Liaoyang and Xingjing far reaching into Korea--winning many to Christ. He set up schools for orphans, educating many children. Moreover, he translated the Bible and wrote several commentaries. To train church workers he founded a theological school; more than a dozen Chinese pastors passed their examinations for ordination. After laboring until he was 70 years old, Dr. Ross returned to his own homeland. Though retired, he continued his ministry wherever he was without ceasing until his death at age 75 years in autumn of 1915. News of his death brought deep sorrow to Christians in China, and therefore the following words are inscribed here with pondering affection to his memory:

Great our good shepherd, kind in nature, faithful to God and loving to friends.

Giving life for Gospel, leaving homeland for thirty-eight years; spreading God's word in Shenyang, Liaoning proclaiming salvation in every direction.

Toiling in sacrifice with diligence and patience; through one, God's blessing to all in region led into broader horizons.

The Gospel preached and churches founded; fragrance of virtue and grace penetrated everywhere.

Retired at 70 and departed with work done. Now in peace rest to God's glory rejoicing in heaven, the great reward; here good example remains forever.

Presence parishioners and students sorely miss; on stone are carved words to memorialize.

Deeply indebted, presence still felt whenever is renewed the good example left behind.

With respect and humble gratitude we dedicate these few words. The Presbyteries of the Three Provinces of Guandong. May 1916 in the year of our Lord.

Translated from the tablet in Dong Guan Church, Shenyang, Liaoning Province by Jean and Franklin Woo. Easter 1999.

Mamie Johnston

Mamie Johnston was a lady missionary in Faku, who served in Manchuria from 1923 until 1952. In 1981, she published a book *I Remember It Well* about her life there; I also had the good fortune to interview her in May that year. The book provides an inside look at an important part of the PCI mission in Manchuria. Of its 91 missionaries, 48 were women, of whom 14 were doctors. Most of the women did not marry and dedicated their lives to mission work; it was an ideal which shocked the Chinese among whom they worked and who considered that marriage and family were the most important duty of a woman. Miss Johnston shared a small house with Sara McWilliams, a lady missionary who had gone to China in 1897 and would remain until 1935. These were women of great conviction and strong character, who endured extremes of climate, physical danger and risks to health that could not be imagined at home.

Miss Johnston's inspiration was Dr Isabel Mitchell, who had visited her home in Belfast when she was a girl of eight, just before Dr Mitchell's departure. "She said to me that one day I might be able to go out and help her. I never forgot that," she told me. She applied to the church to work as a missionary and said she was willing to go to India or China. The foreign mission board decided to send her to China and assigned her to Faku; it did not consult her in advance. She made the six-week journey to Shanghai with six other lady Presbyterian missionaries, four from Scotland and two from Ireland. She went first to a language school in Beijing to learn Mandarin. One day she was riding home in a rickshaw and talking to the driver; when he learnt that she was unmarried, the driver said that he was sorry for her. "How was it possible that your father had let you, a young girl, come out here, not married and not even a marriage arranged?" he said.

After Beijing, she went to work at the Teachers' Training College in Shenyang. In 1924, she set out for Faku for the first time, travelling on her own, taking a cart drawn by three mules. "On the dreadful roads, the cart rocked, bumped, sank in holes and jolted out again; if my teeth were not chattering and rattling too, my head was bumping hard on the bamboo framework, first one side then the other." When they came in sight of humans, the carter drew the curtain so that she would not be seen; at deserted places, he would stop and point with a whip to a clump of bushes or rocks, where she should relieve herself. She stayed in an inn, sharing a kang with the innkeeper, his wife and teenage son; the air in the windowless room was full of incense and the opium her three companions smoked before they went to sleep.

Her new home, formerly occupied by Dr Mitchell, was that she shared with Miss McWilliams. Built around 1900, it was a one-storey structure with a small garden in front; it had no electricity or running water. Water came from a well and was stored in large earthenware vats; the toilet was outside the house. The walls were thin, so that the corridor at the back shone with ice crystals during the winter. The house had four rooms, one occupied by Miss McWilliams and one by five orphan girls whom she had adopted, as well as an amah to look after them. Miss Johnston shared her bedroom with another missionary colleague. In winter, where the temperature fell below zero, they would undress in the warmth of the sitting room, which had an iron stove, and run through the icy corridor to their bedroom. During the summer, the house was invaded by flies; they used a cloth made of goat hair to keep the flies away and a mosquito net at night.

It would be hard to imagine a place more different to the warm and well-equipped home she had left behind in Belfast.

> We lived in the same houses as the Chinese. There was a short, hot summer and, in the winter, the temperature fell to minus 20 F in the day and minus 50 F at night. The winter was the busiest time for us as the rivers froze over and travel was much easier. I do not remember it as being cold. We were well wrapped up, Chinese-style of course. There was enough to eat. I do not ever remember feeling deprived of anything.

At that time, bandits operated in the Faku area, kidnapping people for ransom. One night, the two ladies were having dinner when they heard bandits climbing over the wall of the nearby girls' school. The school sounded the alarm and

In front of Mamie Johnson's house in Faku.

rang its bell. One teacher at the school played the organ, another the flute and the two ladies ran out into the darkness, waving sticks; they were working in concert. Fortunately, the robbers were sufficiently frightened by the noise that they ran away and the two returned to finish their supper. On another occasion, when the bandits attacked the town, the government ordered the school to extinguish all the lights; she told the students to lie down in the dark. "I was sitting on the school steps, seeing the reflections of fire in the town, hearing the shouting and screams and dogs barking – and had not the least idea what to do if the bandits climbed the wall. Fortunately, the robbers left the town."

When they travelled on the long, open roads, the missionaries – like everyone else – ran the risk of being kidnapped; the criminals might believe that a foreign face would bring a larger ransom. Miss Johnston was very clear what this would mean. "As a new missionary, I was told in the most casual way: 'If you are ever kidnapped or captured by bandits, remember there is no ransom. If we went for ransoming people, we would have missionaries lifted every week. It would become too expensive.'"

On November 18, 1920, the Reverend William Gillespie died at Changchun on injuries received when he was attacked by bandits while asleep at his home; he had served for twenty-eight years in Manchuria. Many children of missionaries died, including my two uncles, Patrick and Dermot. When Professor James Haire, the convenor of the PCI's Foreign Missions, arrived in Jilin city in 1922, he saw the graves of two children of one missionary and of three children of another.

Like other missionaries, Miss Johnston aimed to become as close to Chinese people as possible. "In my early years, now with a Chinese name, dressing in Chinese clothes, eating Chinese food, living the Chinese life, I was making myself 'acceptable', as I conformed to the manners and customs." She said that doing missionary work was like being a fisherman.

"They must have their skills, know the fish and the right bait (to attract a person into the church): and themselves to have patience, be prepared often to work in darkness and danger. I was learning the fisherman's skill."

To persuade a person to join the church was not easy; it often faced opposition from his or her family and community; it meant giving up the worship of Buddhist, Taoist and other deities and removing their images from the house, something that other family members were likely to oppose. It meant devoting time, energy and money to the Christian community – and away from the family and other commitments. But this was how Miss Johnston and the other missionaries measured their success – how many people did they attract into the church and how many became regular, long-term members.

She found many aspects of life in Manchuria in need of change.

The average birthrate was about 12-13 births for each woman; of these, only two or three would live to be adults... If a newly born infant was found to be handicapped in some way or deformed, it would be left on the road to die. I have often seen, out on a hillside, a woman weeping her heart out, at her feet a bundle wrapped in straw, her thrown-out baby. They were not buried because people believed in a demon called the "dog-spirit" whose food was the soul of babies;

to propitiate this spirit, the bodies were left on the hill side where the wild dogs roamed and would find them. Little girls did not count for much; "little mistake" or "son coming" was the name of a girl who should have been a boy. Girls would grow up and marry away and be no more use to the family. Ordinary Chinese believed in spirits, demons, devils and a great variety of gods who are to be propitiated to avoid calamity.

She found Chinese religions to be harsh and uncompromising, without the compassion and humanity which she considered the heart of Christianity.

Christianity offered the best qualities of all the native religions. There were two kinds. One was a primitive type of gods as good luck. They would put the gods in a hot place in the market in the summer to punish him if he did not deliver rain at the right time. There was no notion of adoring God. To them, we offered a God who was more powerful than theirs. The better educated believed in Confucianism, a system of humanitarian – though slightly feudal – ethics which I admired . Neither group resisted Christianity. A big part of the growing church was composed of people from the Buddhist sect who had a consciousness of sin, knew self-denial and experienced forgiveness in Christ. A second section of the Christian church came from the Confucianists, who knew the rules of right conduct and deportment in every imaginable situation. Manchuria had two families who were direct descendants of Confucius and bore his name. Both were Christian; the heads of each were ministers in the church.

Smoking opium was widespread in Chinese society, among the poor as among the rich; this was in part a legacy of the arrival of the foreign powers in the nineteenth century. "In one large town lived a doctor of Chinese medicine named Yuan who had great success was helping people give up opium. It was commonly used as a painkiller; there were "social smokers" and addicts, many of them officials in high positions who could afford it. Dr Yuan advised instant and not gradual withdrawal. He organised group therapy during which the members would learn Christian texts by heart and sing."

For Miss Johnston, Frederick and Annie were like a father and mother and their house like her home in China.

Frederick was a great scholar who spoke Chinese very well. He used to criticise us if we made a small mistake. The more you studied, the more you could do. He did not speak gutter Mandarin, so I used to surprise him with that. Annie spoke Chinese well too. Frederick was a great teacher and speaker but not very practical. They lived a very frugal life. I do not think Annie ever got over the death of Patrick, her first born, who died of dysentery at the age of four. It killed many people at that time. She and Frederick were away when Patrick died.

She looked back on her twenty-nine years in Manchuria with great affection:

To my delight, I was sent to Ida Mitchell's station. We went there because God's message was not only for the Westerners, but for all people. We had to bring it to the Chinese too. We were not imposing it on the Chinese, but offering it. It was a partnership between us. How could we impose it when we had only our words? We liked China because it was not a colonial country. We were not at once identified with the ruling power. It was more on equal terms. I was not homesick, except when I was in Ireland on holiday. That (Faku) was where our loyalties were.

Orphan girls

Living with Mamie Johnston were five orphan girls who had been adopted by the mission after the death of their parents in floods. The daughter of one of them is Li Su, born in 1951, whom I met in Shenyang in August 1997; she told me the story of her mother.

She lived in Faku from 1921 to 1927, between the ages of nine and sixteen, when she moved to Shenyang. While she was in Faku, she lived with Miss McWilliams and four other orphans. Frederick was a tall man. He and Annie lived a simple life. In their house, they had a cook and a maid but no car and no bicycle. They walked everywhere. They usually ate Western food, including bread, toast and cakes. They also liked dumplings. They walked everywhere or took a horse cart for long distance. Frederick spoke Chinese very well and gave his sermons in Chinese; Annie was not so serious and looked after us very warmly. They had no telephone and relied on letters and cables for contact with the outside world. For lighting, they used a kerosene lamp.

She said that, in those days, Faku was an agricultural place, with no factories. "The farmers had one harvest a year of crops and sometimes two of vegetables. Life was very simple. It was a stable place. There were bandits but they kidnapped rich people and not missionaries." Her mother became a believer because she saw what the missionaries did. "The Faku people thank him for bringing the hospital and the schools. The missionaries brought science and medicine. Without them, there would be no church."

Frederick spent part of the 1920s away from Faku. He spent two winters – six months each time – in the YMCA in Jilin city, in Jilin, the province north of Liaoning; this was in the winters of 1921 and 1926. During the 1926-1927 school year, he taught classes in theology and Old Testament at the church's Theological College in Shenyang. In 1928, he was selected as one of the China delegation to an international missionary conference in Jerusalem; it had 14 prominent Chinese Christians and 6 missionaries. The conference held its meetings on the Mount of Olives, from which, according to the Bible, Jesus ascended to heaven. Then he spent a period of leave in Ireland. On his return to Manchuria, he was assigned to cover two districts in addition to Faku and lived for six months in one of them, Xinmin. This was a result of a shortage of missionaries.

Gulf between Chinese and foreigners widens

The gap between Chinese and foreigners widened with fatal incidents in 1925 and 1927, which severely affected the churches.

On May 30, 1925, a dozen British policemen in the Foreign Concession in Shanghai faced a large crowd of protestors who were demanding the release of students who had been arrested that morning. The protestors turned violent and pressed forward. The police opened fire, killing 11 and wounding many others. On June 23, 1925, facing thousands of demonstrators in Guangzhou, French and British military police opened fire, killing 52 and wounding 170. These deaths shocked the nation, leading to strikes, anti-foreign protests and emergencies in the foreign concessions. People organised boycotts of British and Japanese goods. Some shouted the slogans: "Down with Imperialism, Down with Christianity".

Missionaries were the foreigners most at risk, because many lived in the interior and had no protection; some were forced to flee to the safety of the big cities with a foreign military presence. Such incidents did not happen in Manchuria, so the reaction was less fierce; but there was increasing anger against the foreign community.

In July, the synod of the Manchurian church – where Chinese had a large majority – held a discussion of the killings in Shanghai and issued a lengthy resolution. Part of it read:

> We firmly believe that the root cause of this tragedy is to be found in the form of government of the International Settlement in Shanghai as well as in the unequal treaties repeatedly concluded with China. We therefore declare the necessity of a fundamental alteration in the regulations of the Shanghai Municipal Council as well as the revision of every article in the treaties which bear unequally on China...
> In proclaiming the Gospel of Christ within the social environment, we do not wish to rely on the special privileges granted from time to time in the treaties with the foreign powers.

In other words, the church was calling for an end to the unequal treaties and the privileges which foreigners enjoyed in China.

This was a much stronger statement than the missionary conference in Shanghai earlier in July 1925 which said that it did not have sufficient evidence to come to any decision about the rights and wrongs of the police action. This conference reflected the views of the foreign missionaries, many of whom were, like the policemen, British and did not want to condemn their countrymen, while that of the synod reflected the views of the Chinese church leaders. The conference also proposed that the mother churches urge the British government to allow missionaries to give up their extraterritorial privileges and be subject to Chinese law, like ordinary Chinese.

Under the unequal treaties signed by the Chinese government in the nineteenth century, foreigners in China were not subject to Chinese law but to those of their own countries. If they committed murder, they would be tried not by a Chinese court but by judges administering the laws of their own countries. But the British government would never agree to some of its citizens giving up this privilege and not others; quite the contrary – at such a time of intense nationalist sentiment, foreign residents of China felt particularly threatened and relied on this extraterritoriality for their protection. The killings and the anger against them showed the ambiguous situation in which the missionaries found themselves – living among and close to Chinese people but seen by many as representatives of a cruel and militarist foreign power.

In March 1927, another tragedy occurred which further drove a wedge between Chinese and foreigners. On March 24, units of the Nationalist army began large-scale looting of foreign properties in Nanjing, including consulates, churches, schools, hospitals and private property. The soldiers killed half a dozen foreigners, including John Elias Williams, Vice President of the University of Nanjing, and a teacher at Aurora University. At the request of the British Consul, British warships on the Yangtze River shelled the city; in response, the Nationalist commander ordered an end to the looting. In total, about 40 people were killed and 10 wounded.

Buddhist priest in Faku

In foreign countries, there was outrage against the killings; but the United States and Japan wanted to avoid action against the Nationalist president Chiang Kai-shek that would weaken his hand against the Communists, whom they feared more. This position of the U.S. and Japan restrained the European powers from taking severe retaliation. The incident further worsened relations between Chinese and foreigners. As in 1925, missionaries were the easiest target of Chinese anger, because they were most accessible, living in the middle of local communities and without armed protection.

In May, Frederick wrote a report on the aftermath of the Nanjing incident:

> Not since the Boxer Rebellion twenty-seven years ago have the church and the missions faced such a torrent of abuse. Sometimes a Chinese pastor with a fool's white cap on his head has been led along the streets by a group of jeering foes of his faith. While looting, wrecking and persecution have not been systematic, nevertheless the Church as a whole in the southern provinces is passing through a fiery trial. The proportion of foreign missionaries who have evacuated the interior is estimated at 80 per cent. Hospitals and schools have had to be closed. All kinds of hardships have been suffered by missionary refugees, men and women. Over wide areas of the country, there has been terror on every side, destruction of church and mission property, hatred of our religion, an attempt here and there to suppress Christianity and the loss of precious lives.

> We are watching the birth throes of a somewhat menacing China, not indeed a monster, but a strange creature, hitherto unknown. Should the Communists gain the upper hand, there will be seen a sustained hostility to what in Russia the present rulers call "the opium of the people", by which they mean religion of any kind. Even if the Communists, a comparatively small minority, are defeated, the outlook for the missions will remain grave. Christianity is, in the eyes of the people, inseparably linked with the nations of the west, particularly Britain, America and France. Britain offered the world a splendid lead in giving up her concessions at Hankou; just now negotiations for handing over the British Concession at Tianjin are proceeding with the northern authorities. Patience, persistent patience under insult and humiliation is the supreme gift needed by the foreign powers.

> In their patience, they will win their souls; they will also win a renewed opportunity and a more secure footing for the

preaching of the Gospel of Christ. Whether from the point of view of foreign trade or of Mission work in China, the policy of retaliation for the Nanjing outrages is worse than useless. Missionaries themselves are, indeed, divided in their opinions as to the course of action their governments should take. But the Chinese Christians are of one mind. They, with the missionaries, are bound to suffer the evil consequences of the line of action advocated by so many of our countrymen, the policy of the "strong hand".

Events like those in Shanghai, Guangzhou and Nanjing drove a wedge between Chinese and foreigners. In some places, the presence of missionaries became an embarrassment: they made the church and its properties an object of criticism and attack and accusations that it was a "Western religion". Most people did not consider Buddhism an "Indian religion", because it had become thoroughly sinicised in the hundreds of years since it arrived from India. So the missionary and his family had to leave and seek safety in the cities with foreign concessions, where he had physical protection, or go out of the country all together.

Frederick reported that this temporary retirement of the missionaries did not lead to a breakdown of the church but rather its strengthening.

Church services, administration and finance have been handled well. Faced with the bitterest opposition and thrown on their own spiritual resources, the majority of the Chinese pastors and other leaders have stood firm. The pressure of recent events has fostered the spirit of independence. The Church has grown in strength. Most of the missionaries may return to their posts but it is felt that their return should usually be on condition that they are invited by the Chinese church. This new development indicates the self-respecting status to which the younger church has now attained.

So China's struggle for political independence had an echo in the churches; just as people wanted an end to the unequal treaties, so Chinese ministers and congregations wanted to run their own affairs.

Frederick and his colleagues in Manchuria were more

fortunate than missionaries elsewhere in China; they did not have to flee for safety because of violent clashes between foreigners and Chinese. They were able to continue their work normally, without the level of hostility directed against foreigners in Shanghai, Guangzhou and elsewhere. The most visible foreign presence in Manchuria was not Caucasians but Japanese and hostility was more likely to be directed against them.

Idol or cultural object?

Like other foreign missionaries, Frederick found himself confronted with many dilemmas. He had brought a religion that had grown in one culture and civilisation into a country with its own distinctive culture, tradition and values; his mission was to persuade its people to accept his religion and its message about Jesus as their own. To do this, how much should he adapt his religion to China's culture and traditions? If he refused to adapt at all, then few Chinese would join. If he adapted too much, he would change the nature of his religion and betray the gospel he came to preach. As the early church grew in an environment influenced by Greek philosophy, the writer of John's gospel used Greek terminology of "the Logos – the Word" being with God and being God and becoming flesh. Was it possible to take classical Christian theology and express it in terms familiar to the Chinese, without distorting the message? How could he translate this into Chinese?

One adaptation that was easy was to separate the men and women in the church, with a curtain dividing them; this was not done in Ireland but was the choice of the believers in Manchuria. Not so simple was the presence of images and idols in the homes of believers. Presbyterian churches have no images, occasionally a cross; it is the same in Irish Presbyterian homes. But people in Manchuria, as in the rest of China, usually lived in large families, with three or even four generations together. The parents and grandparents of the believer could have images of the Buddha, Chinese native gods and their own ancestors; to hang pictures of ancestors was a sign of filial piety, a virtue greatly valued in Chinese society.

Should the believers allow these images to remain hanging or should they remove them? Doing so might deeply offend other members of the family and could cause a serious rift. Missionaries had different views on this question. The stricter ones said that all images should be removed because they were "idols"; those who were less strict considered them cultural items which could be allowed to stay. The same problem occurred later when the Japanese tried to impose Shinto worship in Manchukuo, the puppet state which they established in Manchuria after their conquest in 1931. Was Shinto a Japanese religion or an expression of Japanese culture? When the Japanese imposed it in the church's schools, it was a bridge too far and the church withdrew from its schools.

Another difficult issue was burning incense in front of the tomb of ancestors, a custom followed by the Chinese for centuries; it is a sign of respect and honour, especially for parents and grandparents. Many believe that the souls of their ancestor are alive in another world and can help them in this one. The minimum form of respect is to visit the graves once a year, on the day of Qing Ming, when people honour the dead. Officially, the Presbyterian Church was against this practice; but to ban it would offend the Chinese, especially older people. One solution, as Mamie Johnston described above, was to go into procession to the cemetery wearing red – a symbol of joy – rather than the traditional white and sing religious songs next to the graves. On these two issues, missionaries exercised their discretion; Frederick was on the liberal side. In any event, the most prudent course was not to report them to the mother church, many of whose members – like the Reverend Hunter who accused Frederick of heresy – were conservative and opposed deviation from the strict doctrine. Frederick enjoyed writing and also challenging people; so he was not shy of talking about these matters, even at the risk of arousing controversy.

Chinese worshipping at a temple

One issue on which missionaries, whatever their views, had no discretion was that of monogamy. The church allowed a man to have only one wife; unless he divorced her, he could not take a second one. At that time, polygamy was widespread among the rich and well connected in China and accepted as part of normal life. The church made no compromise on this. In 1915, Sun Yat-sen, the father of the Chinese Republic and a Protestant, wanted to marry Song Qing-ling, an American-educated woman twenty-six years his junior. His wife, Lu Muzhen, begged him to take Song as a concubine, a position which then had legal status in China. It would allow Lu to remain as the only wife; such an arrangement would have been acceptable within the wider society. Lu said that a divorce would humiliate and disgrace her. But Song, a Christian, insisted that Sun divorce his wife, which he agreed to do.

In the early years of the mission in Manchuria, this was not an issue, since most of those who were converted belonged to the poor ranks of society who could only afford one wife. In later years, the church attracted more wealthy and educated people, some of whom had or wanted to have more than one wife. They had to make the choice between conversion and polygamy.

Another difficult issue for Frederick and other missionaries was the standard they required of local ministers. At home, Presbyterian ministers were highly educated, sometimes with two degrees, including one in Theology. But it was impractical for them to set the bar so high in Manchuria, which had few institutions of higher learning; they needed Chinese people together spreading the Gospel. As well as training ministers, they employed full-time evangelists who were educated. But, as Frederick discovered in Faku, many people took this job for the money, not the vocation, and proved unsuitable; he had to dismiss them. Who decided who was eligible to be a minister and an evangelist? Initially, it was the foreign missionaries who had brought the church.

By the 1920s, the Chinese church in Manchuria was largely autonomous and control had passed from the missionaries to their Chinese colleagues. But the question of when and how they passed this control was a sensitive one; some individuals who had long held power were reluctant to give it up. On this issue, Frederick was among those more willing to hand over his authority. In a report in August 1931, he wrote:

> The new status of the missionaries is working very well. Autocratic power is dead and buried... We are all of us under committee control, the essence of the ecclesiastical system of Presbyterianism. The committees and boards are manned by a big majority of Chinese.

In April 1935, Frederick described the funeral of an elder of the church in Jinjiatun, who was the head of a wealthy family. At the request of the family, he pronounced the benediction beside a large coffin, which was under a mat shed in the open air. Then everyone moved into a crowded room inside, where they held a religious service by lamplight. At the end, the twenty members of the family, all dressed in mourning white, knelt on the floor in front of the table behind which Frederick was standing.

> Led by the chief (of the family), they kowtowed to me all together, three times in succession. It seemed so strange and yet behind the Chinese rite lay the solemnity of an ancient tradition. They had done their duty, one more way of completing what was required for the dead chief. Let no-one imagine that the elder has heathen ideas mixed up with his Christianity.

This was an example of something that would not happen in a Western funeral but was acceptable in the Chinese context.

Education

For Frederick and Anne, like other missionaries, the education of their children was of great importance but a major headache. There were few schools in China offering the British curriculum and in the English language. The China Inland Mission ran boarding schools for the children of missionaries and other expatriates. Jack Weir, the son of a missionary in Manchuria and a contemporary of my father

Desmond, attended one of these schools in Yantai between 1925 and 1931. "At that time, it was school policy to keep us largely cocooned from surrounding Chinese society, so I have no memory of contemporary Chinese life," he wrote to me in a letter in 1999. He recalled the Battle of Yantai in 1930 or 1931, when the armies of two rival warlords invaded the town. The pupils were not allowed to leave the school and slept on the floor. Over the wall, they watched the rival soldiers march along the seafront road. The school lost one boy; he set off a grenade left by a soldier and killed himself. When he was twelve, Weir left Yantai and continued his education at home in Belfast.

Frederick and Annie decided that their three sons should return to Ireland for their school from the age of primary school. This was partly out of concern about public health and medical care in Faku, after they had lost two sons to disease there. The other reason was that their sons would have a better chance to succeed in their academic careers if they started at an early age in the main stream. So, like his two elder brothers, my father Desmond only lived in Manchuria for a short time – until the age of six – before being sent back to Belfast to study. My grandparents made the same choice as most British expatriates in China and elsewhere at that time, if they could afford it. In many cases, the government or the companies they worked for covered the school fees; it was part of their terms of employment. Without this benefit, most people – but probably not missionaries – would have refused to work in remote and dangerous countries.

But, while Frederick and Annie made the same decision as their peers, it was very painful emotionally. Their sons would spend their childhood without their parents, except for home visits every five to six years and would stay in the home of relatives; the parents would not have the joy and comfort of seeing their children grow up. It was an era without Boeings and Airbuses, international calling service providers or the Internet; contact between parents and children was limited to letters and, in emergencies, telegrams. The separation would have a lasting effect on both parents and children. This was another price foreign missionaries had to pay for their choice in life. Their children had made no such choice.

14th June, 1932.

Rev. F.W.S. O'Neill,
Fakumen,
Manchuria,
Via Siberia.

Dear Mr. O'Neill,

I have been waiting to answer your letter of
the 12th May until I had had a chance of discussing
Desmond's future with his Science and Mathematics Masters.
Now that I have done so I think I can say that Desmond
has a very good chance of gaining a Natural Science
Scholarship at Oriel in December, 1934, but not in
December, 1933. Our experience here is that in order to
get a scholarship at Oxford or Cambridge a boy needs a
year and a half in the Upper Sixth Form before sitting for
the examination, and as Desmond will still be under eighteen
in December, 1933, I think it will be better for him not to
sit until the following December.

Both Mr. Brierley, who looks after the Science, and
Mr. Martin, who is in charge of the Mathematics, have a
very high opinion of Desmond's promise, and now that they
know your wishes and intentions for him they will both
concentrate on his scholarship subjects. It will be wiser
not to interfere in any way with his programme for the
Senior Certificate Examination. He has eleven periods of
Mathematics a week already, and I doubt if he needs any
more. However, I will see in September whether it is
possible to squeeze in the extra period that you suggest.
Later on, when he is in the Upper Sixth, his time-table
will include fourteen periods of Mathematics and fifteen
of Science each week, together with five of English and
five of French or German.

I saw Desmond the other day and talked the
matter over with him and he seems very keen on going
to Oriel and following in Denis's footsteps. If he
does himself justice I do not see any reason why he
should not do just as well as Denis has done.

I am returning Mr. Tod's letter.

With kind regards and best wishes to you both,

I am,
Yours very sincerely,

Principal.

The principal at RBAI responding to Frederick's letter to the school.

In Belfast, Desmond studied at the Malone Public Elementary school which his mother's father had established. In April 1928, Frederick and Annie applied for Desmond to enter the Royal Belfast Academical Institution (RBAI), where he had studied. The principal of the Malone school had earlier written that Desmond had been in China with his parents for several years and was in consequence badly in arrears in several subjects. "Now he is up to usual standards," he wrote in May 1928. "He has an excellent character and will give no trouble. His proficiency is good for his age and, if he follows in the steps of his grandfather, the Rev Wilson of Malone, and of his father, who were Instonians, he will not disgrace RBAI."

In a letter to a teacher at RBAI dated August 11, 1928, Annie thanked him for offering Desmond a scholarship. She wrote that Frederick had just arrived in Manchuria after a thirteen-day journey on the Trans-Siberian Railway, most of it in hard class. They spent July in Ballycastle, a holiday resort in Northern Ireland: "It is a very beautiful place. We shall look forward to going again when my husband has furlough (leave) – 1931. I am now living for that!"

In August 1931, Frederick wrote from Manchuria to Desmond's teacher at RBAI, asking him to respect his request to drop Greek as a subject in favour of Science, in view of his desire to become a doctor.

Assassination of Zhang Zuolin

On June 4, 1928, Zhang Zuolin, the ruler of Manchuria, was killed in the outskirts of Shenyang when a bomb exploded on a nearby railway line as his train passed. The bomb had been placed there by a Japanese army officer named Komoto Daisaku. Zhang had ruled Manchuria for eighteen years, bringing a level of peace and prosperity unmatched in the rest of China. He had given the missionaries an environment of comparative stability in which they could build churches, schools and hospitals and establish their communities. The assassination was a bad omen for the people of Manchuria, a sign of the anger of the Japanese military against Zhang and its growing ambition in the region. No-one was sure what its next step would be; everyone was full of apprehension.

In his assessment of Zhang after his death, Frederick was largely positive:

> From the point of view of a resident of Manchuria, the chief thing to be said in favour of our late ruler is that, within the bounds of his broad domain beyond the Great Wall, he kept the peace. The three provinces of Manchuria were almost the only provinces of the country of which this could be said. The lives of foreigners were protected. European and American businesses went on unhindered. Marshall Zhang was usually well-disposed to the missionaries. For years, he gave a large annual subscription to the Shenyang Mission Hospital and also helped our medical college, many of whose graduates joined the medical service of the Manchurian army.

Zhang presented a valuable site within the city wall for the YMCA to build a large, modern building; he and his son gave large subscriptions to the building fund.

> At one time, the Young General (his son Zhang Xueliang) was so closely identified with the YMCA that his father became alarmed – so it is said – lest his son should join the Christian church. The fatal step was prevented by arranging for the young man to marry a secondary wife... He did much, especially in the earlier years, for the benefit of Manchuria. Himself without education, he allowed to be established an up-to-date system of primary, secondary and university education, which even his ruinous wars, with their waste of public money, did not make bankrupt. We missionaries owe to our late Governor a debt of gratitude. The work of the Christian Mission, except in special circumstances, proceeded with entire freedom. We have had less police supervision or interference than usual under the Japanese in Manchuria.

Zhang had ruled Manchuria almost as an independent kingdom. Although it was officially part of the Republic of China, it was isolated geographically, with a single pass, at Shanhaiguan, where the Great Wall meets the Bohai

Sea, which could easily be closed. His power rested on his Fengtian (Shenyang) army which had 100,000 men by 1922 and almost three times that number at the time of his death. He paid no revenue to the central government other than from postal and customs income, because these had been promised to the foreign powers by the agreement at the crushing of the Boxer Rebellion; Zhang feared their intervention. The power of his army meant that the central government could not intervene in Manchuria. The main threat to his rule came from the Japanese. After the Russo-Japanese War, they had gained a lease of a peninsula covering 560 square kilometers on the southern tip of Manchuria, which included the ice-free port of Dalian.

The Japanese also managed the South Manchuria Railway, which ran from Dalian via Shenyang and Changchun to Harbin; its army controlled the land on either side of the track and maintained up to 14,000 men there. It was the railway which Frederick and other missionaries took on their regular visits to Shenyang and Dalian; when they went home via the Trans-Siberian Railway, they travelled on it north to Harbin, where they transferred to the Russian rail network. At that time it was one of the most modern railways in the world. The company that ran the railway expanded into coalmines, port facilities and many subsidiary companies; it was by far the largest corporation in Japan, providing over 25 per cent of government tax revenue in the 1920s and with its assets reaching over 1 billion yen in 1930.

During his period of power, Zhang was responsible for significant economic progress. Financial reforms and a new currency enabled Manchuria to pay off outstanding loans to foreign banks and consortia by 1921. His government invited workers and farmers from north China to migrate to Manchuria; it offered them reduced rail fares, money to build a home and ownership of land after five years of continuous occupation. Thousands went to the interior of Manchuria, where they reclaimed land for agriculture or worked in mines or forests. Between 1924 and 1929, the land under tillage increased from 20 to 35 million acres.

The government invested in a large cotton textile mill,

which broke the Japanese monopoly in this sector, and in other enterprises; it also built new railway lines. But these achievements were undermined by military spending, which accounted for up to half the budget. From 1920, Zhang made the first of several attempts to capture Beijing and become head of state; these attempts led to costly wars, with thousands of casualties on both sides. In June 1926, he captured Beijing and, a year later, proclaimed himself Grand Marshal of the Republic of China. But the Nationalist army under Chiang Kai-shek attacked the city and Zhang was forced out.

Frederick was very critical of Zhang's military spending. "During the last six years, Manchuria has either been engaged in wars, largely of its own devising or on strenuous preparation for them." He criticised Zhang's war against two other warlords, Wu Peifu and Feng Yu-xiang. "A life of inconspicuous well-doing is apt to appear tame. Gambling at mah-jong sometimes loses its zest, opium may even begin to pall. One occupation retains its constant thrill. It is war." In 1922, two missionaries negotiated a settlement between the armies of Zhang and of Wu. In 1924, Zhang defeated Wu and gained control of north China. In 1925, his ablest commander with several divisions rebelled; but the revolt failed because of the exhaustion of long winter marches. The rebel General and his wife were captured, shot and laid on the frozen ground, a spectacle for the public of Shenyang.

Zhang was succeeded by Zhang Xueliang, then twenty-seven, the eldest son of his official wife; he had 5 wives in all. He had been educated by private tutors and, unlike his father, felt at ease with Westerners. He loved to play tennis in the fine three-storey YMCA building built in 1925, close to the large family mansion in central Shenyang. It had a well-equipped gymnasium in the basement. It was one of half a dozen YMCAs that the church had built in Manchuria, to provide adult education, sports and social activities to thousands of people; they were the most popular church facilities and an important way to reach the public.

As Frederick reported, Zhang nearly became a Christian. In December 1928, the latter declared his allegiance to the Nationalist government. The Japanese military had expected Zhang to be more pliant than his father. But he proved to be more independent; at a dinner party in January 1929, he had two prominent pro-Japanese officials executed in front of the assembled guests. But he could not control the Japanese's ambition towards his homeland; they wanted its soya bean, coal, iron ore and other mineral wealth, its rich farmland, its empty land on which to settle surplus population and its geographic position as a bridgehead to attack the rest of China.

At 10:20 P.M. on September 18, 1931, Japanese soldiers set off an explosion near the tracks of the South Manchuria Railway in Shenyang, damaging a 1.5-metre section on one side; the damage was so minor that a train from Changchun was able to pass ten minutes later and reach the city's main station. Blaming the explosion on Zhang's army, Japanese artillery next morning opened fire on a nearby Chinese garrison and destroyed the small air force. The Chinese troops ran away and, by the evening, the Japanese had occupied Shenyang with the loss of only two of their soldiers. The Japanese army in Dalian moved its headquarters to Shenyang and next morning reinforcements from its army in Korea landed at the city's airport. That day Zhang himself was not in Manchuria; he was at a hospital in Beijing, raising money for victims of terrible floods on the Yangtze River that had created tens of thousands of refugees.

Unwilling to sacrifice his army against the better equipped and trained Japanese, he ordered them to retreat to North China. Zhang had more than 200,000 troops as well as tanks, 60 combat aircraft, 4,000 machine guns and 4 artillery battalions; the Japanese Kwantung army in Manchuria had only 11,000 troops. But more than half of Zhang's men were in Hebei Province and the rest scattered across Manchuria. Japanese intelligence had long penetrated his army and knew its movements in advance. The Japanese army occupied Changchun easily but faced resistance from local forces in Jilin city and Heilongjiang. By February 1932, it had overrun all major towns and cities in Manchuria. A new era in the region's history had begun; it would change dramatically the life of its inhabitants, including the missionaries and the members of the Chinese church. For Frederick, it would end in his forced expulsion from the country where he had lived for forty-five years.

Chapter 5

From Manchukuo to Pearl Harbour

(1931-1941)

Manchukuo

After its occupation of the three Northeast provinces, the Japanese army implemented a plan to separate them from the rest of China. On February 18, 1932, it declared the new state of Manchukuo – the country of the Manchus – with its capital at Changchun, which it renamed Xinjing, meaning "new capital". It persuaded the last emperor of China, Puyi, to become head of state. Japan recognised the new state in September 1932; it never achieved recognition by foreign governments except allies of Germany and Japan during World War Two. The Japanese built a large palace in Xinjing for the new emperor; the country had a prime minister and a cabinet of Chinese, but real power rested with Japanese vice-ministers, who took all the decisions. Of the population of 31 million in 1934, 29.5 million were Han Chinese, with 700,000 Koreans, 600,000 Japanese and 100,000 other nationalities. Many of the Koreans had fled from the Japanese annexation of their country in 1905 and were bitterly anti-Japanese. Few welcomed the new rulers.

The Japanese occupation and the foundation of Manchukuo marked the start of Frederick's final decade in China. It was the most difficult and most painful period, marked by political control and police surveillance such as Frederick had never experienced during his years in China. The Qing government and the regimes of Zhang Zuolin and his son were, by comparison, benevolent; they largely left the missionaries to their own devices, enabling them to build their churches, schools and hospitals and establish Christian communities. Initially, the Japanese authorities did not interfere. But they gradually came to see the church as an obstacle to their aim of controlling the hearts and minds of the Manchurian people. During this period, despite the fact that he was over sixty, Frederick remained in good health and continued to walk long distances.

The immediate result of the Japanese occupation was a breakdown of law and order outside the cities. The Japanese army was well-armed and ruthless but did not have enough men to control such an enormous area as Manchuria; it concentrated its troops in the major cities and centres of economic activity and around the lines of the South Manchuria Railway. In the rest of the region, the administrative system of the previous ruler, Zhang Xueliang, collapsed. This opened the way for bandit gangs to operate, in an atmosphere of widespread opposition to Japanese rule. In a letter in November 1932, Frederick described how bandits sacked the town of Jinjiatun twice in the space of a month, looting shops and houses and forcing residents to take sanctuary in the church compound.

> Kidnapping for ransom was rife. A motor-bus on the 17-mile road from Guangning to Faku was attacked and 4 Japanese and 68 Chinese killed... for weeks our mail has been disrupted. In July, the new government took over the post office administration. 'Manchukuo' stamps were valid only inside the new state or in Japan and were not recognised either in China proper or abroad.

The British Consul-General in Shenyang advised missionaries not to travel unless absolutely necessary. Bandits controlled movement around Guangning, allowing people to travel to the railway if they paid a fee. Armoured cars accompanied trains. Several Irish out-stations near Xinjing were plundered by robbers and some Christians, including evangelists, were habitually kidnapped and held for ransom. In another place, a trainee minister and young evangelist were abducted by bandits and beaten over a period of several weeks, before being released upon payment of a 200-Manchukuo-yuan ransom.

Lytton Commission

In December 1931, the League of Nations appointed the commission, under the chairmanship of a British peer,

Lord Lytton, to investigate the situation in Manchuria and present a report to the League. It spent six weeks there in the spring of 1932. The key issue was whether the new state of Manchukuo reflected the will of Manchurian people or was a result of Japanese aggression. The Japanese rolled out the red carpet for the five members of the commission – from Britain, France, Germany, Italy and the United States – and made their best propaganda efforts. Many Chinese wanted to express their opposition to Manchukuo; but to do so ran the risk of their opinions being shown to the Japanese and punishment after the commission had gone. The Japanese put police and soldiers around the hotels where the five members were staying, making access extremely difficult. Foreign residents like the missionaries had a certain degree of immunity from Japanese persecution and were a conduit for Chinese to express their views.

According to the records of the Chinese church, Frederick made several visits to the commission, in Shenyang and the north of Liaoning Province, to provide "secret reports of Japanese brutality". In his account of Frederick's life, Minister Hu Changyu said that Frederick and other British missionaries carried these secret reports to the commission. A Communist sympathiser named Gong Tianmin went to Faku to ask Frederick if he could deliver a package of material to Lord Lytton; he said that he would be honoured to carry out such a mission. He left the material in the safety box of the British Consul in Shenyang and invited Lytton and his secretary for a dinner in the home of a Chinese minister in the west of the city. The home was small. When Japanese officials sought to enter, Frederick said the house was too small and that he had not invited them, so they had to wait outside. This enabled him to give the material, which he had removed from the safety box, to Lytton without being seen by the Japanese.

The commission's report, published on October 2, 1932, found that the new state of Manchukuo could not have been formed without the presence of Japanese troops, that it had no general Chinese support and was not part of a genuine and spontaneous independent movement. In February 1933, when the General Assembly of the League of Nations was considering a motion to condemn Japan as an aggressor, the Japanese delegation walked out and left the league. In the end, the report, while historically valuable, showed the weakness of the League of Nations and its inability to enforce its decisions.

In 1935, when Japanese police carried out widespread arrests of Chinese, the first question in their interrogation was: "Did you give evidence to the Lytton Commission?"

Siege

In 1932, Faku was garrisoned by Mongol troops loyal to a Chinese general who had thrown his support behind the new government. His soldiers were fierce and uncouth and despised by the people of the town. The area around Faku was full of bandit gangs, some armed with field guns. On one occasion, the Japanese air force dropped bombs on the town; they were unable to distinguish between friend and foe. In the late summer of 1932, the Mongol troops were posted to the north of Manchuria and left. In September, after they had gone, Faku came under siege by a gang of well-armed bandits. The residents defended themselves by digging a deep trench and covering it with a live electric wire fence, using current from the electricity works that was close to Frederick's house. With the aim of cutting the power supply, the bandits shelled the electricity works, with one shell landing close to the church and two in the vegetable garden next to the mission house.

At that time, the mission hospital had no resident doctor. If Frederick or his wife had been injured, there would be no-one to treat them. The crisis lasted twenty-four days until a brigade of Japanese soldiers arrived on the outskirts of the town to lift the siege. The question arose of how, in a tense situation with the town surrounded by highly armed men, to approach the Japanese and negotiate a ceasefire. The Japanese were as nervous and ready to use their weapons as the bandits. Town leaders formed a delegation to go out and meet the Japanese and invited Frederick to join them; he agreed. Fortunately, the delegation was able to reach the soldiers peacefully and the mediation worked; the Japanese troops entered the town and a period of stability followed.

In a nearby village, an evangelist nearly lost his life. Bandits robbed him and his wife of all their possessions, even what they were wearing, and inspected his church. Seeing no images, they said: "Have you no Gods?" To which he replied that he worshipped the Lord of Heaven who had no image. "What, you have no Buddha! It must be the Japanese religion you are teaching. Come out and I will kill you," said one of the bandits. The evangelist replied that that he did not fear to die but asked: "What harm have I done to you?" Another bandit commented: "We worship Buddha but commit pillage, whereas this man who is well-behaved does not worship the Buddha." Then they let him go – and he later appeared in Faku, wearing a cap and shoes which the bandits had left him, with a big smile on his face. Another Christian, a farmer named Han, was captured by robbers who stripped him of his clothes, beat him and demanded money. One put a gun to his head. "Shoot me dead, if you like," said Han. "That will send me to heaven." The robber replied that he did not want his life but his money. Finally, Han borrowed from a neighbour a horse worth 50 Manchukuo yuan, plus 18 Manchukuo yuan in cash and 2 ounces of opium); the ransom totaled five pounds. After he was set free, Han had to repay the price of the horse, with the addition of 50 per cent interest.

In May 1933, Frederick commented that the town had not seen such chaos and disorder since the Boxer Rebellion of 1900. But, on the positive side, there had been a record number of baptisms – 223 during the year. On Christmas Day 1933, the church had a congregation of 750. An Irish missionary stationed in India who visited Faku in January 1935 found the wire fence still surrounding the town. "This reminded us that Faku is a frontier town and has often been attacked by bandits. More than once, our pioneers (missionaries) saw the gateway leading into the plains of outer Mongolia festooned with human heads, after an attack and the subsequent executions."

Opium

One of the most evil policies of the new government was its sponsorship of opium, morphine and other narcotics. An official report in October 1932 estimated that 5 per cent of the population of Manchukuo, or 1.5 million people, were addicts of opium or other narcotics, making an annual demand of 2 million kilograms of opium. On January 1, 1933, the new government established an opium monopoly. For the next twelve years, narcotics became an important source of government revenue, in the form of product sold by the monopoly and licence fees paid by opium dens and shops.

According to John Jennings' *The Opium Empire – Japanese Imperialism and Drug Trafficking in Asia, 1895-1945*, Manchukuo consumed 75 per cent of Korea's entire opium output from 1933 to 1945: in 1933, Manchukuo also began to import raw opium from Persia and during the 1930s increased the area under cultivation at home. The Japanese military urgently needed revenue to finance their new state; narcotics provided an easy source. There were no legal restrictions on morphine, heroin or cocaine, so shops selling these goods flourished. The military banned its troops from using narcotics – if they were caught, they could lose their Japanese citizenship; but it was content to see them being used by other races in Manchukuo. It would follow the same policy in other areas of China it occupied after the outbreak of the all-out war in July 1937.

This policy undermined any claim that the new regime had to be a legitimate government. According to official history of the PCI in Manchuria, written by the Reverend Austin Fulton and published in 1967:

> One thing in particular destroyed the Japanese effort to win Chinese friends and influence Chinese people... That was their connivance at the widespread trade, in which Japanese and Koreans engaged, in narcotic drugs. Some observers believed that this trade in opium and opium derivatives brought the Japanese into greater disrepute with the Chinese than all the atrocities of their soldiers or the barbaric cruelty of their police.

Fulton himself served in Manchuria from 1930 to 1941 and titled his book *Through Earthquake, Wind and Fire*. Many Chinese believe that this policy aimed to weaken and demoralise the non-Japanese people of Manchukuo, a kind of slow genocide. After they had ransacked the homes of Chinese, Japanese soldiers used to write on the wall: "slaves of a dead nation".

In May 1934, Frederick reported that sales of opium, morphium and heroin were widespread in urban and rural areas: "The misuse is now open and unashamed." Becoming a Christian was one way to break the habit. "A short time ago, the eldest son of the best known aristocratic house in Faku laid aside his opium pipe and, in dependence on God, began to face the misery of determined renunciation." In the nearby county of Xinjin, he said, "the sale of heroin, morphia and other narcotics has become much more widespread since the Japanese occupation and not only does there seem no means of controlling it but there is seemingly no desire or effort to do so. There is a public office in the city for receiving all the opium grown throughout the district and another where it is openly sold to all who want it."

One convert in Changchun was a tax officer named Wang Tzuhou. He made enough money from his work to open two opium shops; they flourished but he too became an addict. In 1935, he converted to Christianity and had to give up his business and the habit. He destroyed his opium pipes, lamps and stocks, a loss of over 3,000 dollars, his entire capital. He became the business manager of the church, for a modest salary, and spent much of his spare time doing evangelical work in the local prison.

The widespread availability of drugs was also noted in a report in 1937 by a Scottish Presbyterian minister, the Reverend A.S. Kydd, who went to Manchuria and visited all the Scottish mission stations and two of the Irish ones. He also met the leaders of all departments of the church and many senior Japanese officials.

> Drug peddling by Japanese and Koreans was widespread and unconcealed. Opium smoking was giving way to injections of morphine and heroin. An injection cost about 1.5 (British) pence was often given free to start the habit. Once the habit was started, complete destruction of the victim was certain within two years. In one town of 20,000 inhabitants, about 17,000 pounds was spent yearly on drugs. The church was becoming poorer. Self-supporting congregations were finding it increasingly difficult to meet their financial obligations.

After the war, The International Military Tribunal for the Far

East found Japan guilty of deliberately promoting drug abuse as a weapon to further its imperialistic aims in Asia

In 1937, areas under Japanese occupation in China accounted for an estimated 90 per cent of world production of opium, as well as a large amount of heroin, thirty to sixty times more than legal requirements, according to a report in the *Missionary Herald* in 1937.

In their daily life, Frederick and the other missionaries saw the daily effect of the narcotics policy in the people among whom they lived – addicts whose health and livelihood was ruined by the habit; their families forced to spend heavily to pay for the habit and care for them – households and businesses sold and families torn apart by the addiction. The church promoted conversion and abstinence as the solution but this required stern discipline and strong family support – easier said than done.

Arrest and torture

It did not take long for the Manchukuo government to move against the Manchurian Protestant church, which they regarded with suspicion: it was an institution with close ties to the Christian Church in the rest of China and foreign countries. The authorities wanted to control all aspects of life in Manchukuo.

The police in Shenyang moved against the church on the night of October 10, 1935, the twenty-fourth anniversary of the Chinese Republic. They arrested many people, among them over 40 Christians and prominent church leaders. The mother church in Ireland could do nothing. Those arrested included ministers, doctors, students and staff at the mission college and hospital; there were as many as 50 or 60 police and detectives in the wards and the clinics at one time. They also arrested Chinese employees of British American Tobacco and the Hong Kong and Shanghai Bank, two of the biggest British firms in Shenyang. Those arrested were interrogated and, in some cases, tortured; one pastor was held in prison for seventy-two days and tortured for up to eight hours a day, before being released two days before Christmas Day.

The head teacher in a women's Bible school was arrested in the middle of the night by two Japanese and one Chinese policeman as she slept in her bed; she was imprisoned for forty-eight days during which she was twice beaten unconscious. The interrogators were looking for links between those they detained and Communist or anti-government activities but had little success; the church was not involved in political or social activism. To save face, the courts sentenced a small number of people, including a theological student who was given a seven-year sentence. For good behaviour, he was released after four years; during this time, he converted the prison warder to Christianity due to his calm and good spirit.

The missionaries were caught in the middle, between the Japanese and their Chinese friends and colleagues who had been arrested. As foreigners, they enjoyed a certain level of immunity, since the Japanese government did not want to antagonize the countries they came from; they would lose this immunity after the attack on Pearl Harbour in December 1941, when Japan went to war with the Allied Powers. So the missionaries did what they could to lobby on behalf of those who had been arrested and try to secure their release; they wrote letters and held meetings with Japanese officials. On October 31, 1935, Colonel Kato, the head of the Shenyang gendarmerie, told the British Consul that he had been ordered to "clean up" Shenyang. "Clean up Shenyang, I will. If I am doing the wrong thing, I am willing to commit suicide."

The Japanese ambassador in Xinjiang, the capital of Manchukuo, said that the missionaries were being used and that mission institutions harboured Communist activities. They argued that the missionaries did not know what was going on within the churches, schools, colleges and hospitals they ran. One day, staff at a church compound in Shenyang found a Chinese translation of *Das Kapital* by Karl Marx in a box of books that had been taken there from a city bookstore that had closed; if the police had discovered it, all their suspicions would be confirmed. So the missionaries decided to burn all the books. When the furnace and fireplaces in the house did not consume the paper fast enough, they buried the other books in the garden and planted a flower bed above it.

In official church history, Austin Fulton said that it was

hard to explain the reasons for the crackdown. One possible explanation was that Tokyo was angry at the inability of its forces in Manchuria to suppress banditry and secure law and order.

This caused the Tokyo authorities to bring pressure to bear on the Manchukuo authorities to take more drastic and effective steps to defeat the guerilla fighters who seemed to operate freely throughout so much of the territory. The Manchukuo government looked around for some group or groups of people who might be suspected of being the inspiring and integrating force behind the banditry. Such a group would be made up of people with education. They turned therefore to the Christian leadership which provided the only educated group among the Chinese in Manchuria... the movement took on an anti-foreign and anti-Christian character. The real power in Manchukuo was the Japanese Guandong army, which was both anti-Christian and anti-British.

He said that the occupation of Manchuria did not work out as the Japanese had expected:

They found colonising Manchuria not to their liking. The numbers hoped for did not come to the new land and many of those who came did not remain long. Their communities, outside the larger cities, were tiny islands in the middle of cold, unfriendly seas (of Chinese). There were many Japanese soldiers in evidence in the cities, towns and along the railways. But their presence did not make good colonists of the people from the mild climate of Japan. The Japanese traders and settlers remained apart. They could never feel part of the total Manchurian community. They worked all the harder to build up a generation of Chinese indoctrinated in their schools and moulded by propaganda, to regard the Japanese as their friends and benefactors and the Emperor of Japan as their Lord and Protector.

The Japanese in Manchuria felt isolated from the rest of the population, especially the new Japanese migrants who had settled on land seized from Chinese farmers.

Any headway that might have resulted from this universal and continuous brainwashing was undone by the short-sighted policies of the army and the stupidities of local administrators... The Chinese were not easy to understand and proved to be unresponsive and unappreciative. It was the opposite of what the simple-minded Japanese colonist had been led to expect. Here, in the promised land, it turned out that only the dope peddlers and the brothel keepers could make an easy living. Everyone else found conditions too hard and business prospects too bleak.

One of Japan's main motives for the conquest of Manchuria was to dispose of its surplus population, especially from rural areas. In 1930, Japan had a population of 64.5 million people, up from 44.4 million in 1900 and nearly double the 35 million in 1870. Japan is a country of mountains and forests; in the 1930s, only 16 per cent of its land area was under cultivation but 45 per cent of households lived off farming. The average farm size was 2.67 acres, compared to more than 150 for the average American farmer. In 1937, the government unveiled a twenty-year colonisation programme, to move 1 million Japanese families or 5 million people to Manchukuo, between 1936 and 1956. It launched a lavish propaganda campaign, presenting Manchuria as a land with rich earth, an excellent climate and a society in which all the races lived in harmony. Between 1938 and 1942, 200,000 young farmers moved to Manchuria; the government arranged the migration of thousands of young Japanese women for them to marry. In addition, 20,000 families also migrated.

When the Soviets invaded Manchuria in 1945, they captured 850,000 Japanese settlers. The migration programme was a failure. The farmers came from the three main islands of Honshu, Shikoku and Kyushu and found it difficult to adapt to the harsh Manchurian climate, especially its winters. Most of the land they cultivated was seized from Chinese farmers; so, far from being made welcome, they discovered that they were islands in an ocean of hostility and had to rely on the Japanese military or their own self-defence units for protection. Many returned home disappointed. The settlers were, like the Chinese, victims of Japanese militarism. When they knew their country would be defeated, senior officers of the Guandong army and the elite of the Manchukuo government prepared their escape to Japan and abandoned the settlers to the mercies of the invading Soviet army after August 8, 1945. Many settlers took their own lives, some in mass suicides in which they burnt themselves alive inside the schools and community halls they had built; women committed suicide to avoid being raped by Soviet soldiers.

The mass arrests and crackdown on the church reflected the unease and anger of the Japanese officials that they could not control their new colony and their need to find a scapegoat. It also reflected their regret that they had not abolished the Christian church in Korea, which they had occupied 30 years earlier; it was the one of the Korean institutions that resisted Japanese rule most fiercely, teaching a system of belief that was incompatible with the Shinto religion and worship of the Japanese Emperor. The Korean church was so strong that it sent missionaries to China and Japan. By 1935, there were an estimated 1.5 million Koreans in Manchuria, of whom 25 per cent are Christians; they far outnumbered the Chinese Christians. So the Japanese saw the church in China as a major obstacle to their totalitarian control. But, while the arrests did not help them to control bandits or improve law and order, they did have one result which the police intended – most Chinese became uncomfortable to be seen with or talking to foreigners. They feared that such contact would bring suspicion upon them. The missionaries reported that this did not apply to Chinese who belonged to the church itself and remained very loyal to it.

From 1935, wrote Austin Fulton in official church history, the authorities brought in the full panoply of totalitarian rule of the kind that was spreading in Europe at the same time. "The Japanese army must know what everyone was being taught, what people were thinking, what they were saying. Draft of sermons to be preached had to be submitted to these police. Letters, especially from the rest of China, were censored. Forms with questions on one's thoughts, activities, friends and hobbies confronted foreigners in a continuous stream. Indeed, almost identical questionnaires had to be filled up for the different police authorities and gendarmeries, which apparently had little dealing with each other and did not pool their information.

The police had to be advised when and where one intended to travel. Sometimes permission had to be obtained. Chinese and foreigners found this very irksome but the Japanese took it as a matter of course; it was similar to the procedures to which they were accustomed in Japan." Fulton described a two-hour interview with a Japanese detective, in which he tried to convince him that the (Presbyterian) Church of Scotland was not part of the British government. "That there could be a distinction between a national church and a government institution was quite beyond his comprehension. He could not conceive of any reason for a missionary leaving his own country other than his government had sent him.

Mamie Johnston, a missionary in Faku from 1923 to 1952, said that Manchukuo was a police state:

It was like the Nazis, I suppose. We needed passes to go anywhere and had to explain where we were going and why. The Japanese saw us as a rival to them. They demanded worship of the emperor who was divine and of Puyi, his representative in Manchuria. We would respect him but not worship him. We had to learn Japanese, of course, as did the secondary school pupils.

Some Chinese Christians and missionaries paid the ultimate price for the totalitarianism of the Japanese and were martyred.

In the autumn of 1936, the Presbyterian Church's Board of Missions sent its chief administrative officer, the Reverend Dr R.H. Boyd, and his wife to visit Manchuria and report on what they found. This is what he wrote about the ordeal of the members of the church:

No-one could imagine the strain and anguish that most of our missionaries have undergone during the last thirteen months. The irritation to which they are subjected is nerve-destroying. Grace has been sufficient for them. Nothing else could have kept them from breaking down. One cannot bear to think of the days of distraction and the nights, the long, feverish nights of sleeplessness that they have lived through. For men, it was a severe trial. For women, it was agony and torture. And yet they have endured as seeing Him who is invisible. If that is true of the missionaries, what more can be said about the pastors, doctors, teachers and others who had physical agony to endure or were in close touch with it through the sufferings of their friends? And yet they too have endured. What a privilege it has been to meet them and see how Christ has been glorified in them. Never shall

we forget H – of Xinjing, L – of Shenyang, S – of Faku and
others like them who have come through great tribulation
and still live to serve the same Lord.

One of the church institutions worst hit by the crackdown
was the Medical College in Shenyang. Initially, it had
been designated by the new government as a recognised
educational institution. In 1931, it was recognised by the
University of Edinburgh as fitting its graduates for admission
to examinations for diplomas granted by the university in
the higher branches of medicine; this followed the excellent
impression made by a succession of its graduates sent to study
in Edinburgh. Founded in 1726, the university's medical
school was and is one of the most prestigious in Britain.

But, in the late 1930s, the police arrested several Chinese
members of the college staff and imprisoned them on political
charges; others fled from Manchuria to avoid the same fate.
This torpedoed the plans of the church to increase the number
of Chinese staff and reduce the proportion of foreign ones to
a minimum. It had to go on a recruiting drive in Europe, to
find qualified people to replace those who had been arrested
or fled; in 1938, 22 of the 37 professors and lecturers were
Europeans. By that year, the number of graduates had risen
to 275 and the number of students were 119 – 97 men and 22
women.

Passing the baton – remarkable Chinese

In his reports, Frederick did not describe such arrests and
torture in Faku. He wrote of the activities of bandits and
kidnappers but at the same time an increase in the number of
members. "Altogether for the year (1933), we have had the joy
of baptizing 82, the largest number on our annual record." On
Christmas Day, the church held a baptismal service attended
by 600 members. Frederick praised the work of his Irish and
Chinese colleagues in preaching and Bible classes. "One
cannot conclude these notes without expressing admiration
for our Pastor Shang of Faku, whose quiet courage and
patience is beyond all praise." On Christmas Day, the church
also chose 14 new deacons (assistants to the minister), one

of whom, a commercial traveller named Sun, had given up drinking and gambling.

In his firm, the manager objected to his pasting tracts on the office walls and tore them down. The subordinate asked why? To this question, the manager could offer no reply and so our Deacon was allowed to have his own way, holding Bible classes in leisure hours among the employees and by his evident sincerity gaining the respect of all.

He described a pastor named Tai, who used his bicycle to criss-cross the district:

Disliking idleness, he flies on his bicycle in and out of streets and lanes, holding cottage meetings and going further, against wind and weather; he appears with a volunteer deacon in one village or another in the neighbourhood. One village about 3 miles distant has a contingent at church early on the Sunday. He had to go 30 miles to Jinjiatun church the day before yesterday.

Another way to spread the gospel was through itinerant sellers of parts of the Bible. One of them, Chin Ta-san, wrote a report of his work to the Faku church in July 1934. He and a colleague entered the house of a woman in Suntzuwopeng:

She made haste to bring a long – stemmed pipe and tobacco. Filling the pipe with frog tobacco – the poorest quality – she lit the pipe at the smouldering end of the rope which hangs down from the roof-beam. Then she handed the pipe to us with the words, "Have a smoke, gentlemen." We replied: "We do not smoke, we are sellers of the Bible." This kind of thing we constantly meet, so that we pay little attention to it. But at first it arouses both dislike and pity.

Chin explained that they had come to show holy books: "the reading of which shows that there is One True God, who wishes us to do good and not evil." The woman and her family interrupted Chin by saying: "Alas, we know about doing good without reading books. We farming people have no knowledge of written words. How then can we read? Gentlemen, move to some other house." But bystanders encouraged the family to buy the books: "Is not your grandson a reader? Buy some books for him to read, lest he become like his father,

Four pastors of the church in Manchuria (from left: Paster Liu, Pastor Liu, Pastor Kao, Pastor C.W. Liu)

constantly reviling you with a carter's tongue."

At last they took five gospels. "Having no cash, they gave two eggs." On another day they went to a district and went to register at the local police station; the officer did not give his permission, which was not granted until late in the afternoon, so that they sold no books that day. In one village of twenty houses, they met a man of eighty years old who encouraged his neighbours to buy; thanks to him, they sold three hundred copies of Biblical writing. It was these people, like Pastors Shang and Tai, Deacon Sun and vendor Chin, who would spread the church in China, long after the missionaries had gone.

In the autumn of 1934, to encourage the sale of electricity, the Japanese authorities arranged a night market in Faku by hanging long rows of bulbs over stalls in the street. Staying open until 09:00 P.M., it attracted a large crowd of young and old.

Frederick wrote:

> It happens that our main street chapel is in the middle of this market street... A better position we could not desire. Hence the usual bedtime for the people find the hall filled with listening throngs, keeping our Pastor and his eager assistants busy explaining and illustrating the Truth of Christ. Hitherto after dark, the streets were almost deserted.

Another remarkable Chinese believer was an elder of the town of Tuchuan, 260 miles from Faku. Named Chao, he was the best-known businessman in the town and often chairman of its merchants' association. "He makes the church his special care," wrote Frederick in April 1935. "You might see him sweeping the floor or tidying the rooms." It was a remote place close to the border with Mongolia; to reach it from Faku required a long journey by cart, train and then bus or cart over a plain of 60 miles, occupied by more antelopes than people. This lonely road was a favoured place of bandits, who sometimes shot to kill. In the summer of 1934, one pastor took four days to cover the 60 miles after rains had damaged the roads.

In 1933, bandits sacked Tuchuan, looting as they went, but not touching the church. The citizens fled, including Elder Chao.

Now the Christian community is thriving and has a large school. The people do not seem to need periodic stimulation to keep their Christian enthusiasm alive. They have no salaried evangelist. From the beginning of its history, they have paid their own way, asking for no help from foreign funds, until lately they pled for assistance in their school with their increasing numbers. A centre of light in a troubled land, the church in Tuchuan, led by Elder Chao, a big, reserved and humble servant of God, holds on its way in perils of robbers, isolated and conspicuously successful.

On Christmas Eve in 1934, a Chinese minister named Liu, who had formerly worked in Faku, gave an address over the radio to the people of Manchuria from a studio in Shenyang. It was the first time a Chinese Christian had broadcast over the radio. He had to submit in advance three copies of his address to the government but they did not change a word.

Frederick wrote in a report home:

Through the cold, quiet streets, I made my way to the office of a coal company and at once was listening to the beautiful, distinct voice of my dear friend... It was wonderful to listen to the preaching once so well known in Faku, the town where he had made his mark, now addressing all Manchuria in the name of Christ. I came away thankful to God that such a man had been chosen and that he had given his witness with such conviction and power.

In 1934, the church in Faku had 355 baptisms, a record since it was established in 1890. Frederick saw a relation between the deteriorating conditions of society and the rise in conversions:

We cannot ignore the possible connection between the present success of our religion in Manchuria and the fear, uncertainty and suffering which resulted from the occupation of September 1931. Social deterioration, accentuated by opium, morphia and heroin, blackens the picture against which shines the brightness of a redeemed community.

The Moderator

In 1936, Frederick was chosen as The Moderator of the Presbyterian Church of Ireland, at the age of sixty-six. He was the church's most senior public representative, a minister who held the post for one year. He was chosen by a vote of the presbyteries of the church; 30 of the 33 met and 21 voted for Frederick, against 7 for the second candidate and 1 for the third. It was the greatest honour which they could pay to one of their peers; it was also a symbol of recognition for the mission work done since Manchuria since 1867 and Frederick's role in it. He was the third foreign missionary to be elected; the two previous ones, in 1867 and 1898, had served in India. Having been nominated by 28 of the 37 Presbyteries, he was elected as Moderator in June 1936. He was clearly a popular choice. "His books on missionary work in the Far East are widely known from their penetrative power, their unfailing grip of essentials and their practical wisdom," commented the *Belfast Newsletter*. "He is a master of Chinese and has an extensive knowledge of the Chinese outlook on life."

Let us consider how this absence would affect the church in Manchuria and Frederick himself. Becoming Moderator meant returning to Ireland for the year of the assignment, during which he acted as an ambassador for the General Assembly and for the PCI as a whole. It meant visiting churches all over Ireland, preaching sermons and attending public events as the church's representative.

In terms of climate and physical comfort, it was a great improvement over Manchuria, as well as an opportunity to spend time with family members and old friends. It was an escape from the stress of living under the surveillance of the Japanese police and their constant demand for reports of his movements, his meetings and the content of his sermons. From being a suspect, he suddenly became one of the most important figures of Northern Ireland society, invited to meet senior members of the government, other churches and civil society. He had a busy schedule – but it was not comparable to the physical and psychological challenges of living in Manchukuo, including the threat of arrest and interrogation by the Japanese and of kidnapping and even assassination by bandits.

However, it did not occur to him to stay on in Ireland after the end of his assignment, despite his advanced age and the risks of life in Manchuria. A missionary like him treated the posting to their new country as a lifetime commitment which was only ended by death, serious illness, incapacity or circumstances outside their control, like arrest or expulsion. "Home" was no longer Ireland but Manchuria. This commitment was shared by those in the church at home who supported him financially and spiritually; they expected the missionary to remain abroad, unless he had a very good reason to come back; one term used at that time for those who ended their foreign assignment early was "returned empties", like an empty bottle of beer or milk that is handed back to the shop which sold it. The bottle has lost his valuable contents – as the minister was considered to have come back without having completed his mission. The members of the church who supported him took the commitment as seriously as he did and expected him to complete it.

This was especially the case with the mission in China, for which each person chosen had to spend years to learn the language, culture and customs before he or she could work effectively. To return after four or five years meant a waste of this hard-earned preparation which the church at home had paid for. This level of dedication was hard on family members whose commitment was not so strong and who wanted to return to be reunited with their loved ones at home; it also meant that missionaries were separated for years from their children, which left its mark on both.

Being Moderator meant Frederick's absence from Manchuria for an extended period, at a time when the church was facing great difficulties and challenges and needed all the help it could get, especially from such an experienced minister as he. To spend a year in Ireland was a culture shock; he met members of congregations concerned with issues very different to those facing the church in Manchuria. At that time, Northern Ireland was a place deeply divided between the majority Protestants who rejoiced in their adherence to the United Kingdom and the minority Catholics who preferred union with the Irish Free State established in the south of the island in 1922.

This division affected many aspects of life, with separate schools, churches, community associations and often housing and places of work; mixed marriages were rare and usually opposed by members of both families. One story which circulated in the family was of a visit by Frederick in 1936 to a church in Fermanagh, a rural county whose population was evenly split between Protestant and Catholic. At the end of his sermon, he said that two Catholic priests from the area were about to leave to work as missionaries in China; knowing as he did the dangers and challenges of such a mission, he asked the congregation to pray for the health and well – being of the two men. After the service, two elders approached him and told him that he would not be welcome in their church again – even though he was, as Moderator, its most senior representative. In Manchuria, relations between Protestant ministers and Catholic priests were much warmer than in Ireland. Far more united than divided them; both were working to build a Christian community in an environment that was difficult and often hostile; the Chinese government and most Chinese people considered them to be the same. During periods of anti – foreign sentiment and persecution, they were both targets of attack:

Frederick O'Neill, the Moderator

After the Boxer Rebellion in May 1901, the Protestant church in Manchuria had sent a moving letter of condolence to the Roman Catholic mission in the region, in recognition of its many foreign and Chinese members who had been killed:

> We venture to approach you to express our heartfelt sympathy with you in the trying circumstances which you have been called upon to pass through in the year gone by. We can never forget that, when one of our number fell seven years ago, the first note of sympathy which we received was from one of you... The whole province of Manchuria is infinitely poorer today in the removal of such witnesses for Christian faith as the wise and just Bishop Guillon, the gentle Pere Emonet, the well-beloved Sister St. Croix and all those others who counted not their lives too much to lay down for Christ's dear sake. Many of us have lost among them kind personal friends and we shall miss their good fellowship and all will ever be inspired by their example and fortitude and heroic devotion to the Christian cause.

Even after such a tragedy as the Boxer Rebellion, such an expression of friendship toward Catholic priests would not have been well received by many at home. It was more prudent for missionaries in Manchuria to remain silent about their feelings for their Catholic friends than to speak of them in their reports back home. What was normal in Faku was not normal in Fermanagh.

With the year as Moderator, the long journey times and other commitments, Frederick and Annie were away from Faku for two years. They arrived back in Dalian in August 1937, after crossing the Atlantic, Canada and then the Pacific Ocean.

Return from leave

While they were crossing the Pacific, the Japanese army attacked Nationalist forces at Marco Polo Bridge outside Beijing and began its all-out attack on China. It was the beginning of the most devastating war in the country's history, in which more than 20 million Chinese soldiers and civilians were killed. The impact of this war would soon be felt by the church in Manchuria.

During Frederick's absence, his place was taken for one year by another missionary, Harold Corkey and his doctor wife, who were then sent to another station. For the second year, no other missionary came, so the job fell onto the shoulders of his longtime colleague, Mamie Johnston, who had arrived in Faku in 1923 and would stay until 1952. The Manchukuo period was one of declining involvement by the PCI. Between 1931 and 1945, 35 missionaries left Manchuria and only 15 new ones came, with none between 1938 and 1944. It was especially hard to recruit medical missionaries; only 2 came, in 1934 and 1937. This decline was a result of the Japanese occupation which made the work of the missionaries more difficult, the increasing physical risk of living in Manchuria and the growing independence of the church, which made the missionaries less important.

Frederick paid the following tribute to Mamie Johnston, who was, after his wife, his longest-serving colleague in Faku:

> The debt of the whole Church to her wisdom and daring is beyond compute. Thinking nothing of her own safety or convenience, she faced all manner of ominous situations with the utmost resources, absorbed only in the protection of the helpless, through faith in the power of God.

Despite these storm clouds on the horizon, Frederick was able to carry on his work in Faku, as long as he informed the authorities. He wrote in a report in October 1937:

> When I paid the necessary calls on the two chief Japanese officials in this town, I was received with courtesy. One of the officials postponed judicial work to come and talk to me through an interpreter. Being told that I had been present at the Coronation (of British King George VI on May 12, 1937), he was very much interested, hoping I could show him some pictures of the ceremony.

Frederick had the good fortune to be in London during the coronation and was able to witness this important event in the life of the British royal family, which occurs infrequently.

Later the Chinese head inspector of schools, who had been educated for ten years in Japan and become a Christian there, told him that he was very pleased with the mission schools in Faku:

> To sum up my present impressions, I should say that the tension which began two years ago has eased very considerably, so that there has ensued much greater mutual understanding. Our aims in Church and School and Hospital are becoming clearer to the authorities. But one cannot tell what a day may bring forth.

One new requirement of the government was that the students spend one hour a day on manual labour, such as gardening, sweeping and tidying the grounds. The church planned to rent land the next year on which the pupils would be trained in agriculture.

Frederick said the authorities put no restriction on the church's evangelising work. Accompanied by a local assistant, Annie regularly visited about fifty households to teach the scriptures and sing hymns. "Everywhere the visitors are received with pleasure and sometimes with joy. The educated Buddhist said to his (Christian) wife the other day: 'You go your way to heaven, I go my way to hell.'" Frederick received a residence certificate for Faku, drawn out in China, after a long but agreeable interview with the Special Affairs Office of the local government. When he was preparing to leave, the Japanese head of the office asked him: "Have you a wireless set?" "No," Frederick replied, "and if I were offered it, I should decline." "Do you possess a gun?" "I do not and, if one were given to me, I should not know how to use it."

Frederick was much in demand as a speaker. On the boat crossing the Pacific, he had given a lecture to a large audience on the situation in the Far East as well as delivering sermons. In the first half of 1938, Frederick went to Shenyang three times to speak at religious meetings. One was at a church, at which attendance averaged from 120 to 150; another was at the Manchurian Christian College and the third an Easter retreat for the Theological College. In the summer he organised a Bible school for a week in Faku. The Japanese wanted to know everything that was going on, even in the church. So they sent an observer to the Bible school for one day to take notes.

One of the greatest successes of the mission in Faku was the boys' school. In 1938, it had a record enrollment of 160 students, including 120 boarders squeezed into a small space; ten boys slept in a small room, 20 feet by 11 feet, with two kangs. One condition for attendance was that every boy had to come to morning service on Sundays. Frederick gave a sermon at this service and was also one of three ministers to give religious instruction to the pupils.

He wrote:

> The chief of the town's police brought a boy, urging that he be received. He was told that the boy would go through the same examination as the other applicants. Clearly the reputation of our school for good education and discipline has spread far. The headmaster is honoured and respected in the community. One result of our present school status is that the headmaster's recommendation for government appointments in the civil service is favourably received; several graduates have already been placed.

> Our boys' high school has a history of more than 40 years and of late has been at the heights of its reputation for good management and teaching. If you could hear the 220 boys, between the ages of fifteen and nineteen, forming one immense choir, singing with all their might in praise of God, you would never doubt the value of your gifts to the Foreign Mission cause. At present I lead the evening worship service of the school on five days of the week, from 06:00 to 06:30 P.M., in our large church.

All the graduates of 1938 secured positions, as teachers, civil servants or in higher education, except for one who had eye trouble. In 1939, the enrollment increased further to 207. He gave an example of the charity of the school. The mother of one of the boys died and his classmates discovered that his father was a poor water-carrier who had donated everything he could for his son's education. The small room his parents occupied did not even have a lamp. So the boys and teachers made a collection and collected 80 Manchukuo yuan, equivalent to four pounds and 14 shillings in British money. Frederick commented that this would only be possible at a Christian school.

Other British people had the same vision of the value of a Western education, such as Frederick Stewart (1836-1889 AD), the founder of the public education system in Hong Kong. He also believed that Chinese would benefit greatly from an education in both their native language and English and a diverse curriculum, including history, geography and science, designed to enrich the students culturally and encourage them to think and analyse. Like Frederick's school in Faku, the schools Stewart established in Hong Kong were extremely popular with parents eager that their children have a modern education that would equip them for the new world being created in front of them.

In 1940, Frederick took part in the ordination of 4 young ministers from Faku, a record number for a single year. "One has shouldered the burden of a dwindling cause in Jinjiatun, where the first Chinese pastor in the Irish mission was ordained thirty-two years ago." He also organised a week-long summer Bible school, attended by 57 men and women. In one outstation, Takungchutun, a principal deacon donated a site suitable for a new chapel.

During the year, the vendors of the Bible sold 31,600 copies of single Scripture books. They were examined by the chief of the town's Japanese secret police, who asked them: "With your energy and spirit, why not help the Japanese Empire? On the borders of the Empire, there is work to be done. Why not do something of use to the Empire?" They replied: "Our preaching of the True Religion is indeed of benefit to the Empire." These words persuaded the chief, who allowed them to continue their work.

In December, Frederick reported that the membership of the Faku church had reached 1,356, with 3 missionaries, 5 Chinese pastors and 32 male and female evangelists. There were 409 pupils attending Christian schools, with 840 attending Sunday school and 1,140 enrolled in Bible schools. The women's hospital had a Chinese staff of 15 and total attendance of 5,014 during the year. Since the death of Dr Isabel Mitchell in 1917, the hospital had been unable to attract a long-term foreign missionary doctor. One of the patients cured by the hospital was a lady named Mrs Tsai, a church member who had become an opium addict. For two years, Annie and others had tried to persuade her to give up, but in vain. Her eldest son was an outstanding teacher at the church's high school; he had used up all his money and felt unable to refuse the money for fear he would be responsible for her death. "Now, thanks to God, Mrs Tsai is free, well and happy," said Frederick.

Harold Corkey, the minister who had stood in for him for one year, reported that many children died of measles every spring. Tuberculosis was also widespread. He said:

> There are no mental hospitals in China, so that all such illnesses usually come to the church if their people have any connection with us. The Chinese lump all such mental and nervous illness together as 'possessed by devils'. It is remarkable too the improvement and even cure which follows when such poor folk get into an environment of love. Some get completely well.

Closing the schools

The sharpest conflict in Manchukuo between the authorities and the church came over its thirty mission schools, which employed 200 teachers and had more than 5,000 students. The ones established by Frederick in Faku were good examples. They were popular and respected by the local community, with parents competing with each other to send their children. It gave the church prestige and status; with the hospital, it was the principal method of introducing Christianity to the public, in Faku as elsewhere in Manchuria and many parts of the world.

But the government wanted control of every aspect of society, including education. It demanded a representative, a "juridicial person", on the governing body of each school; he would report to the government what the schools were doing and be the bridge between the authorities and the church. The church did not want to accept such a person since it wished to retain control over its schools and preserve their Christian character. Then the authorities ordered that teachers and students attend Shinto shrines and worship the Sun Goddess, one of the main

Shinto deities who was said to be an ancestor of the Japanese emperor.

After the Meiji Restoration of 1868, the Japanese government had made Shinto the state religion and separated it from the Buddhism with which it had been mixed from a thousand years. The government turned Shinto into a symbol of nationalism and the Emperor into a divine figure. Fighting for Japan meant not only fighting for the country and its ruler but also a god. The militarists who took over the country from the early 1930s exploited Shinto for their own nationalist purposes. As Japan conquered more and more territory in Asia, so its army needed an increasing number of soldiers to control it; it used Shinto and the worship of the Emperor to convince its people that they were fulfilling a mission that was both national and divine.

The government of Manchukuo used the same methods as those in Japan to try to brainwash the people of Manchuria, through rigid control of education, the media, propaganda and religion and make them believe that Emperor Hirohito was divine. It adopted Shinto as the state religion in 1940. In 1942, it adopted a new anthem, of which the first line reads: "With the universe created in God's light, the vast land strengthens the Emperor's rule." "God's light" in the anthem referred to the Emperor of Japan.

The government's demand that students of mission schools attend Shinto shrines and worship the Sun Goddess provoked an uproar within the church. Some members said that the church should refuse cooperation with the Japanese and close all schools immediately. Others, eager for a compromise that would enable them to keep control of the schools, argued that the law on Shinto shrines was a political rather than a religious law; Japanese Christians, including ministers, said that taking part in Shinto ceremonies had no religious significance and was equivalent to British people standing for the national anthem. In January 1938, the conference of missionaries held a full debate on the issue and voted 100-to-4 in favour of defying the government. A vast majority believed that Shinto ceremonies were completely against the Christian religion.

Another point of dispute with the government was the church's insistence that their schools were defined as Christian institutions, which the authorities refused. In accordance with this decision, in October 1939, the church reluctantly decided to close the mission schools. The government bought five Presbyterian schools in Yingkou, Jilin, Guangning, Xinmin and Yushu and three belonging to the Presbyterian Church of Scotland. The General Assembly of the (Presbyterian) Church of Scotland in 1940 said it received with much regret the news that the two churches in Manchuria "had found it necessary for conscience' sake to abandon their educational work. They express their sympathy with the missionaries in thus being deprived of so potent an instrument of evangelisation and with the Manchurian Presbyterian Church in the loss thus sustained". This marked the end of half a century of missionary educational work in the region and was a tragedy for the church. Education was one of the most important instruments of bringing Christianity to the people of China; it had probably attracted more into the church than any other activity had. Every parent wanted his child to be educated and have a life better than he had; in many places, a church school was the only or one of the few choices available and at a modest price. The missionaries were pioneers in bringing education for girls in China. Giving up these schools was an incalculable loss for the church, the missionaries and for present and future pupils and their families.

The schools in Faku were to close also. Frederick wrote in December 1940 that all had been arranged in an atmosphere of friendliness and mutual respect. "But our Christian basis does not fit in with the clearly defined purposes of the government. Some schools are to continue to function, being purchased by the authorities. Others, freely chosen by the missions, must close down not later than the end of 1942."

After negotiations with the church, the government agreed to pay 641,000 Manchukuo yuan in early 1941 for the schools it purchased. At the official rate of exchange, this was worth about 40,000 pounds. At the rates available in Tianjin which the church could obtain, it was about 12,000 pounds, which the church considered a fair price.

The church's Theological College in Shenyang was more

successful in resisting a government takeover. For five years, the authorities had been pressing it to become a registered institution, which would enable them to exercise more control. But they were not sure under which category they should list the college. It agreed to accept part-time Japanese lecturers, who were Presbyterian ministers, but refused to accept a Japanese as a full-time official on the grounds that he was not Presbyterian. This reason was accepted by the government; but the man gave a series of lectures in which he said that Manchukuo was indissolubly linked to Japan and that everyone in it would worship the divine ancestors of the Emperor at a new shrine that had been built in the capital at Changchun. He said that this was the first religious duty of everyone in Manchukuo, without exception.

Despite this, the college was able to continue its normal teaching and evangelical work, with a student enrollment in two grades of 100, until the end of 1941 and Japan's attack on Pearl Harbour on December 7. In March 1942, a new college board was appointed that was dominated by Japanese and the student enrollment had dropped to 50. The new principal told the students to forget the contacts they had had with the Westerners and that they must fulfil all government requirements. He introduced Shinto national ceremonies and said that these were not inconsistent with Christianity. The newspapers said that the church had been liberated from the evil influence of missionaries who were "agents of Western imperialism".

Conflict and evacuation

In 1937, a senior minister of the Scottish Presbyterian Church named A.S. Kydd visited Manchuria to report on the situation for the church at home. He visited all the Scottish mission stations and two of the Irish ones. He also met the head of the Japanese Military Mission in Shenyang, senior officials of the Ministry of Education, including military advisors and a dozen other Japanese officials. The foreigners in Manchuria were still being treated better than Chinese and could hold meetings without the police being present; but they were subject to surveillance, had to report regularly to the police, needed permission to travel and their letters were opened.

Kydd reported that the church had 20,000 members in fifteen districts extending from Yingkou to Harbin. By July 1940, the number had increased to 21,898, with 14 hospitals, staffed by 50 doctors and 250 nurses. Kydd wrote:

> It is a living force in Manchukuo, the only independent association that is purely Manchurian in outlook and personnel... Under the new regime, it offers a rallying point for thousands of Chinese Christians who would otherwise feel themselves totally uprooted from any kind of communal life.

He said that five of the Christians arrested in 1935 were still in custody in May 1937 but that the torture had stopped. The police had to be notified of all churches meetings and sent observers to them; they had informers everywhere. The church had been forced to sever its connections with churches in the rest of China; radio sets could not receive Chinese stations and it was hard to obtain permission to leave Manchuria. It was dangerous to possess books published in China, including religious ones. Many of those with resources, initiative and education had escaped to the rest of China, before it became too difficult to leave. "The church had lost some of its best leaders. Community life was becoming ever more desolate and the object of educational institutions was being defeated."

He painted a dismal picture of economic exploitation and impoverishment of ordinary people, with vast railway and road construction programmes and the planning of huge cities. Manchukuo had become an important part of Japan's war effort. In July 1937, it had launched a full-scale war against China and in December 1941 would attack the United States at Pearl Harbour. The entire economy was put on a war footing, in which Manchuria played a key role. It produced soya beans, corn, sorghum, pigs, cattle and sheep, cotton and timber; through two five-year plans implemented in the 1930, it produced coal, cement, steel, aircraft, vehicle and fabrics. Heavy investment by state and private companies, with the establishment of a new currency and a central bank, produced a stable business climate and rapid industrial growth. The Manchurian economy was dominated by Japanese firms and geared to serve the needs of Japan, military and civilian, not of Manchuria. Tens of thousands of Chinese were forced to work in mines, factories and vast construction projects, as virtual slave labour; thousands died of illness, malnutrition and maltreatment on the job. Entire communities were uprooted and moved to make way for new roads and railway lines, factories, housing estates and military installations. All this made it very difficult for the church to grow. People were often moved and many of the brightest people, in the church as in other institutions, sought to escape to the rest of China. The church was subject to surveillance and harassment. Kydd wrote:

> It is difficult to see how the Japanese financiers providing the capital will be repaid... Japanese capitalists are not enthusiastic about investing more money in Manchukuo, with cereals and beans, the main farm products, suffering from low world prices. Foreign firms are being squeezed and the Hong Kong and Shanghai Bank is the only bank in which accounts are not subject to Japanese inspection. Japanese middlemen are eating up the profits of the farmers and other producers who receive from them 25 per cent less than they could have done by direct trading... The whole system by which the country is being administered and exploited by Japanese with time-serving Manchurians as their stalking horses and puppets is depressing in the extreme... There is no personal freedom and fear is all-pervasive. The Chinese are resentful and cowed. They are resigned and cautious. The Japanese know how to organise and possess machine-guns and planes.

On October 12, 1940, the United States ordered its citizens in Manchukuo to leave the country and return home. This was because of worsening relations between the United States and Japan and fears that it would arrest American citizens. Shortly afterwards, the British government followed suit, advising its nationals to leave the Far East unless they had a pressing reason to stay. The missionaries were very reluctant to leave; in the past, they had often not followed the advice of their government.

Meeting in January 1941, they decided to take the following measures: those due to take leave in the first half of 1941 should do so at once: mothers with small children should leave at once, if they wished: a medical committee should decide who should leave because their health would be endangered in the rush of an evacuation: and a committee of five missionaries would be set up with absolute powers to decide who should do what. In accordance with this decision, many wives with children left and went to Britain, Canada, Australia, New Zealand, Africa and India. The churches there welcomed them; most quickly found work in other mission fields, in churches, schools or hospitals.

In the autumn of 1941, the government banned all foreigners in Manchukuo from travelling, except with police permission that was difficult to obtain. At the beginning of September, the conference of the missionaries decided to advise all men of military age to leave on an evacuation ship which the British government was sending to Japan. It was becoming increasingly dangerous for Chinese to associate with foreigners; so there was less and less work which missionaries could do, especially in rural areas. So some missionaries of military age took the advice and left. It was a very difficult decision for the missionaries. On the one hand, they had the advice of their government at home to evacuate and could see round them the increasing conflict between Japan and China and the Allied powers fighting Nazi Germany. On the other, they were very reluctant to leave their congregations and their communities; if they left, when could they return?

In September 1940, Japan had in Berlin signed the Tripartite Pact with Germany and Italy, a military alliance between the three countries. One of its clauses read: "Germany and Italy recognise and respect the leadership of Japan in the establishment of a new order in Greater East Asia." They could see that war between Japan and the Allied Powers was becoming more likely each month. They also had increasing restrictions on their own activities and movements, making it more difficult to do their normal work. The hostility of the government towards Westerners made it dangerous for Chinese to associate with them. So, while their head told them that it was time to leave before the war broke out, their heart told them to stay.

In 1941, Frederick was already seventy-one; he and his wife had every right to retire after long and distinguished careers and enjoy the comforts of home and family. But they had spent more than forty years – the majority of their adulthood – in Faku; it was their home. As they walked round the town, they saw their life's work – the church, the schools, the hospital, the chapel in the town centre, their fellow pastors, the members of their congregation and hundreds of friends and contacts they had made. This was the treasure they had built up through years of hard work. Like his fellow missionaries, Frederick felt a sense of responsibility, like a father to his children. His place was in Faku. During the previous forty years, he had survived the Boxer Rebellion, a pandemic, sieges, police interrogations and attacks by bandits, events which would have persuaded a lesser man to give up and go home. He put his destiny in the hands of God, who would decide when he would leave. Like most people in Manchuria, he did not believe that Japanese rule would last long, because it was not based on natural justice or popular support. It could only survive through military power and totalitarian control. Once Japan lost its military advantage, that would be the end of Manchukuo and Chinese would resume control of their country. So he planned to ride the storm until the Japanese had gone home. His feelings were described in a letter by a lady Presbyterian missionary, Marion Young, who served in Manchuria from 1935 to 1943. In a letter home on October 7, 1941, she wrote:

> I often think of the O'Neills, he over and she almost seventy. They face the chance of another war. They have seen a lot in their lives in Faku and lost two dearly loved sons there. They have not been "soured" on China by it all. I think it means home to them much more than any place in Ireland.

On the morning of December 7, 353 Japanese aircraft, launched from 6 aircraft carriers, attacked the U.S. naval base at Pearl Harbour in Hawaii, sinking 4 battleships, 3 cruisers, 3 destroyers, 188 aircraft and killing 2,402. Japan was at war with the United States and Britain. The Chinese rejoiced, believing that it would result in the certain defeat of Japan. Even the naval commander in charge of the Pearl Harbour operation, Admiral Isoroku Yamamoto, opposed war with the U.S., saying that Japan could never defeat a country whose industrial capacity was so much larger; he had also opposed the invasion of Manchuria and China. Both he and the Chinese were correct; the attack on Pearl Harbour would result in the end of the Japanese Empire. But, before that happened, it would change the lives of millions of people, including Frederick and Annie.

Chapter 6

War
(1941-1945)

Internment

On December 8, the people of Manchuria learnt that the Japanese navy and air force had attacked Pearl Harbour and started a war with the United States. Japan was now at war with the Allied nations, including Britain. This would mean the internment of all its nationals in Manchuria.

The Reverend Tom Barker, a missionary in Shenyang who had been in China since 1913, described how he learnt the news.

On December 8, as we were finishing our breakfast, the Reverend C.W. Liu, my colleague and nearest neighbour, came in. "Come in here for a moment, please," he said, motioning to the living room. Once inside the room, "Japan has declared war and fighting has begun," he said. He spoke in an awestruck whisper. Joy and gloom, hope and sorrow, relief and terror were all fighting for expression in his face. He knew what it meant to him, his family and his flock in Manchuria. The outcome was certain – freedom at last from the yoke of Japan and the return of the country to its spiritual home as an integral part of China. But the immediate future was dark with danger. Japanese prison doors were always threatening; the city was thick with spies and traitors; a man's nearest friend might unwittingly be the cause of disaster through chance remark or thoughtless conversation.

If the time was long, the spectre of hunger loomed large in the not too distant future. Food was already a problem in Manchuria, in spite of its natural wealth. The Japanese, with their economic control policies – for which the Chinese farmer had the utmost loathing – were ensuring that the food supply should be diverted almost wholly to Japan, meaning the Japanese armed forces. Even one year of war could well bring slow starvation to his wife and children. "If war breaks out, there are two kinds of death for common folk to fear," it was said: "death by bombs and death by starvation."

The above came from a vivid account which Barker wrote of his nearly four years in captivity, entitled *War: From Behind Closed Doors*, which he circulated to his friends after the war. It provides most of the material for this chapter.

On the evening of December 8, the principal of the Theological College in Shenyang called a meeting of the faculty, announced a suspension of the classes and advised the students to stay in their rooms. During that night, the police arrested several missionaries and doctors at the Medical College and interned them in an apartment at the top of the Hongkong and Shanghai Bank Building in the city.

A week later, they were transferred to a club for foreign businessmen in the city, where they would live for six months. Over the next few days, more Westerners were brought in, until the number reached 60. These included men and women from the Presbyterian Church, Roman Catholic priests and nuns and other missionaries. The club had an open-air swimming pool, a badminton court, squash courts and a bowling alley. It made a fine recreation centre but was not suitable as an internment camp. Most of the men slept in a large reception room and the rest in the billiard room. The ladies slept in what had been the card room. Meals were served in the large room, on tables created by pushing together the card tables. Those without a camp-bed slept on straw mattresses, which filled the rooms, making the club like an emergency hospital ward.

Barker described life in the camp:

Two universal rules of Japanese police procedure might be mentioned here. One: never provide anything the prisoner can possibly procure for himself. Two: never be in a hurry to provide anything at all. They asked us for beds from our own homes, carpets, rugs, cooking utensils – in fact, anything we could want they were willing to provide, so long as it came from us. To this end, they left the Shenyang wives and most of the unmarried ladies at home, not allowing any contact with the Chinese, but strictly limiting their movement to providing for us.

He said that life was tolerable because their wives provided for them, bringing additional food, taking their laundry and doing everything necessary for their comfort. In addition, the French priests from the city's Roman Catholic cathedral brought supplies of food every day; because their country had been occupied by the Nazis, they were not interned. Some of the club servants were retained and were extremely helpful.

For me, the outstanding anxiety of those months was personal. I feared, both day and night, danger to the ladies left at home. One could not tell the day or hour some incident might occur that would land any one of our ladies in a Japanese prison. And there is hardly any thought more terrifying. Nothing of the kind happened. They, and we, were protected. And, though no communication was allowed, we saw each other in the distance daily, when she came with supplies. Above and around us was the eternal purpose of the God, whose Name is Love; and a man in Christ should know that all things work together for good.

Conditions for the internees were difficult but tolerable. They had food, warmth, clothing and companionship of one another. Of the sixty, four were doctors and two were nurses. Barker continued:

Perhaps the outstanding personality was the (Catholic) Bishop. He was our official President and a great strength to us all. He suffered much indignity and comparative insult from the cavalier treatment of the police; but he smiled through it all and never relaxed for a moment his vigilance in caring from his priests and sisters and his sense of responsibility for his diocese. No man could have been more friendly, more cooperative, more helpful to those in any kind of trouble – no matter what his creed... One curious thing about internment is how much it increases your respect for some and your comparative dislike for others.

The people who really suffered those six months were the ladies who were not interned. Their first and greatest test was loneliness. Cut off from their work, confined almost entirely to the house and without the companionship of the husband or the friend, life was an empty thing. It was an anxious loneliness, not knowing what would happen to their colleagues or themselves, with no news available from the camp or other parts of Manchuria and, in the first weeks at least, with constant worrying visits of investigating police, life was a trying thing.

Chinese members of the church, students of the colleges and friends of the missionaries prepared themselves for immediate imprisonment because of their association with the "enemy". Some were arrested and kept in prison for months. "We had hoped that, once we were out of the way, they would have comparative safety. But they knew better." Despite the risk, many went to the Shenyang club during the night to bring news to the internees, carry messages and offer financial and material help.

They knew they were running great risks but no danger could prevent their showing their friendship and love," Barker wrote. "It is such times that prove the power of the Gospel... A friendship and a loyalty that revels in ignoring the risk to freedom and to life is something very precious. It illumines the darkest hours and comforts the loneliest life. And that loyalty was shown in very real ways by numbers of our Chinese friends.

House arrest

Frederick and Annie were more fortunate – they were interned at home in Faku. She described their experience in an account published at the end of 1942:

The news of the outbreak of the war reached us in a brief note from our friend Pere (Father) Gilbert of the Canadian Catholic Mission in the dark of the morning of December 9. Next morning, as we were busy packing, a man passed our front windows. I hastened to open the hall door. He entered stealthily, carefully closing the door behind him. Then, from his shoe, he produced a note. It was from the French sisters: "This morning at eight o'clock, after one hour and a half to pack, our two Fathers were taken away by five special police. Pray for us."

We were hourly expecting to be taken away. Almost daily we were visited by the police. They came and went, always courteous, but never gave us any orders. We knew without their telling us that contact with our Chinese friends could only bring suspicion upon them. We knew that our gate was watched but no guard was posted there. We were cut off from communication with our Chinese friends and unable to learn what was happening to our colleagues in other places. For some months we had tried to accustom ourselves to the absence of news from home. Now no postman came at all. Yet, I must not forget – each Christmas Day brought a cable from our eldest son. We could hope for no cable on this Christmas Day. But, in the late afternoon, who should arrive but our old friend the postman, with a letter from this same son! The date was August. It seemed as if God Himself put this letter into my hand and with glad hearts we so received it.

Her account does not explain why they were not interned with the other missionaries in Shenyang. It was perhaps because of their advanced age – Frederick was seventy-one – and the remoteness of Faku. What part could an elderly missionary couple in this small town play in the war effort? What help could they provide to the enemies of Japan? It was perhaps also due to the fact that he had always enjoyed polite relations with the Japanese officials stationed in Faku: not friendly, but correct and formal. They saw the respect in which he was held by the people of the town and that he was a threat to no-one.

All the same, he and his wife were prisoners in their own home; they could neither go out nor meet their Chinese friends and neighbours without bringing suspicion on them. Their main contact with the world was their servant who met members of the church outside and passed on messages. The servant lived in the same compound, with his mother, a strong member of the church. "In the long, dark winter evenings, she would slip over and bring me news of my women and our sick folk," Annie wrote. After Chinese New Year, in 1942, women from the town came to visit them, bearing gifts, as is the custom at that time of year. They brought so many eggs that Frederick and Annie were able to share them with their many sick friends. Most difficult was the loneliness and isolation. They had almost no contact with their many friends and church members in Faku and elsewhere in Manchuria and no news at all from their family and friends in Ireland. Europe was at war and their three sons were serving in the British military. Were they on active duty? Were they safe and well? Who was winning the war? The winter in Manchuria is the harshest in China – it is dark in the late afternoon and the temperature drops to below freezing. It is the season when you need warmth and companionship, not silence and isolation.

In early April, Frederick and Annie were told that they were to board a ship for Japan in mid-April. Annie wrote:

> Once again, we packed our cases... Greatly daring, (church) Elder Fang said to the Japanese head of the special police: "Pastor O'Neill has been here for forty-five years. Many people wish to see him before he leaves. Can we have a farewell meeting?" To his surprise and delight, the answer was "Yes". The meeting was fixed for the following day. As we had not joined in worship with our people since December 9, you can imagine with what joy we met together in that beautiful church of so many inspiring memories. Just to be among them once more and hear the kindergarten children sing their Easter song and to join in the familiar hymns, which the boys and girls sing so heartily. It was a most moving experience and we thanked God for His goodness. In front sat the special police, reverently joining in the service.

Immediately afterwards, they were informed that the date of their departure had been postponed for a month.

"After this courtesy on the part of the authorities, the tension was lessened and our friends came more freely to see us." Many elderly evangelists visited them and prayed with them; it was a way for them to express their pent – up emotions. On May 21, Frederick and Annie visited the home of Elder Fang and his son, a teacher at a Christian school who had been imprisoned for sixty-five days but had recovered from the ordeal. The son was living in a new house built for him and his five children by his father close to his own home. It had three rooms, the largest of which was being fitted with benches, a table and lamps and would be used for religious services.

Finally, the day of their departure came, May 26.

Our pastor had asked and received permission for the people to come and see us off. At 06:00 A.M., I could see women walking to and fro in the garden. About seven o'clock, I ran across to say goodbye to a patient in hospital, a dear friend of mine. As I passed the front block, the sound of singing reached me. It was the doctor and her staff at morning worship. Just before nine o'clock, the bus which was to take us and our guards away arrived at the gate. This was the signal for our brief parting service. There was to be no sadness, only praise to God for the long years He had granted us to be together. We stood in the compound. First we sang 'Jesus love me'. Then together we repeated the twenty-third Psalm, dear to our Chinese Christians as to us in our homeland. My husband prayed, thanking our Father for all His loving kindness and tender mercies, and our pastor pronounced the benediction. As we climbed into the bus, the little group gathered around the gate and sang: "The Lord bless thee and keep thee, the Lord make His face to shine upon thee and be gracious unto thee; the Lord lift up His countenance upon thee and give thee peace." Those were the last words we heard as we moved off. And so we were parted, only in body, but not in spirit, until the day of glad reunion in the Father's home.

So Frederick and Annie left Faku, their home for more than forty years, not knowing when or if they could return, and were taken to Shenyang. They took only what they could carry and had to leave behind most of their possessions. They did not know the outcome of the war nor their future health. But, like the other missionaries, they intended to return; this was their home.

After Frederick's departure, the Chinese minister in charge of Faku proposed that members of the congregation who had broken away and established their own church be reunited with the main congregation. Both sides agreed to this and the breakaway church became a branch of the Protestant Church of Manchuria.

Transfer to Japan

Back in Belfast, the church had no news of its missionaries in Manchuria. Postal services had been cut since the attack on Pearl Harbour. All the information it had came from other parts of China occupied by the Japanese army. Missionaries there reported that they had not been ill-treated but were forced to live at home and needed permission to go outside. In April 1942, the *Missionary Herald* reported that 13 Presbyterian missionaries and their wives were still in Manchuria. "There is no reason to suppose that they are not being treated with the courtesy which is shown to their colleagues in other areas," it said. Before the attack on Pearl Harbour, one other Presbyterian missionary had escaped into the rest of China and four others had left and were living in Canada and Australia.

In Shenyang, the internees discussed ceaselessly how long they would be detained. Most were above the age of military service; holding them did not help Japan's war effort and only tied up the time of the soldiers and police guarding them. When would they be allowed to go home? Barker described how, at the beginning of April 1942, they realised that something was about to happen.

> We were asked innumerable questions and filled in countless forms. The Japanese official is always happy in printed questionnaires, which are carefully answered, filed and forgotten. When the same man wants the same information, another form is produced and the same routine repeated. When another man in the same office wants the same information, the routine is repeated again. Then another office wants it and again you fill it in, once, twice or many times, as fancy may dictate. The waste of time, energy and paper for the past fifteen years in Manchuria alone has been unbelievable.

This filling of so many forms was because different arms of the Japanese government had their own intelligence-gathering operations – including the Foreign Ministry, the Interior Ministry, the Chief of the General Staff, the Navy, the Military Police and the South Manchuria Railway Company. Usually these arms did not share what they knew with each other.

Filling in all these forms raised their hopes. But May passed with no news. Finally, they were told they would leave Shenyang for Japan on June 6, with a limit of four suitcases per person. They protested at this arbitrary restriction; many had lived in Manchuria for most of their adulthood and their life possessions were there. But this request for more space was refused – it meant donating most of their household goods to the Japanese police.

But we consoled ourselves that we should be together with our wives, that all our colleagues would be with us and that getting out of Manchuria meant at least comparative safety. When the police warned us that the seas were full of danger, we told them we would gladly take the risk.

More than a dozen of the Catholic priests remained in Shenyang. The wives of Barker and his colleague came to the camp and they left in the late afternoon of June 4. At the city railway station, they were joined by other British detainees, including Frederick and Annie, for the long journey, by rail and ship to Kobe in Honshu, the main island of Japan. They were told that they would be put on a ship and exchanged for Japanese prisoners held by the Allied forces.

On arrival in Kobe station, we had the usual Japanese delay. We stood, without breakfast, on the station platform for about three hours. The sheep were divided from the goats. The sheep – supposed to be the more elderly and more tender brothers and sisters – were sent to the Yamata and Kobe hotels; the others – supposed to be the strong – were piled into trucks with their baggage and finally reached a fine building in the suburbs, a new dormitory block of the Canadian Academy.

In July, there were told to prepare for their departure. Hastily and happily, they packed their belongings, ready for a meticulous examination by the Japanese customs.

The bags were to be sent ahead of them to Yokohama, the port of embarkation. Just as they had finished packing, the Swiss Vice-Consul came to the camp in which they were being held. As the representative of a neutral nation, he was the middleman between the two sides. He announced that 20 of the missionaries would not be able to go because there was not enough room on the ship. Frederick and Annie were among the fortunate ones to be chosen. Barker was one of those left behind:

I know that only the missionaries were left behind, that considerable lobbying took part in which the Japanese police played an important part and that many changes took place in the roster. I did not feel justified in trying to pull wires; if ill-fortune came to some of us, I felt Ann (his wife) and I could stand it better perhaps than most of our group; I knew no Swiss or Japanese well enough to appeal for help; I was weak enough to accept the situation.

In the end, seven of the Presbyterian missionaries were left behind. Were they too kind or had they relied too much on the good will of the Japanese police, to be taken on board ship? Other foreigners were not so honest, offering money, goods or other bribes and calling in favours that they had done before the war, to ensure that they got on board. Coming from Manchuria, Barker and his colleagues were ill-equipped for this kind of negotiation; they did not have the network of connections in Japan needed at that moment. Nor did they wish to do the wheeling and dealing necessary to take their place ahead of others.

Later Barker regretted his indecisiveness:

It is a merciful providence that prevents our peeping into the future. If we had known what lay ahead of us, I do not think many of our number would have survived. Everyone assured us that another boat would come in a month or two. If I had known then what I know now, I should have fought like a tiger to get every last one of our group on that ship. It has cost us three long years of enforced inactivity in the Church Militant, heartbreaking anxiety and premature old age. We have all, I think, tried hard to see the value of the "discipline". It may be that our thoughts and prayers, our inner struggles and defeats, were of more value to the Kingdom than we know. It may be we were learning patience, tolerance and sympathy and gaining the power to feel as we have never before "man's inhumanity to man". It may be that we were being prepared for a different line of work in ways we could not understand."

Frederick and Annie were fortunate to be spared this calvary. They were put on the ship in Yokohama, with missionaries and other foreigners. Its destination was Lourenco Marques, capital of Mozambique in East Africa, which was then a Portuguese colony. Since Portugal was neutral in the war, it was the appropriate place for an exchange of Allied prisoners with Japanese ones. Such a swap could not take place on territory held by the Japanese or by the Allies. In September 1942, the ship arrived in Lourenco Marques, with seven Presbyterian missionaries, including Frederick and Annie. From there, they boarded another vessel which took them to Britain and finally their home in Belfast.

Kobe

Barker and those left behind were taken to a small hotel in Kobe called the Eastern Lodge, which had been built for Indian students. There were about 30 foreigners in all, including 14 missionaries. They were frustrated and disappointed. They had no idea if or when another ship would be available to take them home; as the war turned against Japan, there would be fewer vessels available for such humanitarian missions, as every ship was used for the war effort. How would enemy prisoners be treated? Would there be any food left for them and would their safety be guaranteed?

They were held in the hotel; next to it was a building called the Parsee Club, which belonged to a wealthy Indian named Mr Schroff, who had married a Japanese woman and had a little boy of two. He was extremely generous to the prisoners, providing them with good beds and bedding, comfortable chairs and excellent and plentiful food; this abundance lasted for over a year. Their hotel had no outdoor space but the guards often took the inmates for walks in the hills, sometimes twice a day. They also took them downtown for shopping expeditions. They hired a piano for morning worship every day and suffered no hardship. Kobe was probably the best city in Japan for a Westerner to be interned. Opened to foreign trade in January 1868, it had the busiest port in the city and had a long experience of dealing with the outside world, a large foreign population and many Western-style buildings. Its citizens were accustomed to seeing foreign faces; many had worked for foreign companies.

The internees expected their stay to be brief, two months at the most. "We used to speculate on how long the exchange ship would take to reach Mozambique and return, how long they would spend on refitting her and where the next batch of Japanese would come from to be exchanged for us." But they gradually realised that the day of their evacuation was being postponed and settled down to a routine. On September 23, 1943, all the men in the camp without wives were moved to another camp in the city and replaced by 40 women, including 4 American missionaries from Osaka and 35 nuns from local convents. The police appointed Barker president of the camp, by virtue of his age and seniority; he was fifty-eight. He would hold the position for the next two years. Of that time, he spent the next twenty-one months in Kobe.

> I retain a grateful memory of a general atmosphere of kindness. This was due to Mr Schroff, to his hotel staff, to the official in charge of foreign affairs, to the attitude of the guards and indeed of every Japanese with whom I had any personal dealings... At the end of this war, when one meets so many authentic cases of brutality, it is good to pause and remember the shining instances of sheer goodwill and to testify that we found in our enemies so much real kindness. I do not profess to understand the Japanese. I loathe their militarism and I detest the stupid inefficiency of their officialdom. But no-one can persuade me that they are not a kind-hearted people.

They organised a camp academy for the study of Chinese characters, French, Japanese and New Testament Greek. They held concerts, lectures, charades and other forms of entertainment at least once a week. They relied for news of the war on a French-Canadian priest who had excellent Japanese; he listened to the radio and read the newspapers and was able to give his fellow inmates some idea of what was going on in the outside world, albeit through news reports that were highly censored. In September 1943, the Americans were told that they would be put on an exchange ship in a few days. They had to fill in innumerable questionnaires and interviewed, with one all-important question: "Do you really want to leave Japan?" They departed from the camp, leaving the others envious and uncertain.

As the months went on, the war was turning against Japan; they began to fear American air raids.

The net was closing round Japan. Things were tighter and we gradually felt the strain. Our walks were now much fewer, shopping was done by the guards and our appearance on the streets was confined to absolute necessities such as dentistry, when we were taken to a dentist close at hand. Singing at worship was frowned on as something likely to irritate the public. A huge handpump was provided and firedrills held frequently. Dugouts – really holes in the ground – were made in the garden and we had practices at self-protection in case of attack from the air. Food was distinctly less plentiful, less attractive and less appetising.

The central location of the camp turned from an attraction into a danger; it was close to the port that would be a prime target for American bombing. They asked their minders if they could be transferred to a safer location. At the end of June 1944, the head of the Internee Department of the city, Mr Matsumoto, told them that 15 of them would be transferred to another camp in Nagasaki, a port city in western Japan. He promised a plentiful supply of food and a guarantee that they would be well cared for. For Barker and his fellow missionaries, most important was that husband and wife would be able to stay together. "Most of us married folk would not have survived the loneliness and anxiety of separation and the loss and comfort and help of the partner... In all my dealings, I found Mr Matsumoto gentlemanly, courteous and altogether friendly."

Nagasaki

In the early afternoon of July 1, 1944, Barker and his fellow missionaries took the train from Kobe to Nagasaki. The journey took twenty-four hours on a crowded and uncomfortable train. On arrival, they took buses to a stop on a hill, where they got out and climbed a steep hill, through a cemetery, to a monastery. One of its buildings would be their home until the end of the war; it had more than 40 inmates, a Chinese cook and 2 women servants. It was a new two-storey building designed as a classroom block for a boys' school, with a dormitory and chapel upstairs. The dormitory was used by 28 nuns and missionaries.

They found a cow, two sheep, two pigs, fifty hens and twenty rabbits. Three women took care of the cow, providing a little milk each day, although more than half went to the police; internees cared for the other animals. It was a harsher environment than the hotel in Kobe. Its isolation meant that supplies had to be brought by hand up the hill. The four guards who watched over them were hostile and suspicious, of a different nature to the guards in Kobe. Three of them "were without shame and without honour, which was literally a disgrace to Japan," wrote Barker. Camp commander Sergeant Negoto "had a violent temper and was a thorough – going liar." The four received more food than that given to the forty inmates: often they had so much that they threw it away or took it home.

The shortage of food became a preoccupation for the inmates, who prepared and served it; they were also responsible for sweeping and cleaning the house.

> Our ordinary daily diet was two very small loaves of ersatz bread, about a cupful of cooked rice, about one third of a glass of milk, two platefuls of questionable vegetables and some ersatz coffee. I saw people picking up separate grains of rice and picking food out of the refuse. I saw them eating potato peelings, cabbage stalks, fish bones, loquat stones and various kinds of grass. Any leftovers from the guards' food were a particular luxury.

The internees complained to Barker about hunger and lack of energy.

While they were outside collecting grass for the cows, they picked wild strawberries and onions, potatoes and peaches, persimmons and loquats which had fallen from the trees and brought them back to share with their fellows. They were greatly helped by supplies of food from a nearby Franciscan monastery and the International Red Cross. The guards refused to let them have any news of the outside world. But one inmate met a Polish priest in the monastery who passed on news; they learnt of the surrender of Germany on the very day it happened. "Towards the end, however, it became more difficult to learn anything, for the news was concealed even from the Japanese themselves."

They made their own routine – up at five o'clock, with a drink of water, soup or coffee. Cleaning the house began after rollcall at 07:10 A.M., then breakfast just before eight o'clock. They held morning prayers from 09:00 to 09:15 A.M., then classes in French or Greek until a tea break at 10:00 A.M. Then they held Bible classes or cut the grass until lunch at noon. This was followed by quiet time for reading, tea or coffee until 03:00 P.M.; then work in the garden or more grass – cutting and reading until dark. They ate supper at 06:00 P.M. and had free time until rollcall at 08:00 P.M. They put out the lights at 09:00 P.M. or, during the periods of bombing, at 08:30 P.M. "With such a shortage, it became necessary to spread the food over several meals. The snacks kept the hunger from gnawing too severely."

In the first week of August 1944, they experienced their first air raid. In the middle of a very wet night, they were roused by the alarm; with no shelter, they hid in the stream of river that ran close beside the house. They spent hours crouching in the damp stones, while the planes were overhead. The bombs were mostly incendiaries which did not have much effect due to the heavy rain. The city replied with a barrage from its anti-aircraft guns. In the spring of 1945, the serious bombing of Japan began and they rarely enjoyed a night of uninterrupted sleep.

This heavy bombing lasted for four months but Nagasaki itself was only targeted six times; on the other occasions, the planes flew to and from more important targets. But, when the alarm sounded, they did not know this and rushed to their shelter. The four guards went to an excellent shelter in the monastery, which was deep underground, roomy, well-ventilated and well-covered; but they forbad the internees from using it. Considering its strategic importance as a major port and producer of ordnance, ships and military equipment, Nagasaki got off lightly.

The internees knew nothing of the momentous decisions being taken on the other side of the world to end the war. For six months, the United States had used intense firebombing of sixty-seven Japanese cities, to force the government to accept the terms of unconditional surrender in the Potsdam Declaration issued by the United States, Britain and China on July 26, 1945. It was Japan's refusal to surrender that persuaded President Henry Truman to authorise the dropping of two nuclear weapons, one on Hiroshima on August 6 and the second on Nagasaki on August 9. Early that morning, five planes took off from bases in Guam and flew over Kokura, a city in Kitakyushu and their primary target. They made three runs over the city but found 70 per cent of it covered by clouds; under such conditions, their orders did not allow them to drop the bomb.

So they flew on to Nagasaki, their secondary target. At eleven o'clock, a break in the clouds over the city allowed the bombardier in the Bockscar, the B-29 carrying the bomb, to see the target; the commander dropped the bomb. It contained 6.4 kg of plutonium 239 and exploded 43 seconds later at 469 metres above the ground. It had a blast equivalent to 21 kilotons of TNT, generated heat estimated at 3,900 degrees Celsius and winds estimated at 1,005 kilometres per hour. That day would live forever in the memory of the detainees.

Barker wrote:

> We had an alarm in the early morning and the all-clear went at nine o'clock... Shortly before 11, we were in our room having had a visit after morning tea from the nuns who had stayed talking longer than usual. Ann (his wife) was sitting on her bed and I was in the only chair, near the window. We heard a plane and looked out. Ann said: 'That plane looks like business. We ought to get ready.' She was reaching for her shoes when suddenly a blaze lit up the whole sky to the south of us. We both dashed for the door but had not reached it when the explosion came. We had just time to get under cover of some clothes hanging on the opposite wall, which was really the sliding door of the room. Those clothes saved our lives.

> Though the window was open, the explosion blew both glass and frame right across the room, driving the broken glass in some cases deep into the woodwork, scattering everything moveable and everything hanging on the walls and literally covering the whole mixture with fragments of broken glass. The sliding doors fell flat on the corridor outside, the house shook and the ceiling rose, luckily to subside again as the tremor passed. Blood was flowing freely but fortunately only from superficial cuts.

Of the inmates, eight suffered wounded from injuries caused by flying glass. But the Chinese cook and one of the two woman servants, who were out hunting for food, were killed.

> We had no idea of the new weapon. We thought an ammunition dump had blown up in the city. And this idea was strengthened by the terrible fire that started immediately, covering the city with flame and smoke, rising and spreading until the whole sky was darkened. The pall hung over us for days and the flying sparks were falling round our house, so that, in fear of the fire reaching our building, we kept guard constantly that day and the following night... We could not tell whether planes were American or Japanese. So we must keep someone day and night on watch to give alarms when a plane was either seen or heard. We did this faithfully, living all the time in added terror, while we tried to clean up and refit the building with what makeshifts we could find, to carry on our routine and to pray for the destitute and wounded thousands in the afflicted city. Most of us had a pre-sentiment that the end was drawing near. But some of us had not much hope that we should escape in the culmination of disaster in Japan.

Margaret McCombe, another Presbyterian missionary internee, described the day in this way:

> Some of our company who had to take turns watching for aircraft by command of the nervous Japanese police noticed a plane over the sunlit city of Nagasaki and saw something being released from the under-carriage. As the plane sped away, the 'object' exploded high in the air. When it went off, the building was filled with light and those outside who saw it described the flash like 'the sun bursting or like 20 suns'. This set off a series of ear-splitting explosions in the huge ordnance factories, in the munitions of the war factories and in the oil storage tanks. Fires broke out and blazed for days. One and a half square miles of the most densely populated area of the city lay in ruins.

The internees were fortunate. The hill which they had to climb on their first day in Nagasaki protected them from the explosion. Estimates for the immediate death toll in the city ranged from 40,000 to 75,000, with up to 80,000 dead by the end of the year; 60 per cent of the city was destroyed. About 15 to 20 per cent died from radiation sickness, 20 to 30 per cent from flash burns and the rest from other injuries. Most of the dead were civilians; less than a dozen western prisoners of war were among the dead. The bomb exploded over the district of Urakami, just 500 metres from the site of the largest Catholic cathedral in East Asia; work on it began in 1875 and it was completed in 1925.

That day many of the faithful had gathered inside for religious worship; all of them were killed. Nagasaki was the only city in Japan with a substantial number of Roman Catholics, many of them descendants of believers who had practised their religion secretly after the government banned it in 1587. Those who were discovered and refused to recant were tortured and killed. The French priests who went to Japan in the 1860s after the country was reopened to foreigners discovered that the believers had maintained their religion without outside priests or contact with the mother church in Rome for nearly two hundred fifty years. The Pope called it a "miracle". It was these believers who built the Urakami cathedral. It was an extraordinary story of the success of foreign missionaries and the devotion to Christianity in the most difficult circumstances imaginable. What a tragic irony it was that these devoted adherents of Christianity should have been the ones to have been killed.

In the days after the bomb, life became even harder. The internees had lost two of their three servants, no more bread and flour arrived from the city and they were completely cut off from the outside world. Senior police officers moved into the camp and the monastery, a sign that life in the city had become impossible. The inmates feared an invasion that would be worse than the bombing. If Allied soldiers invaded Japan, how much would their lives be worth? "We carried on with the day and night lookout for planes. Many passed during those days but ignored Nagasaki, while our anxiety mounted with the waiting."

Six days after the bomb, they noticed a sudden change in the attitude of their guards; they had become friendly and scrupulously correct. At 01:30 A.M. on August 17, the alarm bell was rung and everyone was ordered to meet in the dining room, whatever they were wearing. The Japanese chief of police, Mr Koyama, addressed the inmates, with a Canadian nun interpreting:

> I wish to congratulate you, your country has won and our country has been defeated. The Americans have discovered a new weapon, a new bomb which Japan could not withstand. While we were willing to fight to the last man for our country, the Emperor has given orders to cease fire and the Emperor must be obeyed. Whatever faults we had to find with our treatment in the camp were my responsibility alone and I alone bear the punishment.

It was a moment of overpowering emotion. The inmates could scarcely comprehend what they had heard. But Barker's good nature came to the rescue; he stepped forward, shook Koyama warmly by the hand and said: "Thank you, we can once more be friends. We have no enmity toward Japan. You and your friends will never suffer any punishment from anything we may say." He called on everyone to stand in silence, to thank God for peace restored and honour the memory of the countless brave who had given their lives for their country in this long weary war. From then on, the internees were treated as honoured guests.

With Koyama's speech, the atmosphere changed at once, as if from night to day. The police produced cigarettes, sake and wine and handed them to everyone. There was a plentiful supply of French wine – which came as a surprise to the inmates; the guards had told them that wine was unobtainable. In fact, they had collected a large stock, in preparation to celebrate Japan's victory. But, even at this historic moment which would never be repeated in the lifetime of those present, Barker and his fellow ministers did not break their vow of abstinence from alcohol. Everyone was so excited that they could not sleep. They spent the rest of the night drinking the wine and strong coffee, eating a great deal of Red Cross chocolate and talking.

Suddenly, they went from being despised prisoners of a hostile nation to being welcome guests. The guards vacated the building at night, leaving two extra bedrooms. The authorities provided rice, flour, meat, fish, tea, salt and sugar – food denied before on the grounds that it was unavailable; they also provided five servants to wait on the guests and do the laundry and workmen to mend the windows and replace the broken glass. The Mayor of Nagasaki paid a visit, bringing gifts of wine, sugar, fish and beans. They were free to visit the city but were advised not to go without a police escort; the government feared a hostile reaction from the public. Barker and his colleagues were content to wait until news of evacuation. American planes dropped food and clothing; the parachutes were too light, so much of the food was lost. But they managed to salvage enough to make a good addition to their already plentiful supplies.

On September 12, they learnt that there were five American ships in the harbour and that they could board the next day.

> We found it difficult to believe but started packing what stuff we had. Next morning a detachment of Australian and American troops arrived, armed to the teeth, and took us down to the hospital ship lying in the harbour. The ships had arrived ten days before the formal occupation of Nagasaki, but the Japanese made no objection. In fact they received them cordially.

They were received on the U.S.S. *Haven* and overwhelmed by every possible comfort – good food, well-appointed beds, luxurious and warm American hospitality.

> We spent ten days in the harbour, while the 10,000 prisoners of war from all Kyushu were brought in, examined and given health checks and put either on transports or on the hospital ship. During those days, we realised what others had endured. Our suffering in comparison with theirs had been negligible. And yet I think that both we and they received wounds in the spirit from which we shall never recover. I know that I am at least twenty-five years older than I was on the eighth of December 1941.

Barker and his party arrived at the port of Liverpool two months later, in November 1945.

In November 2005, I visited Nagasaki. People there told me that there were two main camps for prisoners of war, in addition to the place where the missionaries were held. One was near the city railway station, less than 2 kilometers from the site where the atomic bomb exploded. It housed Chinese, Koreans, Russians and Japanese Communists and opponents of the government; all in the camp died after the bomb on August 9, 1945. The other camp was 10 kilometres away from Urakami, next to what is now the Mitsubishi Shipyard, which has made some of the biggest ships in the world. During the war, it made ships for the navy; Western prisoners, such as British, Dutch, Australian and

Mitsubishi shipyard, Nagasaki

those captured in China, worked in the shipyard.

The site of the camp is now a secondary school, whose principal, a charming lady named Seiko Matsuo, told us that the prisoners of war there were fortunate in being some distance from the bomb: "It had no impact on them as the wind was blowing away from the camp. This took the radiation away and not towards the camp." The Reverend David Busk, an Anglican minister then resident in Nagasaki, said that one prisoner saw the bomb fall and was blinded for ten minutes before he recovered his sight.

> Many Christians in Nagasaki felt sympathy for the prisoners. Since they had no prospect of escape, they enjoyed some freedom and could leave the camp. Many died of diseases, not directly related to their treatment in the camp. One was a Dutch missionary from Indonesia who died of a lung disease that would have been treated in peacetime. In June 2005, his daughter came here and we held a service at the school in memory of her father.

War at home

For Frederick, Annie and other missionaries who were repatriated, the rest of the war was more peaceful. Northern

Ireland was the part of Britain furthest from the reach of German bombers flying from bases in the European continent. Before their return, the city of Belfast had been hit in a terrible raid on the night of Easter Tuesday, April 15, 1941. Two hundred bombers of the Luftwaffe attacked, killing nearly 1,000 people and damaging half of the houses in the city; about 100,000 of the total population of 425,000 were left homeless. Outside London, it was the greatest loss of life during a single night raid in Britain during the war. Belfast was an obvious target because it was a major producer of goods for the war – naval and merchant vessels, bombers and flying boats, anti-aircraft shells, tanks, and ammunition.

But its government made virtually no preparation for the raid; Belfast had only 7 anti-aircraft batteries, making it the most poorly defended city in Britain. It had evacuated just 4,000 of its 80,000 children and built only 200 public air raid shelters. The German planes had the freedom of the air over the city from 10:40 P.M. until 05:00 A.M. the next day; no Royal Air Force planes took to the air to fight them. In panic and fearing more raids, about half the population fled the city. Damage caused to shipyards and aircraft factories were so extensive that they needed six months to resume normal production. German bombers hit Belfast, on April 15 and May 4. But there were no raids after that. One reason was that the government of the south of Ireland, which was neutral in the war, protested to Germany about the high level of civilian casualties in the April raid. Adolf Hitler feared that the Irish Prime Minister, Eamon De Valera, and Irish Americans would encourage the Irish Republic to enter the war on the Allied side. Another reason was that, after the invasion of the Soviet Union in June 1941, the German air force had became engaged in its largest operation of the war and had less resources for bombing Britain.

So, by the time Frederick and Annie arrived there, Northern Ireland was relatively peaceful. Its role for the remaining years of the war was as a major military and agricultural base for the rest of Britain. During the war, Belfast's yards produced 123 merchant ships and 140 warships, including 7 aircraft carriers and 3 cruisers. It produced food for a country that was under strict rationing. The amount of land being tilled increased more than three-fold; the number of cattle and poultry being reared increased significantly. It also became a major base for American troops who started to arrive in January 1942. By June that year, more than 41,000 U.S. were stationed there. Its ports provided valuable bases for the convoys protecting merchant shipping from the menace of German U-boats.

Death of a nurse

One of the missionaries who chose not to leave Manchuria before the outbreak of the war was Ruth Dickson, who had arrived in 1923 as the first trained nurse appointed by the Presbyterian Church. She was appointed matron of the mission hospital in Yingkou. In addition to managing the hospital, she set up a comprehensive nurse training programme and Nurses' Home on the hospital campus. In the spring of 1941, she was given the choice to go to Canada, Australia or New Zealand with other missionaries but declined; she was given the extra responsibility of the Scottish Mission Hospital in Liaoyang. In September 1941, the church's Mission Board ordered her to evacuate via Singapore, also a likely target for Japanese attack. When she reached there, she volunteered for National Service and worked in a military hospital for four months. She was among the last to leave the colony; but her boat was bombed and she was captured by Japanese soldiers. She worked in several camps in Malaya and Sumatra and Banka Island, off Sumatra, that was the scene of a Japanese atrocity on February 16, 1942.

Ten Japanese soldiers found 22 Australian nurses in a shelter with a large Red Cross sign on it where they were caring for the wounded. They ordered the wounded to a headland, where they were shot and bayoneted, and ordered the 22 nurses to walk into the surf. A machine gun was set up on the beach and, when they were waist deep, they were machine-gunned. One nurse was shot in the diaphragm and left unconscious but survived the war; she gave evidence of the massacre at the War Crimes Trial in Tokyo in 1947. Dickson herself suffered severely from fever and malnutrition and died on Christmas Eve, 1944.

Chapter 7

Return to China, Return to Ireland

A new home in Belfast

When Frederick and Annie returned to Belfast, they did not have a home of their own – they had not expected to need one. As they were searching, they did not have to consider space for their three sons; none was living in Northern Ireland. They chose a modest house in Stockmans Lane in a leafy southern suburb of Belfast. Since they had little money, they needed financial help from their children to buy it. It was a short walk from the Malone Presbyterian Church where Annie's father had been minister and in the district in which she had grown up. Facing the house was a large park and a view of the hills round the southern side of the city; it was a beautiful place. They called their new home "Innisfree", after an island in a lake in the west of Ireland and also the name of a famous poem by William Butler Yeats, who described Innisfree as an oasis of peace and tranquility.

The house had two bedrooms, a living room, a kitchen and a bathroom, with a small garden and privet hedge in the front, sufficient for an elderly couple, with a spare room for a son or friend who came to stay. The living room contained books and other items from Faku – a Buddhist statue, Chinese calligraphy and enamelware with gold and silver writing. They had been forced to leave their home and could only bring what they could carry; they had to leave behind most of the possessions collected over forty years. Visitors found the house small for a man who had been Moderator of the church and had had such a long and eventful career; it was a life rich in spirit, not money.

As long as the war went on and the Japanese occupied Manchuria, there was no question of returning to Faku; but its church and members were foremost in Frederick's heart. He was kept busy despite the fact that he was past the retirement age of most people. He formally retired on

Annie and Frederick outside their home in F

June 7, 1945, at the age of seventy-five; it was a month after the unconditional surrender of Nazi Germany. As a former Moderator of the General Assembly and with a long record in the missionary field, he enjoyed a high status within the church and was often invited to preach at churches and attend public events. In the Presbyterian Church, retired ministers retain their seats in the General Assembly and continue to work within the church. Annie came from a large family and worked hard to keep in touch with her aunts, uncles and cousins, as well as a wide circle of friends.

Jennifer Seth-Smith, one of his granddaughters, remembers visiting Frederick and Annie during the war. "Frederick was tall and handsome, about six foot, with red hair that went white. He wore lightweight grey suits, with a dog-collar; he dressed in a formal way. They came back from China with no money. He was a very kind person. Their house was very modest. They brought me gifts of a red kimono, an enamel dish and a Chinese paper parasol. I do not know where they found the money. Sometimes Frederick spoke to my brothers in Chinese to frighten them." She described the two as strict and demanding.

When Annie arrived in Faku, he told her that she must learn Chinese. "If not, you will be useless and will have to go home." She told me that Chinese was very hard to learn. She was very easy to talk to. He was very strict in his demands. He had fierce and passionate feelings. The two had a great affection for Chinese people. Their heart was probably in Faku.

With her parents and younger brother, Jennifer went with Frederick and Annie on holiday to rural areas in the north of Ireland. "In the dining room of where we stayed, Grandfather dressed in a grey suit, with a dog collar. He said grace before meals and sang hymns with us." Jennifer Seth-Smith lives with her husband, a retired surgeon, in Guernsey, one of the Channel Islands.

Marygwen Furneaux is a great-niece of Annie who also visited them in Belfast at that time when she was a teenager. Retired, she lives in Paignton in southwest England. "Their bungalow was small, with a little garden. Six people would fill the sitting room," she recalled. "Above the mantelpiece was a very large photograph of their first-born son Patrick who died in Faku; he had a white cotton culotte on his knees. He had a shock of fair hair, an O'Neill look. Frederick was very respectable, with a distinct quality of someone you could trust. In those days, older people did not talk to young people, so he only spoke niceties to me. Both he and Annie were spare in their speech. They were a very stable couple who had had a rewarding lifestyle in Manchuria." She described Annie as a very affectionate woman who hugged people on sight. "She was very warm and fond of the life they had had in Manchuria. They were happy to be back home in Ireland, especially Annie."

Sons leave the nest

Their three sons had left Northern Ireland and made their life in England.

Their first son Denis, born in Faku in February 1908, won a place at Oriel College, Oxford; after graduation, he went to work in the British Ministry of Transport. He had a distinguished career and became one of the most senior civil servants in the ministry. He served as principal private secretary to several Ministers of Transport and was a senior adviser to Barbara Castle, the Labour Minister of Transport between 1965 and 1968. She introduced major reforms, including the introduction of a breathalyser to test the alcohol level of drivers and the mandatory fitting of seat belts in cars. She also made permanent a speed limit of 70 miles (approx. 113 kilometres) per hour, including on motorways. He played a key role in drafting the legislation for these measures and having them passed by Parliament.

Their second son Terence, born in Faku on January 24, 1910, graduated in Engineering from Queen's University, Belfast and eventually went to live in Sheffield in the north of England. He married and raised a family of four children. He worked for a heavy engineering company and travelled to many countries, including Canada, South Africa, India and Yugoslavia, to install its equipment. In 1964, he was working in India for the North British Locomotive Company which was continuing to make steam locomotives as well as mining engineering equipment. There he was bitten by a snake; the bite became infected and he contracted pulmonary embolic disease. He died three years later in 1968, at the age of fifty-eight, in Sheffield. He was always a very fit person, although he was a pipe smoker. His children describe him as a quiet, even austere man who rarely showed his emotions. He did not believe in Christianity and rarely spoke of Manchuria or Ireland. He returned to Ireland only to visit his mother and never went back after her death.

Their third son, Desmond – my father – graduated in Medicine from Queen's University in Belfast and moved to London in 1938. During the war, he served as a doctor in the Irish Guards, often close to the front line in Norway, North Africa and in France after the D-Day landings in June 1944. He received the Military Cross for bravery. After moving to London, he hired an elocution teacher who trained him to speak with a standard BBC English accent; he did not use his Irish accent except on private occasions. He wanted it to make it easier to join the mainstream medical profession in England. Many people who become members of the British elite did the same thing – like Margaret Thatcher and Edward Heath, children of modest families who joined the Conservative Party and became Prime Minister. One of Desmond's classmates from university described meeting him in London after the end of the war.

I was confronted by what appeared to be a very upper-crust Englishman, bowler hat, umbrella and the accent to go with them. It was Desmond O'Neill, an old friend. He had had a "good war" and been well decorated. Like so many sons of the manse, he was a somewhat wild and flamboyant character.

Desmond qualified as a psychiatrist and went on to work in this field at major London hospitals, as well as setting up a private practice.

The three sons had several things in common: they were well educated and had successful careers in their chosen professions. None remained in their native Northern Ireland, none went into the ministry and none was even a member of the Presbyterian Church. After the death of their parents, they rarely returned to Northern Ireland and concentrated on their professions and families in England. It seems unusual that a couple who devoted their lives to spreading Christianity to China could not bring their own children into the church. Their faith may have been a casualty of an unusual childhood. The three spent their early years with their parents in China. When they reached the age of primary school, they returned to Belfast for their education, staying in the homes of relatives.

In China, there were very few schools available in the English language for children of expatriates, and none in Manchuria. Most expatriates – whether diplomats, businessmen, teachers or missionaries – believed that their sons and daughters would have a better education in their home country. In fact, the sooner they began that education at home, the better chance they would have of getting into a high-quality secondary school and university – the escalator into a good job in the government, business or a profession. In Britain, the country in the world with the biggest empire and the largest number of expatriates at that time, there were hundreds of private schools catering for such children: providing education for the sons and daughters of civilian and military officers in the Empire was a major reason for setting them up. The academic performance of Denis, Terence and Desmond certainly improved as a result of going to schools at home, including the Royal Belfast Academic Institution, where their father had studied.

Their parents gave them the best education they could. But they paid a heavy price in the physical and emotional distance from their children, who lived with relatives in Belfast. They saw them only on rare visits home from Manchuria and, in an era without the Internet and few telephones, communicated by letters which took months to reach the other side. In some sense, they were like orphans who grew up without their parents. Perhaps this was why the three chose not to join the church and make their lives away from Northern Ireland.

When Desmond talked of his parents, he spoke with respect and admiration of their dedication to their mission in Manchuria and commitment in serving in Faku for so many years. But, a non-believer, he did not appreciate the mission in the same way as a member of the church.

Return to China but turned away

Even before the end of the war, Presbyterian missionaries returned to China. Unable to enter areas occupied by the Japanese army, they went to places controlled by the Nationalist government. In 1945, the Reverend Jack Weir went to Santai, Sichuan Province in southwest China, where he worked among students of Northeastern University, which had moved there after Japan occupied Manchuria. He was the son of the Reverend Andrew Weir, who had served as a missionary in Chaoyang and Changchun from 1899 until his death from typhoid in October 1933; he was buried in Shenyang. Andrew Weir had been one of the pillars of the church in Manchuria.

A speech by Frederick to a Presbyterian church meeting in Belfast in November 1944 shows how the church was preparing its return. The meeting was called with the aim of encouraging young people to volunteer to serve as missionaries in India and China after the war was over. Frederick said that, unable to enter Manchuria, missionaries were going to Free China, areas under the government of Chiang Kai-shek.

Because of the courageous and self-sacrificing conduct of the missionaries of all denominations, feeding the hungry, healing the wounded, protecting helpless women against their cruel enemies, the Name of Christ is there held in honour. Away from the iron heel of Japan, the day of Gospel opportunity has arrived. Had our young friends been able to enter Manchuria, what would they have found? Terror on the one hand but encouragement on the other. More than 1,000 teachers arrested on suspicion last year and put to death, another 1,000 sentenced to imprisonment. The reign of terror continues. Through food shortages, the people are on the verge of starvation.

He said that 100 Chinese ministers of the church in Manchuria were, so far as he knew, at their posts, as were the Chinese heads of the Medical College and mission hospitals and that the medical needs of people were such that, despite the training of Chinese doctors, they still needed British missionary ones.

As for our schools, nothing can take their place. Even non-Christian officials beg that their sons may be allowed entrance... The largest republic in the world owes a debt of gratitude to missionaries of all denominations. For thousands of years, China declined to educate the girl, until the Christian strangers overcame that fatal tradition. The revolution of 1911 followed the missionaries' lead by opening schools for girls throughout the land. The result has been almost unbelievable. Within a generation, women have risen in social status to something like equality with men. We broke up the fallow ground, opening the eyes of the astonished Chinese lords of creation. And you, by your prayers and gifts, stand beside us in our continuous and exacting enterprise. Never forget the memorable saying of Dean Farrar, whose grandson is Field-Marshal Montgomery: "Women are more moral and religious than men."

Frederic William Farrar was a well-known Church of England theologian and writer in the nineteenth century. Many Chinese women of today would not agree with Frederick's judgement; they would say that, while they have opportunities and careers not open to their grandmothers and great-grandmothers, they have not achieved complete equality with men.

Another speaker was the wife of the Reverend James McWhirter, who had served in China since 1908.

> When the glad day breaks in which it will be possible to go back to Manchuria, we must have a band of new workers ready to undertake the stupendous task of building the waste places, restarting the educational work, opening the hospital doors wider than even and embracing the manifold opportunities of strengthening that young Church of Christ – left alone today, with any outside help and under the heavy hand of Japan – in that great northern Province.

These speeches show the determination of the missionaries to carry on their work despite fourteen years of Japanese occupation, during four of which Manchuria was completely isolated from the outside world. They were impatient to be back in the field; they felt they belonged there and not in Ireland. They regarded the war as merely an interlude in the work of building the Chinese church. This determination was well summarised by the Reverend Jack Weir, whom I met in a Beijing hotel in 1987 on his first visit to China after 1949.

"We men think in years and decades. God has a longer timetable, measured in centuries."

He sent me this account of his return. From the middle of 1944, he wrote, he had been waiting in Ireland and London for a year for the opportunity to return. Since Japan occupied Manchuria, he would have to go to southwest China that was controlled by the Nationalist government. He would join a programme of Christian fellowship and relief work among students in state universities; it was funded by British and Chinese charities and had eight or nine young ministers, of which he was the youngest.

> Eventually, I set sail in May 1945, having celebrated Victory in Europe (VE) Day in Whitehall (central London) halfway up a lamppost in the crowd, cheering Winston Churchill. Wartime blackout on the ship was lifted as we entered the Mediterranean but restored when we reached the Red Sea. After disembarking at Bombay, I took a fortnight to visit our missionaries in Gujurat (western India). Then it was on by rail to Calcutta to get a flight "over the hump" to Chongqing.

The Burma Road* was at that time restricted to military use. At that time, Chongqing was still being bombed by the Japanese, whereas Calcutta had been secure; but I remember vividly how much happier I felt to be in China, "among my own people" than in "British" India.

After a few days in Chongqing, he went to Chengdu and the campus to meet his colleagues and learn the details of his new posting.

There, one evening, news came through of the Japanese surrender. As often happened, the electricity had failed. A few of us went out to join the crowds celebrating on the streets. Very soon, however, we had to douse our torches, as people recognised our western faces and began to mob us (celebrate with us).

He learnt that he would be posted to the Northeastern University, originally from Shenyang but which had relocated to Santai, 90 miles east of Chengdu, during the war. Within a month, he was struck with a fever, which the doctor diagnosed as typhoid; he had to stay in bed until he recovered.

Eight months later, the wife of a professor died in childbirth in a hospital in Santai. Enraged, a crowd of 70 to 100 students rampaged through the hospital, with the aim of finding the doctor and lynching him. Weir joined the crowd and managed to reach the doctor together with the first half dozen; they started to beat him.

Putting my head down as for a rugby charge, I managed to get through to him and fend off his attackers. If I had time to think, I would have hesitated but, by now being known to many of the students and perhaps with a trace of racist self-assurance, I got him away, shaken but largely undamaged. Not so the hospital, which had to be closed.

Weir worked hard to get to know the students, both Christian and non-Christian, in part through giving lectures in Business English. The time came for the university to move back to Shenyang; Weir had to make his own way there.

*The Burma Road was a road 1,154 kilometres long running through difficult mountain terrain that connected what was then the British colony of Burma with the southwest province of Yunnan in China. During World War Two, it was the only land route connecting China with British-controlled India, over which the Allies transported goods for the war effort in China.

He took a backpack and arranged with the driver of a lorry to ride above the regular cargo with Chinese travellers. The driver took him to Xi'an, where he had two days of sightseeing, before taking a train to Shanghai. There he met officials of the United Nations Relief and Rehabilitation Authority (UNRRA), for whom he would work as an agent among university students in Shenyang. He found a place as the only passenger on a UNRRA-chartered ship taking relief supplies to North China and arrived in Shenyang just ahead of Dr Jean McMinn, the first Scottish missionary to return after the war. He asked the university to set up a student centre, in a building that had served as a hospital but had been plundered during the Russian occupation and stripped of doors and window-frames after their withdrawal. He established the centre on the campus with twenty-two rooms, including a reading room, games, room, canteen and large hall; it offered students recreational, social and study opportunities and provided religious education, including Bible study and prayers. It was a good opportunity for a young missionary to spread the gospel message among a large number of young people.

After fourteen years of Japanese occupation, Shenyang and the whole of Manchuria had suffered a further blow with the invasion by the Soviet Army on August 9, 1945. Joseph Stalin timed the operation perfectly; he wanted to maximise the spoils of war and minimise the military losses. So he waited three days until after the Americans dropped the first atomic bomb on Hiroshima, on August 6. Japan was weak and on the verge of surrender. The Soviets mobilised an enormous army of 1.6 million men, backed by 3,700 aircraft. Against them was the Japanese Guandong army of 600,000 men, many of them new recruits, and 50 front-line aircraft: its best units and most of its heavy military equipment had been moved to fight the Americans in the Pacific War. They were no match for the highly mechanised Soviet troops, backed by airborne units who seized airfields and city centres.

David M. Glantz, a retired U.S. Army colonel, in *The Soviet Strategic Offensive in Manchuria, 1945: 'August Storm'*, said:

> Imperial Japanese Headquarters had withdrawn most formations, including all armour and elite infantry from

the Guandong army, reducing it to a mere shadow of its former self... In April 1945, Stalin abrogated the neutrality pact (with Japan) and commenced a massive redeployment effort that doubled the number of Soviet forces in the Far East to 80 divisions... The Soviet Army commenced attack in darkness under cover of thunderstorms, catching the Japanese completely by surprise. The Red Air Force was able to establish air superiority because the Japanese had withdrawn most air assets as the American air-hopping campaigns got close to the Japanese main islands.

In his account of the invasion, Japanese historian Takahashi Nakayama said that the quality, training and capacity of unity of the Guandong army were inadequate; its forces were concentrated in the south and east of Manchuria, leaving the west open to attack. "Its military forces in the areas near the borders became extremely weak.

During a week of fighting, the Russians conquered large areas of Manchuria and captured Puyi, the Emperor of Manchukuo and former Qing Emperor. Emperor Hirohito made his broadcast ending the war on August 15; but he used formal and archaic language, which ordinary Japanese did not understand, and did not use the word "surrender". Thanks to the poor quality of the broadcast and uncertain lines of communication, many Japanese were confused about what he actually meant. So the Guandong army continued fighting against the advancing Soviet forces. Finally, the Imperial Army Headquarters in Tokyo communicated the ceasefire order to the Guandong army.

This should have been the occasion for rejoicing by the people of Manchuria. But, to their horror, the Soviet troops over the next months looted their homeland; they stripped factories of equipment and materials, including power-generating equipment, transformers, electrical motors, laboratories and hospitals and the latest and best machine tools. They took 3 million U.S. dollars in gold and stripped the generating plants and pumps from several of the largest Manchurian mines, causing severe damage in the shafts from flooding. They also seized large stocks of food. Soldiers even stole furniture and fittings from shops and homes, including even electric wiring and bathroom taps. The Soviets had two motives for this.

One was to obtain reparations for their own enormous losses in the war with Germany. The other was to give 'booty' to its soldiers, to reward them for four years of a war in which more than 20 million Soviet citizens had died. It was a terrible blow for ordinary people, the innocent victims of the Japanese and now the Soviets. They were already suffering from shortages of food, electricity, water and other necessities; now the factories where they hoped to earn a living could no longer function and the region's economic recovery was delayed by several years.

Church delegation visits Manchuria

With the end of the war, the Irish and Scottish Presbyterian churches could begin to plan the return of missionaries to Manchuria. Their first step was to send a five-member commission, to find out the state of the Church and how it could help its recovery after the trauma of the war. The members left Britain by sea on December 29, 1945 and arrived in Qinhuangdao on March 6, 1946. They spent a month in Tianjin and Beijing, consulting with Chinese Christians and their foreign partners on what role the missionaries could play in the new post-war situation. In early April, they set off for Shenyang. "We passed into Manchuria through the Great Wall in the remains of a third-class carriage with broken windows and incomplete wooden seats," reported the Reverend John Stewart, a Scottish missionary and one of the five members.

"Most of the stations were wrecked and many of the bridges had been blown up and insecurely repaired. The places we passed through seemed half-dead." They arrived at their destination on April 5.

As we drove in ramshackle carriages across Shenyang, it looked even more than half-dead. The streets had the traffic of a small country town. There was no electricity and therefore no trams and no light at night. There was little petrol and therefore no buses. There were no goods to sell and therefore the shops were shut.

The commission found widespread physical destruction but, to their surprise and joy, life and energy in the community they had helped to build. "We passed through what seemed a derelict city, with its closed shops and destroyed buildings," it reported.

> On Sunday, we entered the East Church, filled with men, women and children – 900 of them – and were at once conscious of life, throbbing, eager life. In a day or two, we were to hear how that life could not be contained within four walls but was pulsing out into the city and into the country around about, founding churches and preaching stations. Life triumphant and over death – that is the story of the church in this through these four dark years – a story that has thrilled and humbled us.

The Chinese believers warmly welcomed the visitors, as if they had never been away. On April 19 and 20, they met fifty-five representatives of churches and institutions in Shenyang and eight areas outside the city – but not Faku, with which they were unable to make contact. "They received the Commissioners with a warmth of affection that cannot be expressed in words," wrote the Reverend R.H. Boyd, one of the five permanent conveners of the foreign mission of the Presbyterian Church of Ireland.

> They showed their deep gratitude to the home church for sending them so far and, above all, so soon. They recalled the past and thanked us for our share in it and assured us of their ardent desire for the continuation of full cooperation. It was difficult to restrain one's emotion when conveying formally, and for the records, a message of greeting and expression of good will... Our sense of solidarity was even stronger at the end than it was at the beginning.

The members of the Chinese church made it clear that, despite all the changes in the four years since the missionaries were expelled, they still had an important place for them, as doctors, nurses, teachers, ministers and evangelists.

The visitors learnt from their hosts the tribulations of the previous four years. The Japanese had taken control of church institutions and isolated them from China and the rest of the world. They had closed the schools, except for a few kindergartens and one or two smaller ones maintained by local congregations. The overall quality of education had fallen drastically. The Japanese had maintained the Theological College, with lower numbers, under the leadership of a pastor named Ishikawa. Since 1942, 27 students had graduated from the senior class, including 3 women. It was individuals, especially women, who had continued evangelical work; they were followed by police who sat in on meetings and demanded drafts of sermons and lectures. The salaries for the evangelists dwindled and their living conditions became worse and worse. There was little or no money to pay pastors or maintain churches.

As for the mission hospitals, Chinese doctors had continued to run some of them but others had closed. The visitors went to the Shenyang Hospital and were moved by what they saw.

No electricity, no water except what was carried, a great proportion of the bedding gone, very understaffed as to nurses and yet every bed in that great institution – 339 in all – was occupied and the patients looked clean, comfortable and happy. It is just amazing how it has carried on during these difficult years... The hands of the nurses were scarred, some of them were still in bandages, some 70 per cent of them and several of the doctors suffered from hands frozen through working in unheated wards and side rooms.

Doctors and nurses received low salaries and inadequate diet; they said they hoped for the return of their missionary colleagues. On top of all this were the serious consequences of the looting by Soviet soldiers, who had removed plant, machinery and infrastructure; factories stripped of their machinery could not operate. Shenyang and other cities did not have the coal, electricity and other necessities they needed. The visitors saw the physical suffering of the church and its members and, at the same time, marvelled at how they had retained their faith and fervour. In a report on the hospital presented to a synod of the church in September 1946, one Chinese doctor said:

Now the Shenyang Hospital is like an island standing out in the open sea; all other hospitals in Shenyang, big or small, government or private, are either looted or wrecked and rendered poor and disabled. The Shenyang Hospital is the only hospital in the city which has weathered the storm unscathed. What a miracle! Who could do that that? It must be the work of God!

After discussions with the visitors and the home churches, the church in Manchuria in June 1946 asked for the early return of more than a dozen missionaries, including 3 doctors. The outlook for them was uncertain, even more than before the war. They were warned to expect extremely harsh conditions, with food and fuel likely to be in short supply during the harsh winter. All must undergo medical examinations in advance, to ensure that they could endure the cold and the shortages. In addition, they did not know if, in future, they would be able to receive money from outside. Five missionaries of the Presbyterian Church who had served in Manchuria returned, including Dr Tom Barker, who wrote the excellent account of detention in Japan in the last chapter. He was over sixty when he returned. In addition, three new ones came, including the Reverend Jack Weir. While Frederick's heart remained in Faku, his age – he was seventy-five in 1945 – and the difficult conditions in Manchuria meant that he could not return. Due to Faku's remoteness from Shenyang, the church at home had no information on what had happened to the church and its members there after his departure in 1942.

Overshadowing these events was the civil war between the Nationalist government and the Communists, which had resumed in earnest after the end of the war against Japan. In Manchuria, the Communist war effort was led by Lin Biao, one of the party's most talented generals. He built a large army, using in part Japanese arms and equipment given to him by the Soviet army and depots and supply trains abandoned by Nationalist troops whom he had defeated. By May 1947, the American Consul-General in Shenyang reported to the State Department in Washington that the Nationalists were likely to lose Manchuria.

In September 1946, 104 delegates from 11 areas of Manchuria held a synod in Shenyang, the first since the end of the war and the first in which they enjoyed freedom of assembly and of speech. In January 1947, the missionaries who had returned held their first post-war conference in Shenyang, with 11 people present. They received several reports; one on evangelism said that, of 250 churches, including 80 enjoying full congregational status, two thirds were without pastor or evangelist because of a lack of money or manpower. Another, on medicine, said that the hospitals needed money to restore the standards as of 1941 and foreign medical staff, especially surgeons, physicians, gynaecologists and nurses.

By May 1948, Lin's armies had cut off Changchun and Shenyang, which the Nationalist government could only supply by air. In a series of tactically brilliant campaigns in September and October, he captured the two cities, leading to the destruction, surrender or desertion of 400,000 of Chiang Kai-shek's finest troops. On November 2, 1948, the People's Liberation Army entered Shenyang. The soldiers were well disciplined and there was no repeat of the looting and rapes by Soviet troops when they occupied the city in 1945. The army enforced a curfew from sunset to sunrise.

With the start of the Communist era, everything changed. The policy of the new government was to unite all the Protestant churches under Chinese control, with no place for the missionaries. It also brought education and health under government control, so that the churches could not continue to run their own institutions. Accordingly, the Presbyterian Church handed all mission property to the Chinese church. In the spring of 1949, the government took over the Medical College and its affiliated hospital. In the new circumstances, the missionaries came to realise that their presence was a hindrance to their Chinese friends and colleagues. All but six of the missionaries left between September and November 1949. The last Presbyterian missionary to leave was the Reverend Jack Weir, on August 19, 1950. It had been eighty-two years since the Reverend William Burns had arrived in Yingkou to begin the Irish Presbyterian mission in Manchuria.

Passing

Frederick and Annie lived in retirement in their home in Belfast. They saw their three sons get married. A photograph survives of them at the wedding of my parents in the summer of 1948 in northwest England. My father married Mary Pearson, the daughter of a well-known lawyer in Manchester. The photo shows Frederick and Annie in good health and spirits.

Frederick passed away in hospital in Belfast on October 7, 1952, at the age of eighty-two. It was also the 49th anniversary of his wedding. A memorial service was held on October 19 for him at the Malone Presbyterian Church, close to his home and the church which Annie's father

Marriage of my parents, Desmond and Mary O'Neill

had built half a century earlier when he was its minister. The address was given by the Reverend Dr Austin Fulton, a missionary in Manchuria between 1930 and 1945 and the author of the official church history of the mission, *Through Earthquake, Wind and Fire*, published in 1967. Fulton's book has been a major source of material for this biography of Frederick O'Neill, my grandfather.

In his address, Fulton spoke of how Frederick had helped him and his wife after their arrival in Manchuria in 1930:

> When we were appointed to our first permanent station after two years in Manchuria, we wondered how things would turn out. In a strange land, working through a strange tongue, shut out, by the barriers of language and custom, from much that is going on, it is with difficulty that young missionaries approach their first full responsibility.

Frederick provided great assistance to the new arrivals, he explained.

After our appointment, O'Neill volunteered to come with us. Would it be of any help to me? He knew Guangning and several of the church leaders there. So he turned the impossible into the possible. That it took a week of his time and added hundreds of miles of his journeyings did not matter to him but it made all the difference to me.

At that time, Frederick was sixty-two.

Fulton described him as a person:

...a man of eager friendliness, with a strong, though controlled exuberance of spirit, who had not lost – as he never did lose – the buoyancy of youth. He was a man of strong devotional life. While his eager mind ranged over wide fields and followed many lines of enquiry, some things seemed so clear to him that they were practiced, not questioned. I do not think he ever puzzled about the problem of prayer. To him it was no problem but the breath of life, not something to discuss but to do. And he did it; he prayed. Disciplined devotion was woven into his pattern of daily living. From roots in his devotional life, there flowered a certain optimism which never left him. We sometimes thought it was a stubborn optimism. He was singularly free from anxiety. He was certain that God is running His world and ruling its peoples; God controls the affairs of nations and of men.

He also said that Frederick loved conversation and debate and read widely.

With his colleagues and his Chinese friends, he would discuss any matter which interested or affected them. Anyone who approached O'Neill with a problem was assured of a patient hearing. He would spare no pains to weigh pros and cons.

Fulton recalled a debate about whether ransom should be paid to secure the release of those captured by bandits; the daughter of a missionary, the wife of a businessman in Yingkou had been kidnapped and her release secured by the British government. The bandits could easily kidnap a missionary. "We should on no account pay ransom because paying ransom is not good for the bandits," Frederick said. "They were great men and women who pioneered in Manchuria. In that company O'Neill has a noble place."

Presbyterian Herald, the PCI's official magazine, published the following obituary in November 1952:

Few have brought to the service of the church more varied gifts and none have found that service more venturesome. Scholarly, eloquent, a master of languages and utterly fearless, Dr O'Neill penetrated to the most unlikely places and made himself equally at home with the men of all faiths of the East. He could command as much attention and respect from a Buddhist monastery as from a Christian church. His influence was therefore great among men of many races and all walks of life.

He saw great changes in China and lived through the major upheavals of that land from the Boxer Rebellion to the coming of Communism. Independent of judgement, enthusiastic, disarming in his friendliness and a man of great decision of character, Dr O'Neill subordinated all to his calling and thus became an outstanding personality in the church, at home and abroad. He was the author of three books which reflected both his knowledge of the history and work of the Irish Presbyterian Mission in Manchuria and his insight into the life and thought of China. "Although in failing health for some time, Dr O'Neill maintained his interest in the affairs of the Church and Her missions. His passing is deeply regretted not only here but in many communities and lands. To all who mourn his going, the sympathy of the entire Church is extended along with thanks to God for his long life of eminent service.

In the issue of the magazine in December, the Reverend Tom Barker wrote about his memories of Frederick, saying that he had two special gifts:

One was evangelism. For over thirty years, there was no man in Manchuria, either Chinese or foreign, who was in such constant demand as leader for Evangelistic Campaigns or Bible Study Conferences throughout the whole church. In his own district, he was tireless in travelling and all too careless of personal comfort. He had an overpowering urge to preach the Gospel, to lead men to Faith in God through Christ. The second... was the gift of friendship. We all knew that we could consult Fred, no matter what the problem or the cause of the trouble. We knew that he knew, as far as any colleagues could, the general background, the aim, the hopes and the fears of each of us. And we knew that anything he could do to help would be done. For we knew that his friendship was very rich in faith and hope and love.

Annie lived as a widow for four years until her passing on November 24, 1956. This is how the *Presbyterian Herald* remembered her:

The O'Neills will always be associated with Faku, where they lived and worked for so long. She was a member of a remarkable family and was herself a woman of keen intelligence and rich culture. Her quiet strength and courage were a source of comfort in many a perilous day and there was none, in difficult or weakness, who could not come to her for sympathy and the grace of succour.

The missionary house in Faku was a place not only of welcome but also of wisdom and genuine inspiration to all who entered it, both Chinese and foreign; and the youngest recruit to the Manchurian field was made as much at home as the most senior and deeply beloved of colleagues or friends. There, amid the changing fortunes in a turbulent land, Dr O'Neill had in his wife the ideal companion and helper. She loved Faku, where her missionary life was spent; she loved its circle of friends and acquaintances and from there the love went back to Malone congregation, where she had been brought up in the manse.

In her will, she bequeathed "Innisfree" as a home for missionaries on leave. "Cherishing the memory of Fred and Annie O'Neill, we will also cherish 'Innisfree' as the last gift of a deep loyalty and great service."

Self-criticism

In the final chapter of his excellent history of the mission in Manchuria, Dr Austin Fulton described the mistakes made by the missionaries. The book was published in 1967, at a time when many said that, despite more than eighty years of effort, they had "failed". He set out these mistakes in a spirit of humility and self-criticism.

The first was the inextricable link between the Protestant missionaries and the imperialist advance into China. Buddhism, in contrast, arrived in the country after Chinese monks went to India to learn a new religion they admired; they studied it, copied the scriptures and brought them back to China. They translated them into Chinese and began to spread the teachings among the people. It was the Chinese who introduced the religion. Protestant Christianity, on the other hand, arrived on the back of naval bombardments and artillery shells. Until the middle of nineteenth century, Protestant missionaries were forbidden to enter China. Only with the unequal treaties forced on the Qing government by Britain, France and other imperial powers did the foreign missions gain legal access.

So, while missionaries differed greatly from foreign business people and government representatives in their motives and lifestyle, many Chinese saw them as part of the same imperial enterprise and Christianity as a "Western" religion – while they saw Buddhism as a foreign religion that had been sinicised. They saw the missionaries as enjoying the same extraterritorial privileges of their compatriots. This antagonism was less sharp in Manchuria than the rest of China, because few western companies and individuals were based there. The two major colonial powers during the missionary period were Russia and Japan. Fulton wrote:

> In Manchuria, we did not feel the force of this anti-imperialist criticism as full as it was felt in other parts of China... The Russians first, and later the Japanese, so filled the picture that the misdeeds of Britain and America were retired into the background. Further, the American presence was not conspicuous in Manchuria. European missionaries, especially the British, were considered to be friends in the face of the enemies who were nearer at hand and whose presence was felt in force.

The second mistake that missionaries made was "unconscious arrogance". "There was always a dangerous tendency to

The main street of Shenyang

assume that everything Western was superior to everything Chinese. This was one result of acquiring only a smattering of the Chinese language and but a very sketchy appreciation of Chinese culture." Missionaries were less guilty of this than other foreigners, most of whom did not know Chinese. The missionaries were obliged to learn Chinese; most stayed in the country for a long time and lived among Chinese people, sometimes in towns where they were the only non-Chinese.

In Manchuria, the missionaries did all their work in the Chinese language. The missionary had in all cases to be able to express himself or herself in Chinese with a reasonable level of correctness. For most, however, that was as far as it ever went. Life was so full, work was so pressing that very few, though there were some, ever made a sustained effort to penetrate the Chinese mind and deeply feel the rhythm of Chinese life. While knowing that Chinese character and culture should command appreciation, few knew enough to enable them to appreciate. They should not be imprisoned within their own limited Christian communities or institutions, but be alive to the trend of national events, to the political, social and economic background of the church.

In addition, almost all missionaries lived in a Western style and according to Western standards.

The missionary often occupied a two-storey house which might be the only one in the place where he lived. He ate, clothed and maintained his family according to a standard of living which no Chinese minister could hope to achieve. This is a difficult matter. The question of the health of wives and children comes into it... the size and style of the missionaries' house was less important that the spirit and manner in which it was shared... There was still too glaring a difference between the way the missionary lived and the way most Chinese lived.

The third mistake was the many splits among the Protestant churches which the missionaries brought with them; they were divided into Presbyterians, Methodists, Baptists and many other denominations. This was the result of theological and historical disputes in the West that had no relevance or connection to China. "To many Christians in Manchuria, our divisions were without meaning and therefore of little concern. It confused them before they became Christians and continued to puzzle them after they had joined the church."

Another aspect of this was the kind of ministry the missionaries brought with them – academically trained, full-time and professional. The churches in the West had developed this model over centuries but it was unsuitable for China, where levels of education and income were lower. A more flexible system allowing part – time ministers would have been better, especially in Manchuria, where the population was spread over an enormous area and most congregations were small. "In Manchuria, it proved impossible for most congregations to support a full-time trained minister." This problem became acute in times of war or scarcity, when the faithful had less money to pay for a minister. A better model would have been part-time ministers who earned their living in another way and looked after the faithful during Sundays and their spare time. By the late 1940s, the Theological College in Shenyang was raising three cows, teaching the male students to raise poultry and bees; the lady students were trained as midwives.

The fourth mistake was in theology, which was too West-based, drawing on European history and scholarship.

Some attempt had been made to write text books in theology. These were translations produced by missionaries working along with Chinese. They were Western in everything but the script in which they were written. How far it was possible for translators or writers to find Chinese equivalents for the subtle terminology of the Greek Fathers or the verbal precision of the Reformation Confessions?

Everything was written in a European context, not a cultural setting suitable for the Chinese.

Chapter 8

Resurrection

In memory of Frederick, my grandfather

Grandmother and Grandfather in front of their house in Faku in the 1930s (credit: Marion Young)

In memory of Grandfather

It was October 2009 and we were visiting Faku, the third
time after 1986 and 2005. At nine o'clock in the morning,
we left our hotel in Shenyang. The city was in the middle of
a construction boom, with new skyscrapers and apartment
buildings, two new subway lines and other projects. We
saw little of the pre-war city which Grandfather would have
recognised. As we left the city, the apartment buildings and
office blocks gave way to rolling plains covered by long stalks
of corn turning brownish yellow and one-storey brick homes
with two chimneys next to a small yard and a garden; they
would have been more familiar to him.

As we arrived in Faku, we saw large wind turbines on the
hilltops, grain silos with a pointed roof, piles of yellow corn
in the yards of the homes and solar panels on the roofs. The
town was more prosperous than it was during our previous
visit four years before, with a new, modern bus terminal,
supermarkets and dental clinics. We had a rendezvous with
several members of the church, who took us to one of their
buildings.

They explained that, in all of Faku county, there were 8,000
believers and 20 meeting halls, large and small, compared
with 1,000 ten years earlier; there were 3 full-time ministers
and 5 elders. Each year 300 to 400 new members would
join. The church relied on funds provided by the members.
"Your grandfather made a big contribution to Faku, with the
church, school and hospital," said one elder. Faku remains a
predominantly agricultural area, with 450,000 people in the

whole county and 50,000 in the urban area. The main crops are rice, corn and wheat, with one harvest a year. The average annual income was 7,000 yuan in the city and 3,000 to 4,000 yuan in the rural areas. Some residents go to Shenyang and Beijing to work as well as to South China, especially in the winter, when you cannot farm the land. In the last four to five years, the city has installed wind turbines to generate power.

We met one of the three ministers, a lady in her thirties named Zhang Hongxia with radiant eyes. A native of Faku, she entered the Northeast Theological Seminary in 1986 and, after graduation, returned home as a preacher. She was formally made minister of the Faku church on April 12, 2002. I asked her to assess Grandfather's life and work.

> He put all his love into Faku. He had great status here and we thank him greatly. The missionaries planted the seeds and now is the time for the fruit to come out. We have a policy of broad religious freedom. God loves China. In June 2009, we had a service to ordain two new ministers and Frederick was mentioned during it. Why did he choose this poor place and not a rich city? During his time, Faku had private schools; he built the first that was open to the public.

She said that, among her congregation, the majority were between thirty and fifty years old, with more women than men, and that more young people were joining. Then she and the members took us to a local restaurant for a sumptuous lunch. The tables were loaded with more food than we could eat; we were received with great warmth and hospitality. Through the window we saw the first snow of the winter, a reminder of the harsh climate that the residents of Faku endure every year.

Interior of Faku Church to

After lunch, we visited the large compound where Grandfather built the mission school and the church. The walls had been newly white-washed and the seats arranged in neat

rows with a corridor down the middle; the seats were made out of the wooden floors of the original building. There were two large heaters at the back, for use in the winter. At one end, there was a raised platform with a red carpet and four seats for ministers and elders. Above the platform were eight Chinese characters in red on the wall written by Grandfather: *Zhu zhi rongguang, chongman da di* (主之榮光，充滿大地), or "the glory of God fills the earth".

In one corner was a bronze plaque dedicated to the martyrs who died in the Boxer Rebellion in 1900, including Elder Xu, of whom Grandfather thought so highly and whom he perhaps could have saved if he had taken him with him to Russia. As my eyes wandered around the church and saw the devotion of the members, I felt strongly the spirit and presence of Grandfather. This was a building he conceived and designed; the plaque and the calligraphy were his work. It has survived a century of wars, revolution and tumultuous change and is still being used for the purpose for which he intended it. Were he there that day, he would be proud of what he had done and the life he spent in Faku. He would be especially proud that it had become a Chinese church, with the ministers and congregations Chinese and all the services in Putonghua; the faith had taken root in Chinese soil. Reading my thoughts, Minister Zhang stepped forward: "We must thank your grandfather for coming here and bringing us the gospel," she said with a big smile. "It was our great good fortune."

She continued:

> Each Sunday, the church has a congregation of 200 people... We want to build a larger church, with space for 2,000 to 3,000 people, in this compound which Frederick used in his time, but we are short of funds. It is a good location, in the centre of Faku. We have no overseas donations; we can accept them provided there are no conditions attached. It would cost 3 to 4 million yuan. Whatever happens, we will keep the church your grandfather built and not demolish it, as a link to the past.

Her husband is also a Protestant minister. Then we sat on the raised platform with the ministers and the members and took many photographs, as a souvenir of the occasion. Everyone was wearing a thick jacket, as is their habit during the long winter.

Then they showed us the one-storey homes next door. Each had two rooms with a kang on which four to five people sleep during winters. This is a design peculiar to Manchuria; pipes carrying hot water run underneath the kang, keeping it heated day and night and making it the centre of family life during winter. Grandfather lived in a home like this in Faku, before he moved into his larger house. All together, the minister and the members of the congregation received us with great warmth and emotion. It was hard to get onto the minibus to take us back to Shenyang. I felt unequal and unworthy of the weight of gratitude and affection, which belonged to Grandfather and the other missionaries and not to me.

Past and present

As elsewhere in China, the church and its community in Faku had a chequered career after 1949. The church was used for worship until 1966, when it was closed by the Red Guards. It was used as an exercise space, with a straw mat and wooden horse for children to jump over. The ministers were sent to the countryside to do labour. In 1981, the city government returned to the believers their compound, which included a meeting hall for services and rooms for the ministers; they resumed religious services n 1982. About five years ago, the city government handed the church back to the community, which set about restoring it to the condition it is today. Like Christians all over China, they are enjoying the religious freedom provided by the government since 1979 and the changes resulting from the reform and open-door policies.

According to figures from the China Academy of Social Sciences published in August 2010, the number of Protestants in the mainland reached a record 23.05 million; as well, there were 5.7 million Catholics. Non-official estimates put the total, including those in house and underground churches, at more than double that and possibly as many as 70 million. This remarkable growth is due to many factors – the new freedoms provided by the government and active evangelisation by Chinese churches and individuals; the transformation of the economy, which has caused tens of millions of people to move from their home places to work elsewhere and weakened the traditional bonds of the family; a hunger for religious and moral values in a society in which the pursuit of money has become a dominant motivation and caused a large and widening gap between rich and poor; and a desire for a clear definition of the meaning of life and ethical standards.

After the departure of the foreign missionaries in 1949 and 1950, the government set up the Three-Self Patriotic Movement as the single, united organisation for Protestant churches; it has no denominations. Its strategy was to be self-governing, self-supporting and self-propagating, independent of foreign influence and supporting the new government. It was formally established in 1954; it was banned in 1966, at the start of the Cultural Revolution, and reconstituted in 1979. It ran more than a dozen theological colleges across China to train ministers. In addition, the China Christian Council was founded in 1980 as an umbrella organisation for all Protestant churches. The Three-Self Patriotic Movement and China Christian Council are the two national Christian bodies. Foreigners are not allowed to proselytise. The Amity Printing Company in Nanjing printed Bibles for Chinese believers; in November 2010, it celebrated the printing of the 80-millionth Bible. Since 2008, it has been printing 10 million copies a year for domestic and international use. It is illegal to bring Bibles into China from abroad.

The Shenyang college where Minister Zhang studied is one of the theological colleges under the Three-Self Patriotic Movement; it was founded in 1896 by the Scottish and Irish Presbyterian churches to train Chinese ministers, with the Reverend Thomas Fulton, an Irish Presbyterian, as principal; he served in China from 1884 to 1941. In the 1920s, Grandfather gave lectures there in theology and psychology. After the founding of the People's Republic of China, the Presbyterian missionaries who remained handed over all the mission properties in Manchuria to the Chinese church, including the seminary. The new principal of the college was a Chinese minister; it offered Biblical Studies and also "technical" courses, such as those on running a farm to raise bees and chickens and midwifery for lady students.

The college continued to operate until August 1953, when it was merged with the Yanjing Seminary in Beijing; it gave up its premises in Shenyang to a hospital for women and children. In October 1982, it was re-established in line with the government policy on religious freedom, in an office building in Shenyang. In the autumn term in 1982, 47 students were admitted for the four-year course. In the early 1990s, it added two-year programmes for lay church workers and church workers for the substantial ethnic Korean community in Manchuria. In 1995, a new eight-storey building was completed on Yijing Street, Shenyang, where the original seminary once stood; it was funded by churches in the three northeast provinces and Christians in South Korea. Students take a four-year course, whose subjects include Religion, foreign languages, Culture and Politics. It has about a dozen staff and 200 students; it trains ministers for the three provinces of the Northeast – Liaoning, Jilin and Heilongjiang.

After 1949, the government took over the mission schools and hospitals. "In Shenyang, the church set up more than ten educational institutions, including a university, middle and primary schools and kindergartens," said *Religion in Shenyang*, published in 2003 by the city's Religious Affairs Bureau. "They made a contribution to the development of universal education in Shenyang," it said. It especially mentioned the medical school, which produced more than 1,300 doctors between 1913 and 1949; it was one of the few medical institutes in China whose graduates could take the examination for the royal medical academies in Britain.

> This university paid great attention both to the quality of its teaching and moral education. It had rich educational and teaching knowledge and great practical experience. It produced many very talented people for the medicine of China and made a very great contribution to the development of medical technology in China.

The Protestant community in Shenyang now has more than

twenty-five churches, over 130,000 members and several buildings in the city. One of the largest is the East Church, established by the Reverend John Ross in 1889 and now with eight hundred seats. Like other churches in China, it was closed during the Cultural Revolution. In August 1966, Red Guards entered the church compound, closed the building and locked the more than 30 ministers and other staff inside. The older ministers were sent home and the younger ones sent to work in an auto parts factory.

In 1978, the government restored religious freedom and returned the building to the church; on December 25, 1979, more than 200 ministers and believers celebrated Christmas there. In April 1981, the faithful celebrated Easter, with the first lady minister in Manchuria. The 1990s was a period of stable growth, with the construction of new buildings to accommodate the increasing number of believers. The church now has more than 35,000 registered members, with 4 ministers, 2 elders and 40 volunteers, with services every weekday and four on Sunday; it is responsible for more than thirty congregations in rural areas.

At the East Church, thousands now attend services, some sitting outside or in rooms in nearby buildings, where they listen over a sound system. In November 2005, John Dunlop, a minister and former Moderator of the Presbyterian Church of Ireland, visited the church and was very moved to see the numbers and devotion of the believers.

> It was truly amazing to see the churches packed with people on Sundays, for one service after another... In the short term available, we came across three recently completed buildings, all capable of seating about 1,000 people. They will be filled on a number of times each Sunday, with hundreds of people meeting in smaller 'meeting points' which may have between a dozen and a few hundred believers. The survival and growth of the church since the suffering of the Cultural Revolution has established the church as both Christian and Chinese.

> The enthusiasm of the church and its astonishingly rapid growth are in start contrast to the dwindling size and lack

of confidence of the churches in Europe. The church in Ireland is old, small and declining. The church in China is young and professional. Their congregations are growing and enthusiastic. In many ways, they are stronger than we are... The churches in China will join those of South Korea, along with those in Africa and Latin America, which are already becoming the dynamic missionary churches of this new century... The story of the missionaries is one of extraordinary sacrifice, hard work and achievement. They were very impressive people.

The city also boasts a Korean church for the large number of ethnic Korean residents. It consists of a church built by the Presbyterians in 1913 and a six-storey structure built in 1993. It holds services in Korean on the sixth floor and on Putonghua on the fourth floor, with church offices on the other floors. It has 1,500 members, with a further 7,000 attending branch churches. The Northeast Theological Seminary has classes for Korean-Chinese. In 2004, the church received back the YMCA building, which had been used by the city's Public Security Bureau since 1949 as a detention centre. It uses the building as a training centre, such as for volunteer evangelists. The YMCA has opened in many cities in China, including Beijing, Shanghai, Tianjin, Chengdu, Nanjing, Guangzhou and Xian.

After the trauma of the Cultural Revolution, the church in China recovered remarkably, including the church in Manchuria. Its membership has long surpassed that of the Presbyterian Church in Ireland – less than 300,000. It is a church that is entirely Chinese, in membership, ministry and training.

Jack Weir

The last Presbyterian missionary to leave Manchuria was the Reverend Jack Weir, who departed from Shenyang on August 19, 1950. He went on to a distinguished career in the Presbyterian Church at home, serving as a parish minister and its clerk and general secretary for twenty years. He was elected Moderator in 1976. In the 1970s and the 1990s, he participated in talks with paramilitary groups from the

Protestant and Catholic sides in an effort to negotiate an agreement to end decades of violence.

Throughout a busy life, he never forgot his roots as a missionary in Manchuria. He was born in Shenyang on March 24, 1919, the son of two Presbyterian missionaries. He received his primary education in China and returned to Belfast to continue his studies at Campbell College and Queen's University, where he graduated in experimental physics. After studying theology in Edinburgh and Belfast, he was ordained in October 1944 as a missionary to China, following the footsteps of his father, who was buried in Shenyang in 1933. The Reverend Weir first returned to China in late 1983, the member of a delegation from the British churches, led by the Archbishop of Canterbury, Robert Runcie. After his retirement in 1985, the Reverend Weir made a second visit, staying in Changchun, Shenyang and Anshan, where one of his former students was the minister of a local church.

I had the good fortune to meet the Reverend Weir in a hotel in Beijing during this visit; I was working in Beijing at that time and had heard of the visit from contacts in Belfast. I asked him if we could meet, to which he kindly agreed. It was my first meeting with a minister who had been a Presbyterian missionary in Manchuria. I was impressed by his determination, commitment and sense of loyalty to the Protestant community of Manchuria; for thirty-six years, he had been away and had little contact with them, but spoke of them as people close to him. He returned to Shenyang and visited the people and places with whom he had been associated; it was a moving and emotional experience.

The Communist takeover was for the best. It has strengthened the church which has had to stand on its own feet, not under the protection of the missionaries. It was not that they closed the country off from Christianity but closed it in. The faith has spread not by public evangelising but by person to person contact and by good living. When I went back to the Theological College in late 1983, I met 52 students, lively and independent... One should take the opportunity for mission work, since you do not know how long you will have it.

Weir made his final visit to Shenyang in 1996, ignoring the advice of his doctors, who said that he was too ill to travel. "I had come full circle. I had come home," he said. I last met him in the late 1990s, when he was living in a home for the elderly in East Belfast; he had moved there because of his poor health as a result of Parkinson's disease. His apartment was a remarkable sight – it was as if he were living in Shenyang; it had Chinese statues, paintings and calligraphy. Perhaps he wanted to recreate the sitting room of his childhood. He played us videos of his visits to Shenyang, his meetings with ministers and church members and services he attended; he described with great pleasure the details of the visit and could scarcely contain his emotions.

He was proudest of the cover on his bed – golden embroidery with the design of a dragon. This, he explained, was the canopy of Puyi, Qing Dynasty's last emperor; Weir had bought it in a flea market in Shenyang in 1946. After the Soviet army arrested Puyi, the contents of his palace in Changchun were sold. He showed us the photographs of Shenyang's National Northeastern University in 1946-1948, where he ran a Christian Student Centre. He also showed a letter he had written while he was a student at a school for expatriate children in Yantai in the 1930s: it described a visit by a warlord who marched through the city with his army and the students doing their best to see the troops but not attract gunfire.

Jack Weir in his "Chinese" apartm

After we marvelled at the contents of his apartment, he drove us to Church House, the headquarters of the Presbyterian Church, to show us its chapel; he had overseen its refurbishment, in remembrance of his parents and as a memorial to all the men and women who served in the missions of the church. He passed away on September 19, 2000, aged eighty-one, after a long illness. How appropriate, how poetic that he should breathe his last below the canopy of the man who had ruled China and Manchuria.

He did not say so directly, but I felt that he believed his life's work to be a missionary in Manchuria. His early life, parents and education had prepared him for this, but events had decided otherwise. He had an outstanding career as a minister at home, active in national affairs as well as those of the church; but perhaps he had not fulfilled his vocation. Whenever I visited Manchuria, I sent him letters and postcards; he was delighted to receive news and images from there. He gave me a sense of the continuity of missionary work. The spreading of the Gospel across the world is the work of centuries and that, like the other Presbyterian missionaries, he was an instrument of this work; others had done it before him and others would continue after him.

In June 2010, Joey McCausland, the last surviving missionary of the Presbyterian Church in China, died in Belfast at the age of ninety-seven. She had served from 1937 to 1941, including a period in Faku. She told me the following in August 2009, when she was living in a retirement home in Belfast:

> The content of the services there were the same as in Ireland... Men were on one side of the church and women on the other. Mothers fed their babies during the service. Faku was a country place, not sophisticated. Our houses had no electricity and no plumbing. The missionary had no radio in his house and his wife used to read aloud from books in the evening.

Five generations of a missionary family

At the beginning of the story, we mentioned James Hudson Taylor, who founded the China Inland Mission (CIM) in 1865, as one of the most important foreign Protestant missionaries. The CIM brought more than 1,000 missionaries to the country and converted at least 18,000 Chinese.

While none of Grandfather's sons chose to follow him into the missions, the Taylor family has a remarkably different record. Four generations have followed the founder's footsteps, not only as missionaries but as missionaries to China. They have seen the birth, persecution and rebirth of the Chinese church.

The current one, the fifth generation, is James Hudson Taylor IV, the great-great-grandson of the founder. He is Executive Consultant of Chinese Ministries of OMF International, the successor to the CIM. Based in Taipei, he spends half of his time away from Taiwan in other parts of the Chinese world, including the Mainland. He said following in an interview in Hong Kong in January 2011 en route to China:

> When the missionaries left China in the early 1950s, there were 700,000 to 1,000,000 Protestants in China... Many felt that, with the departure, it would be the end of the church. Now there are some 30 million according to official figures; some say 70, 80 even 100 million. The growth of the church has been predominantly Chinese and the role of foreigners has been marginal. God has turned persecution to fulfill His purposes.

The Chinese church is turning outward, seeking to evangelise not only the ethnic Chinese but also people of other races. "For two hundred years, the church has been recipients of God's grace, including missionaries who gave their lives. Now Chinese need to become bestowers of grace and to share it with other races and ethnicities," he said. Within China, the role and prestige of the church, as of other official religions, is improving; Beijing increasingly sees the church playing a constructive and positive role towards the government's goal of social harmony and stability, he said.

Taylor works with the Chinese church in China and abroad. The Overseas Missionary Fellowship has 1,300 missionaries from over twenty countries working in East Asia and East Asians living in other parts of the world, like Chinese and Japanese communities in Europe and North America. After the new government expelled the missionaries of the CIM in the early 1950s, they moved to Asian countries with large Chinese populations, ministering first to the Chinese and then to the local populations. Taylor also works with the church within China.

From 1996 to 2006, he was based in Hong Kong and worked with Medical Services International Professional Services, an organization founded in 1994 by his father, James Hudson Taylor III, Dr Reginald Tsang, an American pediatrician, and Richard Chen, a Hong Kong businessman. They founded it in response to an invitation from the Sichuan government to send doctors and medical professionals to work in hospitals and local communities. It sends Christian doctors and nurses, teachers, youth workers and those who train business administration and management and other vocations for short-and long-term assignments in Sichuan, Yunnan and Chongqing. They include ethnic Chinese and people from Europe, Canada and Australia. Since 1995, Medical Services International has sent hundreds of people on short-term assignments; 70 to 80 are long-term residents, some since 1995. It is a way to live out the Gospel that fits the requirements of the time and the country.

They live out the truth of Christianity by example rather than through preaching. "The propagation of the gospel is restricted," said Taylor. "Let our actions and excellence be the catalyst to open the hearts of people. If people want to know why we come, we are free to respond. If they come to faith, they go to the local community of believers." In April 2007, his father was awarded the honourary citizenship of Zhaojue in Sichuan in recognition of Medical Service International's contribution to the prefecture.

> From the beginning, we want to partner with the government, both at the prefecture level as well as various local levels. We work with existing hospitals and the government sees us as a partner and not a competitor.

Taylor said the government was increasingly aware of the importance of religion and spirituality.

> One good example was the aftermath of the Sichuan earthquake (in May 2008), which led to a flood of money and people pouring in. After the media attention waned, a large majority of those who stayed for holistic service to survivors were Christians.

Taylor said his had not been a smooth path to becoming a missionary. He went to primary school in Taiwan, where his father was working, and became fluent in Putonghua; after high school, he returned to the U.S. for university studies. When he was growing up, he did not want to follow the footsteps of his ancestors. "My prayer was to become anything but a missionary. I did not become a Christian till I was eighteen." At Seattle Pacific University, he studied History, specialising in U.S.-China Relations, with a view to using this knowledge in business or politics. His parents saw the burden of history weighing on his shoulders and put no pressure on him. "I was stubborn to the point that, if they had proposed something, I would have done the opposite."

After university, God worked on him, with the help of a retired CIM minister, the Reverend David Adeney, who became his mentor. "I came to grips with my heritage and had a better understanding of God's calling. There are no grandchildren in the Kingdom of God. Each person needs to be called individually." He said his father struggled with the same issues. Born in Kaifeng, Henan Province in August 1929, he grew up in China and studied at a missionary school in Yantai, Shandong. During the Sino-Japanese War, James III, together with several siblings, was imprisoned for three and a half years in a Japanese POW camp in Weifang, Shandong. Following the war, the entire family returned to the U.S.

"My father also asked himself if he should become a missionary for 'family-sake' or was God calling him to the mission field? He was in part influenced by his wife, who dedicated her life to the missions at the age of twelve after hearing my grandmother preach. Later she met my father at university and they were married in 1953." After completing his theological studies in the U.S. in the 1950s, his parents could not go to the Mainland to serve, due to the expulsion of Western missionaries, and thus moved to Taiwan. Both his parents went on to serve as missionaries there and in other Asian countries, including Hong Kong, for over fifty years. James' father passed away in Hong Kong on March 20, 2009, at the age of eighty.

Taylor said there were no family secrets on how to make a missionary. In some cases, children rebel because they feel their parents love work more than their children. So he and his wife are very careful about their own son, James Hudson Taylor V. "He is the sixth generation, so he has one more on top of him. We do not put parental pressure on him." With his two younger sisters, James V studied at Pui Ching Primary School in Hong Kong; all three children speak Cantonese fluently as well as Putonghua. The family is based in Taipei, where all three children attend the Morrison Academy schooling system. Named after Robert Morrison, the first Protestant missionary to China, the school was established in 1952 to meet the educational needs of the children of missionaries. Will James V follow the footsteps of his father and grandfather? "He has not said much so far. We leave it in God's hands."

Taylor's great-great-grandfather was a pioneer. He founded the largest missionary organization in China and could preach in Putonghua and dialects of Shanghai, Ningbo, and Hangzhou. "We do not have to learn all these dialects today," said James IV. "The Communist government has implemented Mandarin (Putonghua) as the national language. This has facilitated the spread of the gospel. In Fuzhou, I can speak in Mandarin and be understood."

His ancestor first arrived in Shanghai on March 1, 1854 and, unusually for a foreign missionary, wore Chinese clothes and a pigtail, with a shaven forehead, to make himself less conspicuous. After setting up the CIM, he recruited the first 21 missionaries and arrived with them in Shanghai in September 1866. The mission accepted people from all denominations but promised them no financial support; so they had to rely on funds from individual Christians in their home country or China and not from any church institution. He accepted people from the working class, as well as single women – both new practices at the time.

Taylor was not an ordained minister of an existing church; he had studied Medicine at the Royal London Hospital, where he eventually graduated from after returning to England, following six years of challenging missionary service in China, in 1863. During the Boxer Rebellion of 1900, 58 missionaries of the CIM and 21 of their children were killed, more than any other mission. Taylor refused to accept payment for loss of life or property, to show "the meekness and gentleness of Christ."

In 1902, because of ill-health, Taylor resigned as director of the CIM. In 1905, he returned to China for the eleventh and final time and died while visiting CIM work in Changsha. He was buried next to his first wife, Maria, in a cemetery in Zhenjiang near the Yangtze River. During the Cultural Revolution, the cemetery was levelled and an industrial building was constructed on the site. His great-grandson, James Hudson Taylor III, found the tombstone and, with the help of the pastor of a local Chinese church, re-erected it on the grounds of the church in Zhenjiang. His life inspired many others to follow his example, including Eric Liddell, gold medalist of the 400 metres at the 1924 Summer Olympics and subject of the film *Chariots of Fire*. Born in Tianjin to missionary parents in 1902, Liddell returned to China in 1925. In 1941, he ignored the advice of the British government to leave because of the threat of the Japanese military. In 1942, he was arrested and interned in the same Weifang camp as Herbert Hudson Taylor, Hudson Taylor's eldest son, as well as James III and his siblings. Liddell died there on February 21, 1945, having declined an opportunity to leave the camp and given his place to a pregnant woman.

Herbert, born in 1861, followed his parent's footsteps and served as a missionary in China for over fifty years. After spending four of his childhood years in China, he returned to England for his education. He abandoned his medical studies at Royal London Hospital after two years to become a teacher at a CIM school in Yantai, Shandong. After marrying a fellow missionary, he survived tumultuous years, including the Boxer Rebellion, the fall of the Qing Dynasty and the Japanese invasion. In 1942, he was detained in the Japanese prison camp in Weifang, Shandong, at the age of eighty, and remained there until liberation in 1945.

Hudson Taylor's grandson, James Hudson Taylor II, served together with his wife in China as well as Taiwan for nearly fifty years. During their time in Taiwan, they established one of the earliest seminaries on the island, Holy Light Bible School. James II was followed by his son, James III, who was born in Henan in 1929, and received his university and theological education in the U.S. Unable to return to China after 1949, he and his wife went to serve in Taiwan, where their three children were born.

In 1970, he took the position of President of China Evangelical Seminary in Taipei. In 1980, he became the seventh General Director of Overseas Missionary Fellowship and in 1994, set up Medical Services International.

The Chinese evangelise the West

Northern Ireland, along, with Poland, is one of the most religious places in Europe: 45 per cent of its population attend church at least once a month, compared to 17 per cent in the rest of Britain. Belfast has one of the highest concentrations of churches of any city in Europe – Catholic, Anglican, Presbyterian, Baptist, Methodist, Moravian, Jehovah's Witness and other Evangelical denominations.

But religion is in long-term decline and there are too many church buildings; some have been sold to developers or turned into an Indian cultural centre, a Chinese restaurant or a nightclub. The membership of the Presbyterian Church has fallen from 324,000 in 1990 to 250,000 today. Laurence Kirkpatrick, historian of the Church, said that all statistics indicated that it was in serious decline. "Total Presbyterian

Church membership has fallen by 33 per cent in the last thirty-five years... In most congregations, a small number of overworked leaders carry the entire organizational workload," he said. It is the same story in other churches, including the once mighty Roman Catholic Church, whose reputation has been

Former Presbyterian church, now a Chinese restaurant

seriously damaged by scandals. Attendance has been falling in nearly all denominations.

What has happened in Ireland over the last thirty years is being repeated across most of Europe, especially in Britain, France, Germany, Scandinavia, the Baltic states, Belgium, Holland and the Czech Republic. The churches have lost the central role in families, communities and national life which they occupied during Grandfather's era.

But those who go every Sunday to one church hall in a row of red-brick houses in southern Belfast plan to reverse this decline and bring the people of Europe back to Christianity – they are members of the Belfast Chinese Christian Church (BCCC). They have an ambitious plan to do what Grandfather and other missionaries did in their country – evangelise Europe.

The congregation of the BCCC numbers 250 – Chinese from Hong Kong, Taiwan and the Mainland. They are migrants from Hong Kong who mainly work in the restaurant business, with a small percentage of lawyers, doctors and other professionals, as well as students attending the universities and training colleges of Northern Ireland. They were converted to Christianity at home or since their arrival in Belfast and attend the church regularly; it has services in Putonghua, Cantonese and English. The church aims to evangelise the growing number of Putonghua-speakers, who account for half the 30,000 Chinese in Ulster, including its universities' 1,000 new students each year.

The life of the Westerners is too easy and comfortable and they do not need God," said Huang Mei, a restaurant manager attending the weekly Putonghua service at the church. "But the lives of Chinese are very difficult. This forces us to seek spiritual help and comfort.

Huang Jiayun is a young Taiwanese completing a master's degree in Nursing at Queen's University, Belfast. She plans to return to Taiwan and become a Protestant minister. "In the West, human rights have replaced God. In addition, young people are individualist and do not listen to their parents."

The longer-term aim of BCCC and other Chinese churches in Europe is to evangelise local people. The instrument for this will be second-generation Chinese who are born and educated in European countries and have the necessary language and cultural skills. Associate Pastor Symon Wong said:

> Look at these young people, the second generation of Chinese in Europe. They will speak fluent English, French and Spanish. They will evangelise Europe. People in the West are increasingly distant from God, but in China the gospel is filling the spiritual vacuum. The hand of God is more powerful than the hand of man. China is sending missionaries to Africa and the Middle East. We call this the "Back to Jerusalem" movement.

Chinese believers see Europe in moral and spiritual decline. Wong said that people in the West spend a great deal of time shopping and in front of computers and televisions.

> As their material life has become richer, so their spiritual life has declined. Look at the U.S. When it was founded, it was very close to God and the religious spirit played a major part in its establishment. Now that it is rich and powerful, it is in moral decline.

Simon Au, a consultant physician who is chairman of the BCCC council, said that this second generation can speak English, French, Spanish and the languages of the countries in which they were brought up.

They have no burden of being Caucasian. Spreading the gospel is part of our responsibility. That is why we need an English ministry. Since China is developing fast as a country and there are so many Chinese around the world, we have a role to promote God's kingdom. Chinese are good messengers to spread the gospel to other races. All the Chinese churches in Europe have this vision.

One organisation carrying out this task is the China Overseas Christian Mission (COCM), which was founded in 1950. Headquartered in Milton Keynes in the United Kingdom, it has offices in Hong Kong, Malaysia, Singapore, the U.S. and Canada. Its mission is "Reaching the Chinese to reach Europe." Its primary mission is to evangelise the Chinese in Europe, including long-term and new migrants and students; its secondary mission is to evangelise the native people of Europe and other continents.

The second and third generations of Chinese in Europe are moving away from the restaurants and laundries where their parents work into professional and white-collar jobs, giving them the skills and self-confidence to operate easily in mainstream society.

In his 2010 Annual Report, the Reverend John Wallis, chairman of the COCM Council, said:

> After a long period of gestation, Chinese professionals are now bursting on to the higher echelons of all professions, business and government... COCM is justly proud of the fruit of years of gospel work to see that many of those occupying positions of significant authority and influence are mature Christian men and women. The mission is confident that its work will spill over to blessing to the indigenous people of Europe and is already praying and preparing workers to cross cultures to reach them for the kingdom of God and the reviving of the churches that first sent them the good news to China and the countries of East Asia. There is a desire to repay the debt they owe for the dedication of the army of European missionaries who brought their ancestors freedom from sin and death.

That the Chinese plan to evangelise Europe is an astonishing and dramatic turn of events. Less than two centuries ago, the missionaries from the cradle of Christianity in Europe could not get legal access to preach the gospel to the world's most populous country. They only received this access after military victories by the governments; then their early efforts were met with hostility, disbelief and violence from the government and the public.

Europe was the place where Christianity became a mass movement; but now the religion is declining and its churches have fewer and fewer believers. In France, for example, the number of local priests fell from 26,000 in 1998 to less than 20,000 in 2008, according to church figures. Replacing them are more than 1,500 foreign-born priests from Vietnam, India, Congo and other countries. This decline seems to be irreversible.

As some people put it, God has left Europe and gone to other continents where He is more welcome. It will be up to believers from these continents to bring the religion back to Europe, among them the Chinese. It is not an outcome which Grandfather and his fellow missionaries could have foreseen – but would they not be proud that the people to whom they brought the gospel are spreading it around the world? Is this the Great Plan of God?

Saying goodbye to a Presbyterian missionary in front of Faku Church, 1930s.

Thank you

There are very many people to thank for this book. First are Grandfather and Grandmother for their work and their writings. I never had the opportunity to meet Grandfather and, as a young boy, met Grandmother only a few times. So I know them through their clear and vivid writings that are the basis of this biography. I must thank the other missionaries to Manchuria who have left us such an excellent account of their work, also an important raw material. The one I knew best was the Reverend Jack Weir, the son of missionary parents who was born and worked in China; I met him in Belfast and in Beijing. He was most generous with his time and his wisdom; the reader can find in this book his words and pictures.

The reports of the missionaries were published in the *Missionary Herald*, whose issues dating back more than a century can be found in the Gamble Library of the Union Theological College of the Presbyterian Church in Ireland, in Belfast. We must thank the library staff for their kind and thoughtful cooperation; they provided access to the documents, enabling us to gather a great deal of written and visual material in a short time. We were also helped by the Reverend Dr Laurence Kirkpatrick, Professor of Church History at the Union Theological College, who wrote two excellent books on the church and the mission in Manchuria and graciously allowed us to use photographs from them. We also owe a great gratitude to the Reverend John Dunlop, former Moderator of the Church and a missionary in Jamaica, whom I was fortunate to meet in Liaoning province in October 2005, when he was making a television documentary about the Reverend Colin Corkey, one of the Irish Presbyterian missionaries. There and in Belfast, he gave graciously of his time and wisdom, enabling me to gain a better understanding of the church and its foreign missions and of the Ireland of Grandfather's era. Declan Kelleher, Ireland's ambassador to Beijing, has strongly supported this project and encouraged me to apply for funding from the Department of Foreign Affairs; it graciously provided a grant. Since then, Mr Kelleher has continued to provide help and encouragement.

I always wish to express my thanks to the ministers and congregations in Shenyang and Faku during our visits there. In the 1980s, it was not a simple matter to meet a foreigner, especially one interested in religion. But they received us with warmth and sincerity, explaining the complex history and present of the Christian community. They spoke of Grandfather with love and gratitude, one of the motivations to write the book: it is not only about the past but also about the present and future. I would especially like to thank Zhang Hongxia, current lady minister of the Faku church which Grandfather built, for her warmth and affection. I must also mention Mu Jingliang, a long-term friend in Beijing, who helped me to understand Chinese history and the place of the missionaries in it.

I must mention Frances Thompson and Helen Sinclair, the daughters of two Manchurian missionaries. They provided vivid accounts of their parent's work and fine photographs for this book. The members of my family also provided invaluable material about Grandfather, Grandmother and their children. I must also thank Gillian Bickley, a cofounder of Proverse Hong Kong, who did an excellent job of the initial editing.

This book would not have appeared without Joint Publishing (H.K.) Co. Ltd. I must thank all its staff who helped in the production, especially Anne Lee who had the faith to sign the initial contract and Stella Cheng and Amy Siu, who are responsible for the English editing. They were unfailingly polite, sympathetic and meticulous in their work. We thank them very much.

Finally and most important, I must thank my wife Louise, who accompanied me on the trips to Faku and Shenyang and encouraged me to see the project through even when it seemed most improbable. She has shared all my joys and disappointments. Without her, the book would not have seen the light of day.

Mark O'Neill
Hong Kong, January 2012